MINNESOTA THEATRE

Other books in the Pogo Press Arts and Popular Culture Series:

MUSEUM OF THE STREETS
Minnesota's Contemporary Outdoor Murals (1987)
BY MOIRA F. HARRIS

ART ON THE ROAD
Painted Vehicles of the Americas (1988)
BY MOIRA F. HARRIS

Other books by Frank M Whiting:

HUCKLEBERRY FINN
A Dramatization Taken from the Mark Twain novel adapted for the stage.
Anchorage, Kentucky: The Children's Theatre Press (1948).

AN INTRODUCTION TO THE THEATRE
New York: Harper & Row (1954, 1960, 1967, 1978).

PLAYREADERS REPERTORY
(With Melvin R. White)
An Anthology for Introduction to the Theatre
Glenville, Illinois: Scott Foresman (1970).

ONE OF US AMATEURS
Provo, Utah: Stevenson's Genealogical Society (1980).

MINNESOTA
THEATRE

*From Old Fort Snelling
to the Guthrie*

FRANK M WHITING

ISBN 0-9617767-2-2.
First Edition 5 4 3 2 1
Library of Congress Catalog Card Number 88-060421.
Produced by Stanton Publication Services, Inc., Minneapolis.

COVER PHOTOGRAPH: Annie Enneking as Alice and George Muschamp as
Humpty Dumpty in *Alice in Wonderland*, a 1982 production of the
Children's Theatre Company. Photo courtesy of The Children's Theatre
Company, George Heinrich, photographer.

LINE DRAWINGS: by Jack Barkla.

Contents

Preface

MINNESOTA, home of Sinclair Lewis, Garrison Keillor, and so many others, can also take pride in its theatre. At least it was no accident when Tyrone Guthrie and his associates, Oliver Rea and Peter Zeisler, after surveying the entire country decided to locate their theatre in Minnesota. It was no accident when America's most exciting new playwright, August Wilson, decided to move to Minnesota because it offered a healthy and stimulating climate for good theatre. There seems to be something about the very air in Minnesota, despite the frequent 50 degrees below zero wind chill, that makes Minnesota a good place to live.

The general consensus (never proven) seems to be that there is more theatrical activity per capita in the Twin Cities area than anywhere else in the nation, New York City included. Visitors, at least, can scarcely avoid being impressed by the abundance and variety of the activity. A recent Kudos (local equivalent of the Academy Awards) Celebration reported that one hundred and six groups, many of them professional, had produced plays during 1983, and there are other claims to distinction. Located on the Mississippi River at the head of navigation, the area attracted early professionals, who (mistakenly, perhaps) pictured Minnesota as a cool, healthy environment for summer theatre. A few decades later, during the age of the great road companies, Minnesota's L. N. Scott gained recognition as one of the most important commercial theatre managers between New York and San Francisco. By 1930 Minnesota's Bainbridge Players had become the oldest and most successful stock company in the nation, and three years later its owner and manager, A. G. (Buzz) Bainbridge, was elected mayor of Minneapolis. Today Minnesota celebrates The Guthrie Theatre's twenty- fifth anniversary, but it also prepares to celebrate the Old Log Theater's fiftieth anniversary. Minnesota's Chanhassen Dinner Theatre complex has been called "The Cadillac of Dinner Theatres." The Children's Theatre Company is known worldwide as the nation's leading theatre for the young at heart. Theatre in the Round Players

(TRP) certainly rates as one of the nation's leading community theatres; and the listing of theatrical achievements in the area could go on and on.

Many today seem to believe that The Guthrie Theater arrived full-blown from nowhere — an instantaneous milestone in the art of the theatre — nothing like it ever seen before. Yet without detracting from the importance of The Guthrie (and I for one take pride in the fact that I had a small role in the founding of it), The Guthrie is only the latest and most successful in a long series of struggles, dating all the way back to 1857, to establish a resident theatre of professional excellence in Minnesota.

MINNESOTA THEATRE is therefore a humble attempt to make us a bit more aware of our theatrical heritage, for our generation is not the first to have dreamed big dreams.

I have made no attempt to cover all of the theatrical activity that has taken place around the headwaters of navigation on the Mississippi. The book is concerned only with some of the highlights. In fact, it seems appropriate to sound a warning. Although much of the book is based upon solid research, and although most of this research measured up to strict standards of scholarship, Ph.D dissertations, especially those dealing with human beings are not infallible. Let me cite one example from my own almost 700 page thesis. When I began my research the only fact that everyone seemed to agree upon was that theatre began in Minnesota in August, 1851, with the arrival of Placide's Varieties from New Orleans. The Christmas holidays, 1940, found me trying to check a few dates and facts in my almost completed thesis. I had a wretched cold; aching joints, sore throat, and a temperature. I should have stayed in bed, but few graduate students, especially during the Great Depression, could afford such luxury. Despite bleery eyes and runny nose I made out a call slip requesting the librarian at the Minnesota Historical Society to bring me the *Weekly Pioneer and Democrat* for June, 1857. Whether I or the librarian made the mistake, I will never know, but in any case she brought me the issue for 1856 instead of 1857. Had I not been so miserable I would probably have noticed the error at once. Instead, I opened the newspaper to page two where the entertainment notices usually appeared and my astonished eyes fell upon a heading, "The Drama in Minnesota Thirty-five Years Ago." A stupid error had led to the greatest discovery in my entire dissertation. Since then I have often wondered how many other important facts remain undiscovered.

Those who may feel that this book gives undue emphasis to the theatres in the Twin Cities are probably right. Information about most other areas simply is not as readily available. Some readers may also resent the fact that The Guthrie appears to get special billing, but The Guthrie is the theatre that is nationally known, and 1988 just happens to mark its 25th anniversary as well.

The material has been arranged in four chronological divisions: Part One takes us from the soldier shows at old Fort Snelling to 1883 when not one but two Grand Opera Houses were constructed, one in Minneapolis and the other in St. Paul. Part Two ends with 1933, the date when Buzz Bainbridge gave up his theatre to become mayor. Part Three covers the thirty year interval between the demise of the Bainbridge Players and the opening of The Guthrie, while Part Four is concerned with the explosion of activity that immediately preceded and followed the opening of The Guthrie.

But the above dates and divisions are more descriptive than they are rigid. As Algernon in *The Importance of Being Earnest* observes, "The truth is rarely pure and never simple." For example, simple truth could suggest that the professional theatre dropped dead between 1933 and 1963. It did not. The Theatre Guild still continued to tour a few important New York plays into the Twin Cities, and the Old Log Theater was born in 1940. Moreover, the unruly amateur theatre which I have confined primarily to Part Three, actually sprawls everywhere. Continuity of subject matter has been regarded as more important than dates.

FRANK M WHITING
Salt Lake City, Utah
May 15, 1988.

Acknowledgments

So many people have contributed to the production of this book that no ordinary list of acknowledgments seems adequate. To begin with there is my daughter-in-law, Marian Sax Whiting, whose faith in the book, hard work, and determination finally found a publisher. Next comes my gratitude to Pogo Press and especially to my editor, Moira Harris, who collected much of the basic information on which the final chapters are based and who, with the help of her husband, John, collected almost all of the photographs.

On another level this book was begun as a tribute to a number of graduate students who with endless patience and care assembled most of the historical information on which Parts One, Two and Three are based. Their names and the titles of their theses will be found in the Notes and References. It was primarily to prevent their excellent research from lying forgotten on library shelves that this work was undertaken.

On yet another level my gratitude is due to John Harvey, Mike Steele, and Jean Brookins who read an earlier version of the manuscript and kindly offered valuable suggestions and corrections. Special thanks are also due to Robert Collins who read portions of the present manuscript and also provided information concerning the Kudos, and to Jack Barkla for his fine line drawings.

The number of persons who helped in the collection of information and photographs is legion. They include, especially, Sheila Livingston, public relations director at the Guthrie, and Truly Trousdale Latchaw, an untiring bundle of energy and information. Also, Linda Twiss, Lynn Lohr and Lance Belville, Great North American History Theatre; David Kwiat and Lori Ann Williams, Actors Theatre; Lance Brockman, University of Minnesota; Kent Neely and Dennis Faustino, University of Minnesota Theatre; Lou Bellamy, the Penumbra Theatre; Sherry Tarble, Lakeshore Players; Don Stolz, Old Log Theater; Aprylisa Schneider, At the Foot of the Mountain; David Moore, Jr.,

Playwrights' Center; Jack Reuler, Mixed Blood Theatre; Steve Antenucci and Dr. Richard Fliehr, Theatre in the Round Players; Jeff Bartlett, Southern Theater; John Montilino, Illusion Theatre; Patty Lynch, Brass Tacks Theatre; Ann Knutson, Dennis Behl and Annette Garceau, The Guthrie Theater; Sean Dowse, Cricket Theatre; Stephen Kane, Theatre 65; Richard Cook, Park Square Theatre; Britta Bloomberg, Chanhassen Dinner Theatres; Lucinda Anderson, In the Heart of the Beast Puppet and Mask Theatre; Miriam Must, Red Eye Collaboration; Lyndel King, University of Minnesota Art Museum; Barbra Berlovitz Desbois and Robert Rosen, Theatre de la Jeune Lune; Dudley Riggs, Dudley Riggs Theatres; Corinne Lauterbach, Duluth Playhouse; George Keyes, Minneapolis Institute of Arts; Janette Helgeson, American Swedish Institute; Alan Lathrop, Performing Arts Archives, University of Minnesota; Lee Haugee, Children's Theatre; Audio-Visual Library, Minnesota Historical Society; Hennepin County Historical Society; Minneapolis Collection, Minneapolis Public Library; Duane R. Sneddeker, Missouri Historical Society; Robert Booker, Minnesota State Arts Board; Darla Cordes Schnurrer, Brown County Historical Society; Dave Hawley, St. Paul Pioneer Press-Dispatch; Mike Paul, Act Two Photography; Barbara Barber Brown; Jean Jory Anderson; Martha Boesing; Jeff Sherman, Cherry Creek Theatre; Lee Adey and Rowena DeWeese, Paul Bunyan Playhouse; Susan Speers, Theatre L'Homme Dieu; and Anne Charlotte Harvey.

And finally, my deepest gratitude goes to Dave Moore, former student and fellow actor, for his Foreword. To conclude, of course, there is my partner in life, Josinette, whose endless patience, encouragement and typing, all the way from my M. A. thesis through my numerous publications, has made it all possible.

Foreword

ALTHOUGH the intervening years have obscured the fine points of the moment, to this day I cherish the memory of a setting in the summer of 1940: I am a 16 year old apprentice stagehand lounging on the front porch of the original Old Log Theater, an awed interloper on the easy conversation of two of the summer theatre company's actors, Paul Luttio and Helen Seal. A wispy breeze fans the tall pines, just enough to make the baking rays of the sun acceptable. The picture is idyllic, and Luttio, a handsome, muscular, beach-type in his mid-twenties, says, "God! How I love this! Perfect! To earn a living acting in such a setting! Why is New York the only place?"

Commiserating, Helen Seal recounts several years of acting joy in such concealed theatre havens as Cedar Rapids, Topeka and Spokane. But alas, New York! That's where it all is. New York's "the only place."

No more. Wherever they may be, let us hope that Luttio and Seal are aware that, as Frank Whiting points out in his Preface, the Twin Cities have become a veritable mecca of theatre activity, rife with more theatre opportunity than any place in the country — including New York.

Chauvinism it may be, but it's supported by fact and Frank Whiting explains how history has made it so.

Growing up in Minnesota I became witness to and a slight participant in a smidgen of that rich history. The memories are indelible: at the age of eight I saw my first stage play, a Bainbridge Players production of *Snow White*, starring Victor Jory and Florence Rice. My first experience on stage was as "Small Boy", a non-speaking role in the melodrama, *The Drunkard*, at the grand old West Hotel on Hennepin Avenue in Minneapolis. At twelve, my first speaking role was Joe Harper in a Better Drama League production of *Tom Sawyer*, which toured local schools and starred Arlene Dahl as Becky Thatcher. The play's director was Clement "Tim" Ramsland, as imaginative and inspiring as he was eccentric and perplexing. I was a junior high school student when David Thompson, playing the title role in a University Theatre production of *Johnny Johnson*, provided me with a spellbinding acting performance I have seen duplicated but once since — by Richard Hilger in a Cricket Theatre production of Mark Medoff's *Red Rover*.

And so from early youth through adolescence the Minnesota theatre bug was nibbling away at me. In 1942 it took the biggest bite of all. Just four months out of high school I landed the title role of *Billy The Kid* in a University Theatre green room production directed by Doc Whiting himself, who also played the villain, Boyd Denver, opposite me. The play ran several weeks on and off campus and it was my initiation into true ensemble acting which Doc masterfully altered to fit the dimensions of whatever stage we happened to be using. What a wonderful thing it was for an 18 year old freshman to be a part of that small and privileged group of University Theatre people! To this day I can name all and the roles they played. It will be to Frank Whiting's everlasting credit, and is certainly the ultimate measure of respect for him that many of his staff and students carry on his legacy in their own careers as professors in the University of Minnesota theatre department.

I am elated that Dr. Whiting has assigned a prominent place in this documentary to Don Stolz and The Old Log Theater. It was fortuitous and fortunate for Minnesota that these two were contemporaries, working in contrasting fields of theatre toward the common good. While Whiting was laboring as both administrator and artistic director to maintain the purity of academic theatre in a land grant university — the budget of which was determined by an only remotely concerned and inaccessible legislature — Stolz, in the same dual capacity was fighting off the bill collectors and critics in the area's then only commercial theatre, in a remote village often rendered inaccessible to audiences by torrential rains and antiquated highways. Testimony that each persevered to unprecedented success is the presence of the Whiting Theatre on the University's West Bank campus, and that The Old Log Theater has become, in its fiftieth year, the oldest continually producing theatre in America.

Does it beg the issue to mention the Playwrights' Center in Minneapolis? I think not, particularly since I write this in a week when two of the Center's most celebrated participants, Lee Blessing and August Wilson, have been nominated for Antoinette Perry Awards. Imagine! Two Minnesota playwrights with plays running in New York simultaneously!

And so we have come full circle. New York! The very name still breathes magic, doesn't it? But today, it's not "the only place."

DAVE MOORE
Minneapolis, Minnesota
May 19, 1988.

PART ONE

The Early Years
1821–1883

1

From Old Fort Snelling Through the Booming Fifties

EVEN if we ignore the drama to be found in the ancient geology of the Minnesota region with its glaciers, its lakes, and its natural beauty; even if we ignore the dramatic life of its native inhabitants with their hunting skills, their warfare, and their great religious rituals; Minnesota can still claim the distinction of having been one of the first areas west of the Allegheny mountains to witness a theatrical performance.

With the beginning of modern recorded history the vast north central region of this continent found itself "protected" in turn by the flags of France, Spain, England and finally of the United States. It was largely to protect the American claim that a military outpost, eventually to be named Fort Snelling after its first commandant, was established near the headwaters of navigation on the "Mighty Mississippi." This fortress, built in 1819, was manned by soldiers who soon found themselves battling neither the red men nor the British but a more persistent enemy, boredom; therefore, like the GI's of World War II and Korea, they soon discovered that one of the most effective anti-boredom weapons available was the theatre. We can pick up the story in the words of one of the first actual participants, none other than Joseph R. Brown, that colorful frontier jack-of-all-trades: fur-trader, lumberman, land-speculator, legislator, newspaper editor, founder of cities—the man after whom Brown county is named—and apparently Old Fort Snelling's first leading lady! Brown's theatrical achievements might have drifted into oblivion had he not lapsed into a mood of reminiscence following a performance of *Pizarro, or the Death of Rolla* at St. Paul's Market Hall. "The representation of this tragedy," he mused in his newspaper, "caused our mind to wander back to the winters of 1821 and 1822 when a thespian corps used to murder Rolla in the barracks at the mouth of the St. Peters. [Fort Snelling is located where the St. Peter's or Minnesota River joins the Mississippi.] We were one of the performers: we done Elvira." [*Henderson Democrat*, June 12, 1856.]

Brown's contemporaries seized upon the item with unrestrained glee. The

3

View of Old Fort Snelling, about 1850. Oil on canvas, attributed to Edward K. Thomas (1817–1906).

Courtesy of The Minneapolis Institute of Arts, The Julia B. Bigelow Fund by John Bigelow. A soldier artist did this view of the Fort, seen from what is now known as Pilot Knob hill.

editor of St. Paul's *Weekly Pioneer and Democrat* responded with: "He measures nearly six feet in height and about as much in circumference . . . We don't think that even thirty-five years ago he was very delicately formed or strikingly handsome. The idea of his representing tragedy at any time in his life, in any character, strikes us as being sublimely ridiculous, but to attempt the impersonation of a female character . . . why, Brown, this was the most graceless, impudent imposture ever perpetuated." [*Weekly Pioneer & Democrat*, June 26, 1856.]

Records indicate that Joseph R. Brown was indeed a Fort Snelling drummer boy, about sixteen years of age at the time of the Elvira performance at this isolated northern outpost which, in all its history, is said never to have fired a shot in anger save on the stage.

The record of dramatic presentations at Fort Snelling is very incomplete, but enough fragments remain to remind us how fundamental the theatrical impulse is. Major Lawrence Taliaferro, the well-known Indian agent, made

Joseph R. Brown.
Photo courtesy of the
Brown County Historical Society.

the following entry in his diary on October 1, 1836: "Attending to see the soldiers perform *Monsieur Tonson* and *The Village Lawyer* . . . The whole went off well." Colonel John H. Bliss, who spent his boyhood at the Fort, remembered that "The soldiers would get up theatrical performances every fortnight or so, those taking female parts borrowing dresses from soldiers' wives and making a generous sacrifice of their cherished whiskers and moustaches." Charlotte Ouisconsin Van Cleve, who arrived at the Fort while still a baby, recalled years later that "I know the women of the plays looked very tall and angular, and there was much merriment about the costumes which were eked out to fit them. It may be that the performances were as much enjoyed as if everything had been more complete, for I know there was a great deal of fun and jollity at their theatricals." [Van Cleve, 1888:43.]

At least one reasonably important American actor, Harry Watkins, began his career at Fort Snelling. From a biography of Watkins written by Maud and Otis Skinner, we learn that:

At far away Fort Snelling on the banks of the upper Mississippi he had his first taste of drama at the age of fifteen . . . He had been a soldier up there, a regimental fife player . . . to rescue themselves from boredom the troopers organized amateur theatricals, and for his graciousness and good looks young Harry was elected leading lady, appearing as the love-lorn Juliet, and the soulful Pauline in *The Lady of Lyons*. [Skinner, M. and O., 1938: 1.]

Watkins headed south along the Mississippi to New Orleans and a long career as an actor, producer, playwright and manager. On a page in a well-worn prompt copy of *Othello*, Watkins had scribbled: "This book belonged to the Post Library at Fort Snelling, Minnesota, (then Iowa Territory). I joined the Fifth Infantry in 1838 (Company I). The library was an excellent one and I was its best patron. It contained a large number of plays from which we selected all we needed for representation in the Post theatre . . . I played the principal female characters. We gave a performance every fortnight. Major Plympton commanded the Post. His daughter loaned me her dresses . . . From this book I studied Iago to play with Forrest as Othello - studied Othello to play with Junius Brutus Booth, the elder, as Iago. I have played every part in *Othello* excepting only Brabantio, and including Desdemona and Emilia. Harry Watkins." [Skinner, M. and O., 1938: 250.]

Nor were these soldier amateurs content to confine themselves to their own home ground. They eventually grew bold enough to invade the domain of the professionals: they appeared in St. Paul in 1857 with Bulwer-Lytton's *The Lady of Lyons* and in Minneapolis in 1868 with Schiller's *The Robbers*. The Minneapolis performance, however, appears to have marked their last attempt to go "big time", for as the *Tribune* critic on February 13, 1868 wryly observed, "Their forte is Fort Snelling."

The Professionals Arrive

As far as professional theatre is concerned, the first Minnesota event of importance occurred on August 12, 1851, when a company from Placide's Varieties in New Orleans opened a two week engagement at Mazourka Hall in St. Paul, which at that time was a growing river town of about 1200 people. No record has been found concerning how or why this tour originated, but motives are not hard to imagine, for this summer adventure, all the way to the head of navigation on the Mississippi, promised escape from southern heat and infection, as well as a chance to pay for the "vacation" by performing along the way. The vacationing nature of the trip is indicated by the fact that the company consisted of five married couples, plus George Holland, star and manager.

Like so many early "American" actors, Holland had been born in London. He made his American debut at the Bowery Theatre in New York in 1826, and by the time he appeared in St. Paul, had earned a reputation as one of the nation's best-loved comedians. Following the tour to St. Paul, he became a

Mazourka Hall, 3rd & Exchange Streets, St. Paul, about 1890.
Photo courtesy of the Minnesota Historical Society.

close friend of a rising young actor named Joseph Jefferson, a friendship that was to result in the naming of The Little Church around the Corner, in New York City, where Jefferson, searching for a church where his old actor friend might receive a burial service, was told, "Try the little church around the corner."

As to Holland's acting ability even Jefferson admits that "his effects were broadly given." Newspaper editor James M. Goodhue who attended Holland's first St. Paul performance, described him as, "A wonderful protean actor, whose versatility is such that he alone amounts to a dramatic company," an evaluation verified by the fact that George Holland in *A Day After The Fair*, one of the short plays presented on that first evening, played six different characters, ranging from a grouchy old man to a French maid! [*Minnesota Pioneer*, August 14, 1851.]

Mazourka Hall, where this first company performed, appears to have been a typical pioneer hall of the period, offering entertainment in a large room on the second floor above a store. The hall was supported by huge wooden columns and was lit by either "smoky kerosene lamps" or "candle lanterns," according to various sources. The stage itself appears to have been nothing more than a platform at one end of the hall; there was also a front curtain of some kind that is reported to have "billowed in the wind." Hard, uncomfortable benches served as seats, both when arranged in the center of the hall for stage shows, or when set back against the walls for dances. Such halls were usually heated by huge wood-burning stoves in the winter, and cooled by open windows, and sometimes skylights, in summer. That they were fire traps is obvious; that there were other limitations may be seen by the following letter, undated, but written sometime during the 1850's by Miss Sara Fuller:

> There was no windows, excepting in front, and the staging took those off, and all the air there was for the audience were the skylights overhead. We had been there about ten minutes when it commenced raining and they closed the skylights, and it was an oppressive warm night and they had been closed about five minutes when I began to grow faint and Sam went out for a tumbler of water for me and when he came back I had fainted and fell upon the doorstep. . . . My bonnet was completely covered with mud, (I) lamed one side of my face and had to wear a patch for more than a week. I did not attend any more theatre parties. [Undated letter, *The Fuller Papers*, Minnesota Historical Society.]

Uncomfortable or not, the visit to Mazourka Hall by George Holland and his friends scored a great success with the entertainment-starved settlers of St. Paul. And so the first professional company to play in Minnesota Territory came up the river, played for two weeks, and departed. In the century which followed, thousands of other "road companies" would arrive and depart, at first via the river, later by rail, and finally through the air. Some, especially towards the end of the nineteenth century, would perform a great cultural service making it possible for Minneapolis and St. Paul to see such stars as Edwin Booth, Joseph Jefferson, and Sarah Bernhardt. But such road companies also had their limitations: they seldom paused long enough to sink roots in a community, seldom paused long enough to discover local talent, and many of them also found it difficult to avoid the temptation to "play down to the provinces." Nevertheless, in spite of such limitations, real or imagined, touring companies were destined to provide the lion's share of Minnesota's first-class theatrical entertainment until well into the twentieth century.

Several other companies paid summertime visits to St. Paul during the early 1850's, but only two appear to be of importance. The first of these came from St. Louis. The name of the company varied but it was obviously essentially the same group of players. It first appeared in 1854 billed as The St. Louis Varieties. This troupe of nine professionals (sometimes supplemented by St. Paul amateurs) played a season of fifteen performances at Market Hall.

a hall very similar to, but obviously slightly superior to, Mazourka Hall, since most future companies also preferred it. Star of the company was Miss Charlotte Crampton, who, like George Holland and most other stars of the day, felt obliged to display her versatility, for the company during its St. Paul run featured Miss Crampton's portrayals of both Hamlet and Richard III.

The St. Louis Varieties returned the following year with an enlarged company that included a new star, Sallie St. Clair, who ignited real theatrical excitement in 1855. Sallie, born in England in 1831, had come to America with her parents and had made her debut at the Park Theatre in New York as a child dancer. During her Minnesota engagements of 1855 and 1857, she was at the height of her popularity. Young men fell in love with her, critics lauded her, and the public flocked to see her. The extravagance of the praise heaped on her is well illustrated by a long article in the June 22, 1857 issue of the *Daily Minnesotian*, a small portion of which reads:

> The highborn genius of Miss St. Clair flings a glory upon the drama . . . To all these she adds a perfect physique and charming grace — a fine musical voice, and clear enunciation — which makes her the embodiment of that ideal, which only one in a thousand of candidates for histrionic honors can ever attain.

That not everyone in St. Paul held such a high opinion of the lady may be seen from the following by Joseph Wheelock, another St. Paul editor, who responded to the high flown rhetoric of the above with:

> If she has enthusiastic admirers . . . it is not the first time that an enchanting figure and a ravishing ankle have created a sensation among very young men . . . She simply capers gracefully. She holds her head well, with a superb arching of the neck, and prances with a splendid curvette through the routine of the Thespian menage . . . If her powers had been concentrated in a particular line of characters, instead of being squandered in ambitious but shallow displays of versatility it is not impossible that she might have become an artiste. [*St.Paul Financial, Real Estate and Railroad Advertiser*, June 27, 1857.]

The truth about Sallie St. Clair's talent undoubtedly lies somewhere between the above extremes. There is ample evidence that she, like most stars of her day, loved to indulge in what Wheelock termed "shallow displays of versatility," since it was not uncommon for her to don male attire for the portrayal of such dashing heroes as Claude Melnotte, Jack Sheppard, and Pizarro, but although Sallie St. Clair may not have been an actress of the first rank, she was unquestionably a stage personality. Her companies prospered. At the close of her first season in 1855 the prominent citizens of St. Paul, including Governor Willis A. Gorman, gave her a great farewell benefit. At Muscatine, in 1856, a gentleman offered to fight a duel on her behalf. In 1857 her power over young men became a choice topic of local gossip. In a letter to her sister, a youthful St. Paul belle remarked that Joe Rolette was suffering from "Sonny Dayton's disease," a malady the nature of which may be surmised when one learns that "Sonny" had followed Sallie as far as Galena, Illinois, before being persuaded to turn back. Clara Morris, one of America's best known nineteenth century actresses, described her as "the lovely blond star," and said, "I adored Miss St. Clair, as everyone else did." Sallie married Charles Barras, author of America's first great musical extravaganza, *The Black Crook*, and many people believed that her husband's death, which followed closely upon her own, was not an accident but the deliberate suicide of a grief-stricken man.

Sallie St. Clair was undoubtedly the most dazzling theatrical star of the period, but she was not necessarily the most important. In fact, not a person, but growing economic prosperity was the underlying factor behind the booming theatrical development of 1855–1857. Immigrants were pouring into or passing through the area in ever increasing numbers. During the summer of 1855 The Packet Company estimated that it had transported 30,000 persons into the territory. Travelers jammed hotels and boarding houses and even camped in the streets. Businesses prospered as immigrants heading westward spent money for wagons and supplies. Blacksmiths and mechanics worked night and day. Speculators and financial sharpers flourished. Money was plentiful, with much of it in the hands of free-spending, entertainment lovers—a fact frequently lamented by the clergy.

Given such a climate, it is not surprising to learn that the St. Louis Varieties of 1855 scored a success. But what was surprising, was the newspaper war that erupted concerning the company after it had left. The article which ignited the fireworks was a short piece by T. M. Newson, editor of the *Daily Times*:

> That Theatre Has Gone!—A gentlemen remarked to us yesterday, that let the influence of the Theatres be what it might, there had been more drunkenness and dissipation in the city during the sojourn of the one just left us than there had been for double the same time in any other period. [*Daily Times*, July 18, 1855.]

This slap at the theatre was too much for *The Daily Pioneer*'s Mr. Charles J. Henniss to bear. He struck back on July 19th by inquiring how long the "argus-eyed gentleman" from the *Times* had been on the watch, and added that Newson's article was a "miserable and unjust innuendo against a very good dramatic company . . . " and also "something of an insult to the very large and very respectable portion of the community (including Governor Gorman) that chose to attend." Newson struggled to remain calm as he replied in the next issue of the *Times*, but anger broke through as he maintained that *The Pioneer*'s defense of drunkenness, dissipation and the theatre simply indicated that "like begets like." "Many young men," he still maintained, "for the first time became dizzy with the poisonous beverage." He ended by advising Henniss to "inquire of the bar-keepers how much extra rot-gut they sold" during the theatre season [*Daily Times*, July 20, 1855.]

Following this, the elaborate sarcasm of both Newson and Henniss became almost incoherent. Henniss complained about Newson's "vinegar-faced article," about his "want of courtesy as remarkable as it is to be censured," and about his "holier than thou" attitude. [*Daily Pioneer*, July 21, 1855.] Newson, not to be outdone, suggested that the "brains of *The Pioneer* editor must be somewhat blurred," since he "dashed off all sorts of quilimagigs, which sound very much like those heard in 'low groggeries'." He, however, concluded with clear, though hardly diplomatic advice, "Very well then; mind your own affairs and do not interfere in ours. If we choose to speak of the evils that flow from the theatres, it is none of your business . . . " [*Daily Times*, July 23, 1855.]

Emotions in those days could run high, off stage and on, and such arguments could lead to actions as well as words. It was only a few years earlier, in 1853, that Minnesota's first outstanding editor, James M. Goodhue, had been seriously wounded by a knife, while trying to gun down his antagonist with a pistol.

The following season, 1856, was a very good one. Sallie St. Clair did not return, but Lionel Bernard, who was with her in 1855, came back as manager of the Hough and Myers Troupe which played a long and successful season at Market Hall in St. Paul from May 7 through August 6. The entire company appears to have been a good one, with the outstanding portion of the season featuring the appearance of C. W. Couldock. Today Couldock is best remembered as the actor who created the role of Dunstan in Steele Mackaye's *Hazel Kirke*. But even when he first visited St. Paul in 1856, a quarter of a century earlier, Couldock enjoyed a national reputation as a tragedian. His visit not only meant good acting but good plays. *Othello, Macbeth, Hamlet* and *The Merchant of Venice* were among those performed to packed houses. Couldock, who returned to Minnesota many times, was noted for his ungovernable temper, but this probably lent fire and conviction to his playing.

The greatest evidence of the success of the Hough and Myers Troupe in 1856 was the explosion of theatrical activity that followed in 1857. According to one old timer, "I can remember going the rounds of the amusements on the Fourth of July in 1857, and I can tell you that I had to be mighty spry so as not to miss any of the shows. There were three theatres, a negro minstrel show, a big circus, and an acrobatic tent show — all running full blast on that national anniversary." [*St. Paul Pioneer Press*, April 8, 1888.] Although not literally accurate, the old timer was accurate in spirit. As a matter of fact, not three but four theatre companies appeared that summer in St. Paul, although one of them seems to have stayed for only one night.

Sallie St. Clair's troupe was the first to arrive; it opened at Market Hall on May 20. This was undoubtedly the finest company that St. Paul had yet seen. Sallie was at her best; others in the troupe included Claude Hamilton as leading man and John Templeton, who became a prominent figure in the theatre of the Twin Cities after the Civil War. Guest stars were C. B. Mulholland and C. W. Couldock. But the high point of the season came after the regular guest stars had departed when *Uncle Tom's Cabin* opened for what proved to be a record run which lasted from July 27 to August 4. The star of the production was the five year old Katie Putnam, or "La Petite Evita" as she was sometimes called. Her performance as Little Eva created a sensation. On July 28, 1857 the *Daily Minnesotian* described her as "a prodigy and her acting prodigious." She was the "chief attraction" of the play, causing "handkerchiefs to be used freely" by both men and women as she died and ascended to heaven. Katie Putnam was destined to return to St. Paul in 1876, 1879, and again in 1890 with her own companies, but never again would her press reviews be quite as extravagant as they had been for her Little Eva. The "afterlife" of a child star can be a problem.

There were other notable features about the St. Clair Varieties of 1857. The company began to sink roots into the community in a way that resembled a resident company rather than a touring company. Lionel Bernard, the manager, was highly respected; this was his third season in St. Paul, and he was openly looking forward to the day when the city would construct a "real theatre" that could support a permanent company on a year round basis. The growing Minnesota roots of the company were also apparent in the music which was provided by The Old Gent's Band, a local unit consisting of W. H. Munger, violinist, P. C. Munger, cornet, R. S. Munger, cello, and D. W. Ainsworth, flute. If a second violin was needed Dan Emmett or George Siebert was employed. The Munger brothers with their music store and musical talent held a prominent place in the community for years to come, and in the following decade R. S. Munger served as manager of St. Paul's Opera House. George Siebert became one of Minnesota's first important musical conductors, while Dan Emmett gained national fame after writing "Dixie", reportedly while in St. Paul during the summer of 1859. Also working for the Varieties was a young scenic artist, Albert Colgrave, whose excellent work soon began to attract newspaper attention. After the Varieties departed, young Colgrave joined Henry Van Liew at the People's Theatre. Then, after the People's Theatre closed he tried painting for a living. Finally he enlisted in the Sixth Regiment, and on March 4, 1863, died of typhoid fever at the age of 24.

Any dreams Lionel Bernard may have entertained regarding the establishment of a permanent theatre in St. Paul were cut short by the unexpected competition of two other theatres plus the financial panic which struck during the last half of the summer of 1857. But before the company left Minnesota, never to return, it established another historic "first" by playing for two

Broadside for Woodman's Hall, Washington and Second Avenue South, Minneapolis, April 18, 1860.

Photo courtesy of the Hennepin County Historical Society.

weeks in Minneapolis, the only professional theatrical troupe to appear in that city prior to the Civil War.

Minneapolis and St. Anthony had a combined population of slightly over 5,000 persons at that time, while St. Paul had grown to over 10,000. In analyzing other reasons why theatrical companies avoided the city by the falls, Don Woods pointed out in his thesis that managers probably reasoned that if business was good in St. Paul, why go further; if bad, why stay? That there was also continuing moral opposition in Minneapolis is indicated by a report in the *Falls Evening News* on June 19 which suggested that several persons had considered bringing theatrical entertainment to the area only to change their minds when they found that "People (in Minneapolis) are wedded to the folly of paying their debts, before they hire somebody to tickle their ribs." But in spite of moral, financial and other obstacles, the St. Clair Varieties obviously made a wise decision when they decided to play an engagement at Woodman's Hall, a brand new hall on the third floor of a brick building located on the corner of Washington Avenue and Helen Street (now known as 2nd Avenue South), for in Minneapolis they faced no other theatrical competition. Moreover, the idea of dividing an engagement between the "Twin Cities" was obviously a good concept, upon which future companies, both resident and touring, would learn to capitalize. In any event, the Minneapolis season, which opened on August 7, played to "crowded" and "over-flowing" houses. A note in *The Minnesota Democrat* on August 15, 1857 reads:

> SALLIE St. Clair's VARIETIES. This company have been giving their perfor-
> mances at Woodman's Hall during the past week and have met with great success.
> On Tuesday night Bulwer's celebrated play of *The Lady of Lyons* was performed;
> the hall was crowded to repletion; many persons, we are told, were compelled
> to leave without gaining admission to the hall.

The best evidence of all that business was good is indicated by the fact that although the company had planned to close on Wednesday, August 19, with *Uncle Tom's Cabin*, they extended their season through Saturday, August 22. Although the St. Clair company gained popular support, a few Minneapoli-tans continued to resist, as is indicated by the following portion of a long editorial in the *Minneapolis Republican* on August 20, 1857:

> Within a few weeks the people of Minneapolis and St. Anthony had invested
> several thousand dollars in the support of itinerant play mongers, circus perform-
> ers, and theatrical actors. Especially for the past few evenings has the dramatic
> mania raged. Woodman's Hall has been jammed with delighted audiences,
> gathered to witness the exhibitions of a travelling troupe about whose morals
> they knew little and care less.

A more severe attack came a few months later when the Rev. Charles Sec-combe, pastor of the First Congregational Church of St. Anthony, published his "Sermons to Young Men." A portion of one reads:

> The men and women who appear on the stage, are usually persons of bad charac-
> ter, and the tendency of the audience is to render it like minded. This is especially
> true of the tendency upon the young wanderer . . . whom no one befriends but
> to seek his ruin. The theatre abounds with such emissaries of Satan, as watch to
> make him their prey. The consequence is that it becomes one of the great charnel
> houses of death to immortal souls . . . to say nothing of the tax which this form
> of amusement makes upon a young man's purse. [*Falls Evening News*, December
> 16, 1857.]

As Woods observes, almost every Minneapolis attack upon the theatre begins by lamenting its effect upon a young man's morals but ends (in keeping with the city's true Yankee spirit) by lamenting its effect upon his purse. Attitudes towards the theatre such as the above may partially account for the fact that no other theatrical companies seem to have appeared in Minneapolis - St. Anthony until after the Civil War, when, as we shall see, the attitudes mellowed.

Henry Van Liew and the People's Theatre

Although one could, if he or she wanted, question how seriously Lionel Bernard considered the possibility of sinking permanent theatrical roots into the soil of Minnesota, there can be no doubt concerning the motives of his chief competitor, Henry Van Liew. The latter made his objectives clear from the very beginning. According to one newspaper:

> It has been a matter of wonder, that with all the enterprise of St. Paul people, they have as yet no building, properly suited for the Theatre, or Public Concert Room. Mr. H. Van Liew, of the Julien Theatre, Dubuque, is now in this city, with letters of introduction to some of our prominent citizens, for the object of getting up a joint stock company, for the erection of a Theatre building. We think the work a commendable one, and trust Mr. Van Liew may be successful in his effort. [*Pioneer and Democrat*, May 9, 1857.]

His efforts were successful, and on May 24, the public was informed that Van Liew had begun construction of The People's Theatre. It turned out to be a crude, barn-like affair intended merely as a temporary structure until Van Liew could complete the organization of a syndicate to construct a first-class theatre building, but unforeseen difficulties, including a financial panic, a devastating fire, and the Civil War, all destroyed the dream. Consequently Van Liew's temporary playhouse, crude as it was, held the distinction of having been St. Paul's only building constructed primarily for theatrical purposes until an opera house was completed in 1867. According to Manton H. Luther, who wrote many years later about theatres in old St. Paul:

> The building cost the modest sum of $750.00. The sides were of rough boards, the roof of canvas . . . The interior of the theatre was as primitive as the days. There were no galleries. The floor, raised gradually toward the rear, was seated with benches. The stage was cramped and small and there was little attempt at decoration. [*St. Paul Pioneer Press*, January 22, 1888.]

The auditorium seated somewhere between eight hundred and twelve hundred people. Nothing is known of the lighting although there were probably footlights, since *The Daily Minnesotian* on September 7, 1857, reported that Nat-Tam-Ab, a Chippewa Indian, "walked to the footlights" to present Miss Henrietta Irving with a $75.00 diamond ring. Information concerning the stage and scenery is almost as meager. Luther said that Van Liew brought an "extensive and costly wardrobe, good properties and stage settings" from

Dubuque, Iowa. This is confirmed by the fact than when the theatre burned in 1859, Van Liew's loss in scenery was estimated at $1,500 by both *The Minnesotian* and *The Pioneer*. We know that in 1858 the stage was enlarged and new scenic pieces were prepared for the production of *Mazeppa*, but there is no definite information as to just what these changes were. Towards the end of the first season in 1857, two large stoves were set up to warm the building. Again, according to Luther, the canvas roof also made history when a portion of it ripped off during a storm, "nearly drowning some of the audience."

The building was finished ahead of schedule and the opening performance took place on June 27, 1857. The first advertisement contained much useful information:

PEOPLE'S THEATRE

Corner of Fourth and Saint Peter Street.
Lessee and Manager ....Mr. H. Van Hew. (sic)
Stage Manager ....W. S. Forrest.
Prompter...R. E. J. Miles.
Leader of Orchestra ....Mr. Freberthyser.
Artist ....Mr. S. Guleck.
Machinest..Chamberlain.

FIRST NIGHT OF THE SEASON

Saturday Evening, June 27, 1857, Will be presented the favorite Tragedy of

DAMON AND PYTHIA

Damon ....Mr. H. W. Gossen.
Pythia..Miles.
Calanthe ....Mrs. Leonard.
Hermine...Mrs. Canter.

Favorite Dance - Miss Azlene Allen.
Song - "Red, White and Blue" - Mr. McMannus.
Overture by the Orchestra.
To conclude with the favorite Farce of
FAMILY JARS.

Old Delph —Mr. W. S. Forrest.
Doors open at 7½ o'clock.
Curtain to rise at 8¼ Precisely.
Admittance — 50¢ reserved seats — 75¢.
[*Daily Minnesotian*, June 27, 1857.]

W. S. Forrest, stage manager of the company, was the brother of the great tragedian, Edwin Forrest. He returned to St. Paul in 1858, 1864, and 1867, and became a favorite in both Minneapolis and St. Paul. *The State Atlas* expressed it well with "W. S. Forrest brings down the house whenever he appears on the boards. That serio-comic old face of his is an inexaustable (sic) source of fun." [*State Atlas*, February 27, 1867.] Probably of all the names appearing in this first advertisement, the one best known today is that of R. E. J. Miles, the prompter, who eventually became nationally famous — thanks to some help from a well-trained horse. Special mention must also be made of Miss Azlene Allen, the daughter of Mrs. Van Liew by a former marriage. She appears to have been a "beautiful and spritely" young dancer, a "fine singer" and a very effective actress in soubrette roles. We shall meet her again as star of some of the entertainments during the Civil War years. But her stepfather's financial misfortunes plus an unhappy marriage ruined her very promising career. Later she travelled with a circus and by 1888 was reported to be "a broken down actress" in Cincinnati.

All in all it was a good company, and reviews for the first year were generally favorable, although as August wore on, the financial strain began to become apparent. Possibly in an effort to rekindle audience excitement, in the way that Katie Putnam's Little Eva had done for the Varieties, Van Liew designated the week of September 7, as "Juvenile Week", featuring the playing of Azlene Allen and Master Moses, a juvenile prodigy. Both the *Pioneer* and the *Minnesotian* gave the young man good reviews, even though he appeared in such mature roles as Shylock, Richard III and Claude Melnotte. "Master Moses" was really Louis Aldrich who, even after becoming a well-known American actor, always remembered with gratitude the generous reception St. Paul had given him during that difficult late summer of 1857.

In spite of hard times Van Liew and his company carried on, giving nightly performances. On October 13, 1857, the *Minnesotian* reported that the People's Theatre was still "Dragging out a kind of existence" but that the curtain was rising nightly on a "splendid array of empty seats." Finally, on October 19, cold weather and empty seats forced the theatre to close. The bill that night included *Bob Miller in Distress* and *Cool as a Cucumber*.

Even so, Van Liew had managed to play two months longer than any other company had; moreover, he managed to revive and keep his theatre alive during the summers of 1858 and 1859, during which time The People's Theatre became a resident company in the best sense of the term. Newspapers rallied to his support, praising his determination and perseverance and reminding St. Paul that Van Liew's theatre was a permanent institution with the life and "interests of its proprieter . . . centered here." Actions, however, provided the best evidence that Van Liew was forging a bond between his theatre and the community. The Old Gent's Band and scenic artist, Albert

Colgrave, formerly with Sallie St. Clair, joined his organization. Mr. A. M. Carver, a printer for the *St. Paul Times*, frequently filled in as an actor. There was still one source of professional competition, Dan Emmett and Frank Lumbard's Minstrels, but the spirit of community neighborliness that characterized these troubled times is nowhere more apparent than in the rousing benefit performances given by Van Liew for Emmett on June 19, and for Lumbard on August 7. In turn, the German Society, the Fire Department, and the St. Paul Dramatic Club gave benefits for Van Liew. Benefit performances in the nineteenth century usually raised money for actors while in the twentieth century benefit funds usually raised money for worthy causes or outside groups.

The best players in the company (Miles, Forrest, and Gossin) remained loyal to Van Liew and returned for the 1858 season. Two productions, *Uncle Tom's Cabin* and Boucicault's *The Poor of New York*, aptly sub-titled *Or the Panic of 1857*, ran for a week each. The outstanding event of the year occurred in the sensational production of Lord Byron's *Mazeppa* (probably the William Dunlap dramatization) when a trained iron grey charger with Bob Miles strapped to its back, dashed wildly across stage and up a specially constructed ramp. This feat won such acclaim from both audiences and critics that Bob Miles decided to repeat it in theatres all across the country, and it made him famous.

The People's Theatre closed on September 28, 1858, but opened again on April 23, 1859, almost before the ice was off the river. That Van Liew was determined to make 1859 a banner year is indicated by the fact that from May 9 to June 2 he featured the playing of Mr. and Mrs. James W. Wallack in the best season of drama and tragedy Minnesota had ever seen. In addition to eight productions of Shakespeare, the Wallacks included such plays as *William Tell*, *The Iron Mask*, and *Richelieu*. Unfortunately when such outstanding guest stars are employed the remainder of the season usually becomes a let-down, and so it was after the Wallacks departed. Attendance declined dangerously. Moreover, the depression seemed to be entering its darkest final phase. Newspapers printed extra pages to cover the foreclosures. On June 30, Van Liew was forced temporarily to give up his lease, allowing some of the actors to assume control of the theatre. A week later, on June 6, he somehow managed to resume the management, but nothing he could do checked the downward trend; and so the theatre's last regular performance took place on July 21, although special benefit performances continued intermittently throughout August.

The final blow came on September 8. A Republican political rally was in progress, with Schuyler Colfax and Galusha A. Grow as the speakers, when flames were discovered under the stage. The cause of the blaze was never determined. Van Liew believed that sparks from lighted cigars had fallen onto combustible material underneath the stage; some radical Republicans openly accused the Democrats of having set fire to the building in order to break up the rally. In any event a heavy wind soon swept the flames out of control and, although the audience escaped, nothing else could be saved. Van Liew lost everything—building, properties, costumes, scenery and effects.

During the following winter he and his stepdaughter, Azlene Allen, danced, sang and entertained in clubs and saloons—wherever and whenever possible in order to make a living. Finally Van Liew gathered up his few remaining belongings and started down river on a barge loaded with sand. Somewhere along the way the barge sank, leaving Van Liew penniless; but, in spite of everything, he went to Memphis and started over again. It is little wonder that, upon learning that he had become the proprietor of a Memphis burlesque opera house, a writer lauded Van Liew as a man of irrepressible "courage and enterprise." [*Pioneer and Democrat*, September 13, 1860.] Many years later "a St. Paul gentleman ran across him at Deadwood, South Dakota, gray and grizzled but almost as cheery as in the days when he catered to the elite of St. Paul in the amusement line." [*Pioneer Press*, January 22, 1889.]

With the passing of Van Liew, the first period in the history of Minnesota's professional theatre came to a close. The Civil War soon intervened and eliminated most thoughts of entertainment, even though amateur theatricals, as we shall see, especially those produced by Minnesota's German settlers, continued to flourish. It was not until 1864 that a regular theatrical company was again seen in St. Paul; and by that time most of the old plays, the old players, and the old playhouses that had stirred audiences with excitement, laughter, and tears during the 1850's had disappeared.

2

Those Incredible Germans and Early Amateurs of the Nineteenth Century

IN writing about German theater in Minnesota, Hermann Rothfuss quoted a comment made by a writer for the *Minnesota Volksblatt* that "hardly have they erected their houses in the forest or on the shores of a river, when a few singers will band together and soon the old folksongs will be heard in the new country. And quite naturally a 'hall' is soon discovered to be necessary, — and it is built . . . The next step is even more ambitious: A German theatrical performance is given." [*Minnesota Volksblatt*, December 10, 1869, quoted in Rothfuss, 1951: 100.] Theater was clearly deeply embedded in the character, culture and traditions of the German immigrants. For the Germans, as well as for other ethnic groups, the foreign language theatre like the foreign language press helped immigrants adjust to their lives in a new country. Another factor seldom realized is that although English was always Minnesota's official language, the German settlers outnumbered the English, the Irish and even the Swedish during most of the nineteenth century in Minnesota. In any event, less than one month after Van Liew had closed the doors on his first season at The People's Theatre, the following notice appeared in St. Paul's German newspaper, the *Deutsche Zeitung*:

> It (winter) will last several months, and during this period hard times will oppress us like a bad dream if we do not prepare to drive the spectre away. An organization has taken this task upon its shoulders and within a very short time intends to blaze a trail by establishing an amateur theater. [*Deutsche Zeitung*, November 7, 1857.]

One week later the following appeared in the *Daily Minnesotian*:

> Deutsche Theater. We have before us a programme headed thus, which we suppose to mean that our German friends have got up a theater, in Irvine's Hall. The institution is to be opened on Monday, the 16th. The pieces are *Der Sprung durchs Fenster* [The Jump Through the Window] and *Einer muss heiraten* [One must mar-

ry] . . . P. S. We do not want complimentary for this puff as we nix sprechen diche. [*Daily Minnesotian*, November 13, 1857.]

Although the writer of the *Daily Minnesotian*'s announcement may have avoided this event because he could "nix sprechen diche" others did not. According to Rothfuss, "More than 400 people attended the first performance. The spacious hall was so well filled that many late arrivals could not be admitted." There were about 3,000 German speaking settlers in St. Paul at that time; the plays were performed in Irvine Hall and the admission was twenty-five cents. Herman Memmler provided intermission music with his St. Paul city band and Dominic Troyer presented the actors with a keg of beer for refreshment during and after the play. At least as far as the actors were concerned, the German theater in Minnesota was off to a great start.

There were other factors, in addition to the German enthusiasm for entertainment, that also contributed to this performance. Although Van Liew himself appears to have had nothing to do with the affair, two members of his company, Otto Dreher and Julius Schmidt, did. Rothfuss even suggests that both probably came to Minnesota as members of the Van Liew company. It was Schmidt who directed the plays for this first evening "because of his practical knowledge and stage experience" and it was Otto Dreher who became a stalwart of St. Paul's German theater during the years to come. Moreover, the People's Theatre also appears to have provided curtains, properties, and other theatrical equipment that was needed.

Two weeks later a second production was apparently presented. If the time interval between these performances seems short according to modern standards, it would not have seemed so in 1857, since plays during the nineteenth century were rarely rehearsed for more than one week. As the *Daily Minnesotian* on December 1, reported the event "Our German friends had a delightful time last evening at Irvine's Hall. We dropped in there a moment and found the Hall crowded and everybody enjoying themselves." At least six plays were given between December 1, 1857 and February 6, 1858. The next two years not only saw many more productions, but also the construction of an important building, The Athenaeum, in 1859.

The Athenaeum was a proud achievement which resulted from the combined efforts of the German Reading Society and the Thalia Society, but there were limitations. Its location on Exchange Street next to the lot where Governor Alexander Ramsey later built his home was a bit too far from the city center to be easily accessible via the primitive transportation of its day. The Athenaeum, so named in honor of ancient Athens, the seat of learning, science and the arts, was destined to function as the chief home of St. Paul's German drama for twenty-seven years. It was destroyed by fire on May 3, 1886.

Another important event took place during the late summer of 1859; a

The Athenaeum (1859–1886), Exchange & Pine Streets, St. Paul, about 1885.
Photo courtesy of the Minnesota Historical Society.

remarkable man, Professor Phillip Rohr, arrived in St. Paul. His credentials
were impressive; they included experience as a musical director and newspaper publisher in Philadelphia. Nor did his talents and energy diminish during
his years in St. Paul. In addition to his stage work, mostly musical, he soon
began issuing a German newspaper (the *Volksblatt*) and was elected to the State
legislature. Although this book tries to avoid the discussion of music and opera, it has been unable entirely to do so in the case of Rohr. His first production on September 2, 1859 included *The Love Spell* (Donizetti) in which Azlene
Allen, Van Liew's stepdaughter, appeared. This was followed a week later by
an act from Verdi's *Il Trovatore*. On November 19, 1860, *The Pioneer and Democrat* announced, "We are promised by Mr. Rohr to have this elegant entertainment the entire winter." This "elegant entertainment" lasted even longer.
During the two years that followed, *Bohemian Girl*, *Daughter of the Regiment*,
Cinderella, *Preciosa* and *Maritana* were among the operas presented, most of
them more than once. Nor did all this musical activity by Professor Rohr seriously dampen the enthusiasm for legitimate theatre. During 1859–1860
twelve legitimate plays were presented, including a production of Schiller's
Die Rauber.

The outbreak of the Civil War and the shock of the early Northern reverses naturally inhibited theatrical enthusiasm. The St. Paul German community was quickly saddened by the news that Julius Schmidt had been killed at Bull Run. Fortunately the report proved to be an error. He had been wounded and captured. Otto Dreher and other stalwarts of the German theatre were also deeply involved in the Northern cause. Minnesota's German theatre would probably have disappeared had it not been for the fact that when professional theatres closed in cities like St. Louis and Detroit, a few of the unemployed actors migrated to the Twin Cities. For example, in 1861 Rohr was able to add Peter Richins and his daughter Caroline to his group. Peter Richins, born in London, had played at the Park Theatre, New York, and had been stage manager (director) at the National Theatre in Philadelphia. Consequently, during the summer of 1861, St. Paul was treated to an impressive group of operas, together with such legitimate pieces as *The Old Guard* and *Blind Man's Daughter*. Azlene Allen was still a member of this group and Rohr was still the magnet that held things together. Then, without explanation, Professor Rohr returned to Germany in 1862, where he soon began publishing a newspaper. In 1875 he served a term in prison. Apparently some of his American democratic ideas were not welcome in his native land.

But as far as legitimate German theatre was concerned, Professor Rohr's loss had already been cushioned in 1861 by the arrival of three actors from the German theatre in St. Louis: Theodor Steidle, Johann Dardenne, and his wife, Marie Hummel. Their opening production, given with the help of St. Paul amateurs, took place on July 30, 1861, on a day when the temperature reached 105 degrees, and only $5.00 was collected. But in spite of the difficulties of the times, Steidle and the Dardennes refused to be discouraged. They persisted in their plan to present a play almost every week in either St. Paul or St. Anthony, and soon began to attract an enthusiastic following. Unfortunately, other groups (mostly amateurs), seeing the Steidle-Dardenne success, also decided to begin producing, and the market quickly became so overcrowded that in January, 1862, the Dardennes decided to leave. Fortunately, Theodor Steidle remained.

Steidle was more than a good actor; he was a painter, carpenter, theatrical handy-man, and a director. Under his leadership the St. Paul amateurs began to do excellent work. The war took its toll, but the German theatre refused to die even though it steadily declined. Rothfuss records 34 productions in 1861, 15 in 1862, about 12 in 1863, and 9 in 1864. In the last year Theodor Steidle gave up and left for New Ulm where he reopened the theatre burned during the Sioux attack of two years before. Steidle spent two years in New Ulm, then moved to Mankato where he helped another German theatre develop. He was later active in St. Peter and Winona as well. There were apparently no special farewells when he left St. Paul—nothing to indicate the fact that Steidle's contribution to the history of Minnesota theatre had been extremely important during these early years.

Only six productions are known to have been given in 1865, but in 1866 there was a revival of activity. This was especially heightened when Carl Ahrendt arrived in St. Paul from Germany, and Captain Otto Dreher returned from service in the Civil War. Of all the nineteenth century Minnesota actors who eventually became professionals, Carl Ahrendt was the most outstanding. By 1860 he had become a member of the Huey and Hardy Ensemble; by 1881 he was with Thomas Keene; he next joined the Clara Morris troupe, and eventually became a major member of Edwin Booth's company, playing Polonius to Booth's Hamlet and Joseph to Booth's Richelieu. Ahrendt spoke German and English with equal skill and was also fluent in Italian, a gift which made him especially valuable as a member of the great Tommaso Salvini's tour in 1889.

Although Otto Dreher came to St. Paul as a teenager with a theatrical troupe, he did not remain a professional actor. In addition to his military service he edited a German language newspaper, ran an upholstery firm, and belonged to six German singing societies. He was, as already mentioned, a pillar of strength in St. Paul's German theatre. He was also moderately prominent in local politics, serving for years as first deputy to St. Paul's city treasurer. From 1875 to 1881 he was Register of Deeds, and from 1884 to his death in 1889 he served as the first permanent secretary of the School Board. Nor was he the only local actor to enter politics. In 1873, for example, three members of the group ran for city offices: Otto Dreher for Register of Deeds; Carl Ahrendt for City Treasurer; and H. P. Gabrielson for Coroner. Fortunately Ahrendt lost, which, as already mentioned, caused him to leave the city and become a famous actor nationally. Only one year after leaving St. Paul he returned with a professional troupe — to a city very proud of the fact that Ahrendt was now earning the splendid salary of $40.00 a week.

There are a number of highlights in the long and abundant history of the German theatre, which was still active up to and even beyond the first World War; its major period, however, seems to have been during the early 1870's. It was in the late summer of 1871 that Gustav Amberg arrived from Detroit with a group of professional actors and began to produce plays, supplementing his company with local amateurs such as Carl Ahrendt. To show his appreciation for the community's early enthusiasm, Amberg made an unprecedented response; he presented two comedies to the public "absolutely free," and the *Staatszeitung*, St. Paul's major German newspaper, concluded on September 7, 1871 with cautious understatement, "I believe Mr. Amberg has succeeded in creating in St. Paul, Winona, and Minneapolis a better opinion of actors and acting." As the winter of 1871–1872 approached, most of Amberg's professional actors from Detroit departed, but Amberg himself re-

Carl Ahrendt.
Photo courtesy of the Pictorial
History Collections, Missouri
Historical Society, St. Louis.
Falk, New York, photographer.

Gustav Amberg.
Photo courtesy of the Pictorial
History Collections, Missouri
Historical Society, St. Louis.
Wilhelm, New York, photographer.

mained. He continued to produce plays, but supplemented his income by giving lessons in singing and acting. The plays he produced were not literary heavyweights; they were mostly entertaining pieces or children's plays, but an entertainment of some kind could be seen on almost every Sunday evening and seen without being disguised as a "sacred concert." Disguising theatre as a "sacred concert" was an old American custom dating all the way back to Colonial days.

In the summer of 1872, Amberg made a second attempt to establish a professional German theatre in the Twin Cities. He imported Emil Lasswitz, director and character actor from Milwaukee, to perform as a guest star in such classics as *Die Rauber*, *William Tell* and *Faust*. This experience with Lasswitz was so successful that Amberg quickly imported another professional star, Mme. Anna Wagner-Martens. Enthusiasm continued to run high during her performances, and so did Amberg's close relationship to the community as evidenced by the benefit performances he gave for the family of August Hees, at Christmas time of 1872. Hees, a laborer, had been killed while digging a well, and although the temperature at the theatre on that December night stood somewhere between -30 and -40 degrees, enough people came to provide $125.50 for Mrs. Hees and her seven children. During the following year of 1873, Amberg brought Heinrich and Hildegard Dobelin as his stars. Competition unexpectedly developed when Mme. Wagner-Martens returned with Lasswitz, and proceeded to establish a second German theatre, but to her obvious dismay, the great character actor, Lasswitz, deserted her and joined the Amberg company. Nevertheless she refused to give up and with the help of local talent like Carl Ahrendt she began to compete. Moreover, there was also competition from a Czech group, a Scandinavian group, and one or two English groups plus strong competition from the professional American theatre at the Opera House (later the new Grand Opera House).

The Dobelins left, but Amberg secured Madame Maria Methua-Scheller as his guest star. Methua-Scheller was well known in Germany and America, having created a sensation in 1867 when she played Desdemona in the Booth-Dawison production of *Othello*. Since Edwin Booth spoke no German, and Bogumil Dawison spoke no English, Madame Methua-Scheller alternated, speaking "perfect" English to Booth and "perfect" German to Dawison. But in spite of such stars (or perhaps because they were so numerous) the glutted market for theatre collapsed almost overnight. The imported stars departed; Otto Dreher and Carl Ahrendt, as already mentioned, became involved in politics and Gustav Amberg abandoned the struggle. For awhile Amberg worked at St. Paul's Grand Opera House, then went to New York where he eventually became one of the leading figures in the German-American theatre. It was in Amberg's New York theatre, for example, that the first American performance of Ibsen's *A Doll's House*, was given under the title of *Nora*. According to Rothfuss, "Amberg was undoubtedly the most important man, Ahrendt, not excepted, to be connected with the Athenaeum." [Rothfuss, 1949: 83.]

As Rothfuss points out, the achievements of these German thespians become even more astounding when one considers the long hours they undoubtedly worked at their regular nineteenth century jobs. He also discovered an interesting pattern, one not entirely unknown to good amateurs elsewhere. Each time the dedicated local amateurs fanned the spark of theatre into a flame, professionals would appear. Then, after an initial flurry of excitement and publicity, the professionals, unable to maintain the great expectations, would depart, leaving the amateurs to once more fan the spark into a flame. With "amateurs" like Ahrendt and Dreher in the local group it is not difficult to see how and why this could happen.

One other reason for the vitality of the German theatre may have been related to the playhouses (the halls) in which most of these plays were performed. Ironically most of these, including the Athenaeum, were frequently criticised by contemporaries as small, unimpressive, and limited in their abili-

Madame
Maria Methua-Scheller.

Photo courtesy of
Brown County Historical
Society.

ty to accommodate "big productions," yet these very defects may have been strong factors in their favor. Their "inadequate stages" eliminated the financial burden of expensive scenery and their relatively small size provided an environment where friends with a common heritage could assemble, could see and hear, and could share in the joy of creating a play. Rothfuss found that these incredible Germans produced about 1,600 plays, some 150 of them classics by such literary giants as Molière, Shakespeare, Goethe, Schiller and Lessing. Records exist of German stages in twenty-five Minnesota communities.

One of these stages, the Turner Hall in New Ulm, was part of Minnesota's theatrical history for almost a century. Members of the Turner Society in New Ulm built the first Hall for meetings, sports, plays and other events in 1858; it burned down during the Sioux Uprising of 1862. A second Hall, built in 1866, lasted until 1901. The third and last Hall, built to replace number two, was destroyed by fire in 1952.

Over the years the various Halls hosted numerous theatrical performances ranging from visiting professionals to local amateurs. Among the many early stars was Mme. Maria Methua-Scheller who was invited to sing in New Ulm in 1873. Her husband, a painter, was commissioned to paint scenes of German castles in the Turner Hall Rathskeller. From August to Oc-

Fred Spoerhase as Simerl in *Im Austragestuberl* (1894), appearing at Turner Halle, New Ulm, Minnesota.

Photo courtesy of Brown County Historical Society.

tober of 1873, while her husband was painting, Mme. Methua-Scheller produced seven plays with the help of local amateurs.

After Mme. Methua-Scheller's visit the Turnverein (or Turner Society) ruled that only local amateurs could use their stage. The Bavarian folk-play, *Im Austragestuberl*, was typical of the productions presented by the New Ulm German players. Later the Turnverein allowed road companies to use its theatre. Under the management of Fred W. Johnson, many important theatrical troupes played in New Ulm. In 1904 DeWolf Hopper brought his 66 member company to perform *Wang*, a visit that was long pleasantly remembered both by New Ulm citizens and by Hopper himself. The road companies came because New Ulm not only had a stage adequate for the largest productions, but the city allowed Sunday shows. Thus a stop in New Ulm made sense for a company whose schedule was planned with stops in the Twin Cities, Iowa, Omaha, and the West. After the coming of the movies the Turner Hall was used mainly for conventions and political meetings. Its last major event was a speech by Senator Hubert Humphrey on January 9, 1952. The following morning the old building burned.

Hjalmar Peterson as "Olle
i Skratthult."
Photo courtesy of Maury Bernstein.

The Olle i Skratthult Company

Although not a resident company, one special group deserves attention,
the Olle i Skratthult (Olle from Laughter-ville) Company. This Swedish-
American troupe was the only Swedish language theatre in America where
the performers were paid and paid rather well over an extended period of
years. Olle (real name Hjalmar Peterson) came to Minnesota in 1906 and by
1911 was gaining a local reputation with his songs and comic monologues;
by 1916 he had organized a small company that performed in and around
Minneapolis; by 1920 the company had been enlarged and appeared with
great success in Chicago. Shortly thereafter, the Olle i Skratthult troupe was
touring from coast to coast, appearing in Boston, New York, Chicago, Salt
Lake City, San Francisco, Seattle, or anywhere in between that could provide
a Swedish speaking, Swedish loving audience. Tours were strenuous. They
began in the autumn, paused for a short break at Christmas, and ended when
summer heat began to become oppressive. Olle's home base was Minneapolis,
but he also owned a large cabin at Grand Marais on the North Shore, where
many of his group spent memorable summer vacations.

The performances offered by Olle's company were perhaps closer to variety or vaudeville than to legitimate theatre although a popular Swedish farce

or melodrama was normally included in the program. The best loved performer, however, was Olle himself who usually appeared between the scenes rather than within the play itself. Although as a human being he was described as rather shy and very sensitive, he was a superb manager. Anne Charlotte Harvey writes, "His appeal was universal: he performed not just for Swedes but for Danes, Norwegians, Americans, even Ojibway Indians." Whether he appeared in the plush opera houses of great cities or in the humble halls of rural towns he was loved and welcomed. Legend even has it that one man in Lindstrom, Minnesota, actually died from laughing at Olle.

The Great Depression, motion picture competition, and the declining population of Americans who understood Swedish finally caused the company to melt away during the nineteen thirties. Olle himself, however, did not retire. In characteristic fashion he continued to give solo performances helping to raise funds for the Salvation Army.

Not all Swedish actors, of course, performed in their native tongue; many performed in English using a Swedish accent. One of the most successful of these dialect actors was Charles Lindholm from Stillwater. His own one act play, *The Man From Minnesota*, in which he himself loved to play the chief comic character, Charlie Lutefisk, is thought to have earned him a small fortune.

Other Amateur Dramatic Societies of the Nineteenth Century

Amateur dramatic activity was by no means limited to German settlers during the nineteenth century. After all, it should be remembered that Minnesota's theatrical history had begun with amateur soldier shows at old Fort Snelling. Fragments of information indicating widespread amateur activity are scattered throughout the newspapers, but until more groups (ethnic, social, religious, artistic or scholarly) can search out and assemble the pieces of their puzzles, as Rothfuss has done for the Germans, their story must remain largely unrecognized.

Theatrical offerings by ethnic groups (other than the Germans) included productions by French-Canadians, Czech, Irish, "colored" and Scandinavian thespians. In addition to such ethnic productions, churches, temperance societies and GAR posts offered works that used drama to promote some patriotic cause or moral lesson. And finally, there was the continued use of drama as a recreational activity.

The reader should also bear in mind that no attempt has been made to cover the extremely complex field of general entertainment; minstrel shows, dime museums, lectures, recitals, and concerts such as those given by the famous Hutchinson family, originally from New Hampshire. The Hutchinsons appeared in St. Paul as early as 1855. Their story is told by Philip Jordan in his book, *Singin' Yankees*. In this age before movies, radio, and television the hunger for entertainment was complicated and intense. Living theatre only partially satisfied it.

3

Revival After the Civil War:
The Early Opera Houses and
Attempts to Establish a Resident
Theatrical Company

Other than the theatrical activity discussed in Chapter 2, which was often amateur and mostly by Minnesota's German settlers, the theatre disappeared from the Twin Cities between 1859 and 1864. This is not surprising. The initial excitement of the Civil War, followed by its anxiety and agony, plus the violent Sioux Uprising during the summer of 1862, rendered drama on stage superfluous. By the summer of 1864, however, the war's outcome seemed reasonably certain, and, with normal life beginning to return, the A. Macfarland company arrived, on July 12, for a short season that lasted until August 3. Other than breaking the long absence of professional theatre, there was little noteworthy about Macfarland's 1864 visit. His troupe resembled those of the 1850's: it came up the river, billed, of course, as "The best company that ever played the west"; it played the same standard repertory that the companies in the previous decade had done; it stayed for two weeks, and then it departed.

No companies are known to have played the area during 1865, but in 1866 there was a decided revival of activity when two reasonably important troupes played extended engagements. After a brief appearance in St. Paul, John Templeton's company, sometimes called the Union Theatre Company, moved to Minneapolis for a season which lasted all summer from May 22 to September 10, while Charles Plunkett, with his "Great Star Combination" reigned successfully in St. Paul from May 19 to July 30.

John Templeton had been with Sallie St. Clair in 1857 and was highly regarded in the area as a Southern gentleman, actor, and manager. His wife, Alice Vane, was the company's leading lady, and his daughter, Fay, who eventually became a well-known opera star, was, according to an article written years later "a toddling infant, the pet and plaything of the entire company." [*Minneapolis Tribune*, November 13, 1881.] John Templeton might have carved a very important niche in Minnesota's theatrical history had his bid, the following year, to lease the new Pence Opera House in Minneapolis been successful, but for some reason it was rejected, and so, except for an occasion-al note about his good work in other cities, plus a couple of unfavorable reviews about his singing in road companies, John Templeton disappeared from Minnesota's history. Accordingly, the attempt to establish a theatrical base in the Twin Cities was left to two rivals: A. Macfarland and Charles Plunkett. But, before we consider their struggles, some background seems necessary.

By 1867 the deep wounds of the Civil War had healed sufficiently so that a general wave of prosperity and progress was beginning to emerge especially in the Twin Cities where transportation and milling were making great strides. A telegraph line reached the Twin Cities in 1860 and in 1862 a rail-road was established between St. Paul and St. Anthony. The completion of a railroad in 1867 linking the Twin Cities, via Iowa, to Chicago and from there to most of the nation was obviously of especial importance. But the ma-jor event of 1867 in Minnesota's theatrical history was the construction of not one but two "first class" theatres, the Opera House in St. Paul and the Pence Opera House in Minneapolis. Prior to these, only Van Liew's "barn" had been constructed primarily for theatrical use. Otherwise, companies had impro-vised, as best they could, in the various halls.

It was in February 1866, that a corporation with riverboat owner W. F. Davidson as president, was formed in St. Paul for the purpose of constructing a first-class theatre. Ground was broken in March, and, a little less than a year later, the building, completed at a cost of approximately $50,000, was ready for dedication. It was located on Wabasha between Third and Fourth Streets. Patrons entering from Wabasha via "magnificent doors" found themselves in a long corridor which ran the length of the building. There were niches for statuary near the entrance, while an ice cream parlor and a ticket office were included among the spaces along either side of the corridor. A pool hall oc-cupied the basement. At the far end of the corridor a grand staircase led to the auditorium, which was located on the second floor. Large fire-escape doors were at the foot of this stairway.

The Opera House appears to have been a pleasantly attractive and func-tional playhouse, typical of its period. Its auditorium, which seated approxi-mately 1,000 patrons, was described in the *Daily Press* of February 26, 1867 as follows:

> The walls are handsomely frescoed in panel, while the ceiling, and arch over the front of the stage is frescoed in a very elaborate and highly artistic manner, in what is called the Grecian style. The auditorium is divided into the parquette, dress and second circles, like other opera houses. The second circle is supported by ten fluted iron columns, surmounted with carved brackets of very handsome workmanship . . . The top of the parapets are upholstered with crimson silk

plush. The painting is 'dead white' tipped with gold. The orchestra will accommodate thirty pieces.

The proscenium arch was flanked by four private boxes on either side of a wide apron. The stage was 60 feet wide, 30 feet deep, with a 32 foot proscenium opening. The entire theatre appears to have been sensible in size and proportions.

The dedication on February 22, 1867, was a gala event. Musical societies from both Minneapolis and St. Paul participated; free transportation was offered by both The Valley and the Central Railroads, while Cook and Webb carried the visitors from the station to the theatre in "splendid omnibus sleighs." St. Paul now had a first class theatre.

Only four months after the Opera House opened in St. Paul, a similar and slightly larger playhouse, the Pence Opera House, opened in Minneapolis. It was also located upstairs — on the third floor of a stone building at Hennepin Avenue and Second Street. Credit for its construction rested almost entirely upon the shoulders of Mr. John Wesley Pence, and it is therefore proper that it carried his name. As in St. Paul, the newspaper accounts were primarily concerned with the elaborate decoration of the auditorium. For example, around the dome of the auditorium ceiling danced "eight angel children holding hands." Above the proscenium was an American eagle from whose beak floated a streamer bearing the words "J. W. Pence, dedicated June 1867." Full length portraits of Washington, Lincoln and Jackson adorned the walls.

As in St. Paul, the dedication was an event of importance. Thirteen hundred people attended, including Governor William R. Marshall, Lieutenant Governor T. H. Armstrong, and Senator Alexander Ramsey. W. D. Washburn gave the dedicatory address.

That rivalry between the cities already existed became apparent when the *Minneapolis Tribune* complained that, while Minneapolitans filled fully one third of the house for the dedication of St. Paul's Opera House, only eleven tickets had been sold in St. Paul for the dedication of the Pence. The situation was not improved when the *St. Paul Press* explained that the *Tribune* was in error. Twelve tickets had been sold.

Even though St. Paul snubbed its opening, the "Little Old Pence", as it came to be known, proved to be one of the most important theatre buildings in the area's history. Improvements and changes were made as the years went by. Gas lighting was added in 1870, and a sewage system installed in 1873; a sloping auditorium floor and electricity were added a little later. The name was changed to The Metropolitan in 1879, to The Criterion in 1880, and back again to the Pence in 1881, but, regardless of the name, this theatre provided a home for major Minneapolis stock companies and for much of the city's

The Pence Opera House (1867–1952), Hennepin Avenue and Second Street,
Minneapolis, during 1869.

Photo courtesy of the Minneapolis Collection, Minneapolis Public Library.

popular priced entertainment until it was dismantled as a theatre in 1908. The
building was finally demolished in 1952.

At the time of its dedication, of course, the long and important life of the
Pence could not be foreseen, but its immediate importance to the community
was obvious. As Woods points out, it was born at a time when cows and pigs
still wandered the streets, when public drinking cups hung on street hydrants,
when creaking Red River ox carts with wildly drunken drivers made annual
appearances, and when fine ladies stepping from carriages might find themselves mired ankle deep in the muddy streets. Minneapolis like St. Paul now
had a "first class" opera house, a theatre capable of attracting important road
companies—even perhaps capable of hosting its own resident company.

The A. Macfarland Company

Even before the opera houses were opened, their attraction was apparent.
In order to be first on hand and therefore available to occupy the new build-

ings, the A. Macfarland company, defying Minnesota weather, opened for a run at Harmonia Hall in Minneapolis on February 20. Macfarland's prior appearance in 1864 had been a temporary visit, but this time, like Van Liew before him, he had dreams of establishing a permanent home in the area. On March 1, the press announced that he had rented the new St. Paul Opera House for a period of six months at $600 per month. Although not scheduled to move to the Opera House until May, he was obviously eager to try the new house because on March 21, 22 and 23, he deserted Minneapolis long enough to play three performances at the new playhouse in St. Paul. On the first of these performances, he made his only known Twin Cities appearance as an actor when an old St. Paul friend, W. S. (Billy) Forrest, who had been with Van Liew, was suddenly stricken with paralysis, and Macfarland had to go on as a substitute. [*Daily Press*, March 22, 1867.] Forrest did not recover. He died at his home in Brooklyn a little over a year later.

Following this brief St. Paul engagement, the Macfarland troupe returned to Minneapolis and for the next two months enjoyed a very successful run, especially after the middle of April, when a petite young actress–dancer–singer, Miss Emilie Melville, joined the company. Women in America may have been treated as second-class citizens generally, but not so on the stages of the Twin Cities. Emilie Melville captivated the public just as Sallie St. Clair had done. April storms and muddy streets could not deter the audiences that crowded Harrison Hall, the Macfarland company's location at that time, to see and hear her. Friends showered her with bouquets and jewelry. Her last two performances during this first Minneapolis run were so crowded that many were unable to find seats. Her success when the company moved to St. Paul was just as great. According to one report:

> Miss Emilie Melville was as bewitching as the grace of youth and the charms of a melodious voice could make her . . . Her pretty bird-like carrolling is a good thing to hear, and any young fellow who does not enjoy listening to her song and prattle, and seeing her merry, childlike ways, must be hard to please. [*Daily Press*, June 27, 1867.]

Miss Melville was not the only special attraction that Macfarland provided during his 1867 season. Numerous guest stars joined the company for limited appearances, and in July, Macfarland offered St. Paul its first leg show (in tights!). This show, *The Black Crook*, was a spectacle that held the Opera House for an unprecedented run of three weeks. But being a success was not enough. In typical American fashion, Macfarland felt that he had to be a bigger success. Accordingly he split his company into two: a St. Paul company under his own management and a Minneapolis company under the management of his very capable leading man, George L. Aiken, who is still remembered as the author of America's most successful dramatization of *Uncle Tom's*

Cabin. But Aiken was more than a leading man and an author, he also proved to be a shrewd manager, which was indicated by the fact that Emilie Melville chose to join his company rather than Macfarland's St. Paul troupe. The chief evidence of Aiken's managerial ability was that the Minneapolis unit continued playing to crowded houses, whereas the St. Paul company began experiencing financial difficulties. Even the *St. Paul Daily Press* indicated envy and admiration. "Nothing is more beautiful than the (Pence) Opera House interior, when it is thronged with people and the beautiful Emilie Melville singing and dancing on the stage." [July 9, 1867.] But, in St. Paul, Macfarland, in spite of sensational projects such as *The Black Crook*, continued to suffer from declining support. However, the rivalry that was beginning to emerge between the two halves of his company was cut short on July 20, when the Minneapolis city council resolved that the company at the Pence would thereafter be required to pay $60 per month for a show licence, a fee charged for all attractions. The press joined with others in crying, "Outrage," but the decisive action came from Mr. Pence himself who simply closed the Minneapolis unit. Some of the unemployed players lingered in town and gave a few benefit performances, but essentially the Minneapolis season of 1867 came to an abrupt halt. In St. Paul, Macfarland struggled on with dwindling success until October 16. After that he disappeared from Twin Cities history. Perhaps, as so often happens in the theatre, he had simply been over-ambitious. The press, which at first had lent generous support to his efforts, turned against him as soon as he left town, taking some nasty swipes at "the last theatrical performances, which so disgusted all respectable lovers of drama." [*Daily Press*, December 27, 1867.] An unfair evaluation perhaps and yet it does seem likely that the company became discouraged and demoralized towards the end of its season.

The Charles Plunkett Company

With the demise of Marfarland's attempt to build a theatrical home in the Twin Cities, the stage was set for Charles Plunkett to make his bid. It will be recalled that "Plunkett's Great Star Combination" had already played a successful season in 1866. Although we know little about the personal life or physical appearance of either Henry Van Liew or A. Macfarland, Charles Plunkett stands before us in comparatively clear colors thanks to two wordportraits. One of these, written years later, contributed the following:

Of Charles Plunkett not much can be conscientiously said in praise of his acting, but he was a whole-souled, jolly, hale-fellow well met, and he knew good acting when he saw it. Poor old man; he was a good fellow but he couldn't act—not

even a little bit . . . Well, he weighed a little less than three hundred
pounds . . . and had the asthma. It was excruciatingly funny to see him rush
up and down the stage wrestling with the lines . . . puffing and wheezing like
a disabled engine. [*Minneapolis-St. Paul Evening Journal*, March 31, 1883.]

The above comment about Plunkett's acting should be taken with a grain
of salt. After all, he had been good enough, in earlier years, to appear as Shylock at London's Drury Lane in his native England; he had also played Othello
opposite Couldock's Iago at the old Bowery Theatre in New York. But the
Journal's comment about his personality is reinforced from this comment from
the *Minneapolis Tribune*:

> A week ago he (Plunkett) rolled into our business office and introduced
> himself—"Plunkett, Sir!" — a broad, bland, jolly man with a benign visage.
> "Havn't (sic) you a bill against me?" he asked. "Guess not" was the reply; "Never
> saw you before." "You're mistaken; I owe you something — My company was
> up here five or six years ago. Nothing outlaws in my family. Hunt it up"; and
> he vanished. Putting our bookeeper detective on the track of the old bill, it was
> eventually caught and presented — $68. — and paid. Let us hope that Plunkett
> is the first of a new race. [June 17, 1873.]

Whether this payment of the old bill was due to Plunkett's innate honesty
or to his sense of showmanship and public relations is unclear. In any event,
on December 23, 1867 Plunkett opened Minnesota's first winter theatrical
season at the Opera House. A report written on January 12, 1868 for the *New
York Sunday Mercury* by its St. Paul correspondent, appears to give a reasonably accurate picture:

> St. Paul Minnesota.— The Opera House is now open, and under the management
> of Mr. Plunkett, who enjoys a good reputation as both manager and actor. Of
> his ability as the latter, we have no doubt, for seeing is believing; but of the form-
> er we wish as yet to reserve our opinion. He has taken a theatre under the worst
> possible circumstances. The times are hard, the public is suspicious and doubt-
> ful . . . The community of St. Paul is mostly composed of people of wealth
> from eastern and European cities; men and women who have traveled, who have
> seen the world, and who know what good acting is . . . Manager Plunkett
> promises us a galaxy of stars after New Years. If they are his equal we shall be
> satisfied. The attendance at present is rather slim.

The "Galaxy of Stars" that Plunkett promised to bring after New Year's
turned out to be unimpressive; for example, they included Marietta Ravel, a
French tight-rope artist, but none of the promised stars did much to increase
attendance. Plunkett tried moving his company back and forth between Minneapolis and St. Paul, the way Macfarland had done; he also tried short tours

The Academy of Music (1872–1884), Washington and Hennepin Avenues, Minneapolis. From the *Illustrated Historical Atlas - State of Minnesota* (1874).

Photo courtesy of the Minneapolis Collection, Minneapolis Public Library.

to other communities in the area, but with limited success. Although the Plunketts themselves, Charles Sr., Mrs. Plunkett (Carrie Storms) and Charles, Jr., remained above criticism both as artists and as human beings, the same could not be said of some other members of the troupe, who were sometimes referred to as "sticks" on stage and some of whom, on at least one occasion, became so drunk off-stage that the rise of the curtain had to be delayed for over an hour. Plunkett, like Van Liew before him, did not give up easily, but on October 3 the company gave the last of its performances and departed.

Five years later, on June 9, 1873, Plunkett returned. By then the Twin Cities had become an important center in the road company business that, as we shall see in the next chapter, was beginning to feature such stars as Laura Keene, Frank Mayo, and Joseph Jefferson. Moreover, Minneapolis had constructed a second theatre. The Academy of Music was larger and more elegant than the "Little Old Pence" which now lay idle and deserted. This was a situation on which Charles Plunkett wisely decided to capitalize. He moved his actors into the Pence as a resident company. This time he avoided the use of expensive guest stars. Instead he simply presented good standard plays at popular prices. The plan almost succeeded. During the first few months it was the "great road shows" at the Academy of Music rather than Plunkett's company at the "Little Old Pence" that suffered from the competition. Plunkett's season, with its usual interruptions for tours to other cities such as St. Paul, Duluth, and smaller towns of the area, lasted from June 19, 1873 to July 25, 1874. Towards the end of the season, competition from the Academy, which had begun booking such attractions as Lawrence Barrett, W. J. Florence, and the Furbish Fifth Avenue Combination, proved too much for Plunkett. Except for a brief appearance in 1875 with a travelling troupe, Plunkett once again disappeared from the Twin Cities.

But although Charles Plunkett had failed to give the Twin Cities a lasting resident theatre, he was able to make his exit with dignity. The press of both cities treated him with respect and understanding. According to the *Minneapolis Tribune*:

> Mr. Plunkett never brought a poor company to this city, and he has been steadily improving the character of his troupe until now they equal any company that travels. [April 16, 1875.]

After leaving the Twin Cities, Plunkett played in numerous smaller communities of the region. Finally he followed the frontier to the west. By 1880 he was in Central City, Colorado, playing much the same repertory that he had featured during his years in Minnesota, which inevitably included an appearance by Charles Plunkett himself as Othello.

The Murray-Cartland Company and its Successors

After Charles Plunkett abandoned his dream of establishing a permanent resident company at the Pence, four years went by before another, and even more determined, attempt was made. In the meantime the road companies continued to do a lively business at the St. Paul Opera House and at the Academy of Music in Minneapolis. It was early in July, 1878, when one of these road companies, under the management of John Murray, visited Minneapolis, playing such standard pieces as *Rip Van Winkle*, *East Lynne*, and *The Octoroon*. No record has been found of how, why, or by whom the idea of establishing a regional stock company originated, but on September 7 the company was back in town. Picking up where Plunkett had left off, it opened as a resident company at the Pence Opera House. Earlier troupes, including the Plunkett company, that had tried to establish a home in the cities had been repertory companies; such companies normally offered a different play every night. The Murray-Cartland Company, on the other hand, was a stock company. In other words, it attempted to produce a new play every week — unless the play was such a success that it could be held over for extra performances.

From the first the *Minneapolis Tribune* sensed the beginning of something important and threw strong support behind the project. The leading lady of the company was Grace Cartland (Mrs. John Murray) and the troupe was usually referred to as the Murray-Cartland Company, although its official title was much more imposing, "The Great Metropolitan Theatre Company." During its first weeks at the Pence, the company scored a solid pattern of successes, and Mr. Pence, realizing that he might once more have a paying company in the premises, repaired the seats, added some fresh paint, and made other limited improvements in his theatre. Best of all, from the company's standpoint, Peter Gui Clausen was employed to provide the scenery. Clausen, a Dane by birth, began his artistic career as a painter and decorator but eventually gained wide recognition primarily because of his work as a scenic artist. In the months and years to come, it was often Clausen's spectacular scenic effects that helped to restore the company's flagging fortunes. But John Murray's greatest stroke of good fortune occurred toward the end of October when Frederick Bryton, the leading man of Charlotte Thompson's touring company, deserted the road to join Murray at the Pence.

Bryton made his debut at the Pence in *Rosedale*, on October 28, and, with the support of a good company plus Clausen's scenery, scored such a success that its run was extended to eleven performances. Just as Emilie Melville and Sallie St. Clair had captured the male hearts of the area, so Frederick Bryton entranced the ladies. He became Minnesota's first matinee idol. The *Tribune* exulted in the fact that Minneapolis could now support a theatre of its own and soon began down-grading other managers at other theatres who were importing "peripatetic theatrical companies" at exorbitant admission prices. "Other theatres" could only refer to the Academy of Music in Minneapolis and the Opera House in St. Paul where top prices were sometimes as high as $1.50 while top prices at the Pence rarely exceeded $.50. In keeping with the true Yankee spirit said to characterize Minneapolis, the *Tribune* article [November 12, 1878] ends with a reminder that the Murray-Cartland Company " . . . is not a financial drain on our people . . . its receipts being largely disbursed in our own city, and the money kept at home."

Not only the Academy of Music, but also the St. Paul Opera House began to feel the effects of the competition. Ordinary touring companies became reluctant to include the Twin Cities in their itineraries, or, if they did, usually suffered financial reverses. Only the companies with well-known stars seemed able to compete with the local stock company at the Pence. Even the international star, Fanny Janauschek, after being largely ignored when she played to poor houses at the Academy of Music on March 13 and 14, 1879, avoided Minneapolis thereafter, preferring to play in Stillwater and other medium sized Minnesota cities. Some of the Murray-Cartland success was, of course, a matter of local pride. In fact, rivalry between the cities once more

Playbill of the Academy
of Music, dated
September 13, 1882.

Photo courtesy
of the Minneapolis
Collection, Minneapolis
Public Library.

reared its head when the *Tribune*, on November 30 observed that the present theatrical situation was "bad for St. Paul, but fun for Minneapolis." The same paper took pride in the fact (questionable) that Minneapolis now possessed one of two true stock companies in the entire country.

With such a successful beginning, it may seem difficult for anyone unfamiliar with the ways of show business to understand why the Murray-Cartland Company did not become a permanent fixture at the Pence. Of course, as we shall see, it did become more permanent than most, but only by comparison. Competition with traveling troupes, which during 1878 favored the local company, finally began to swing back in favor of the road companies, which, during 1879–1880 included such stars as Mary Anderson, Fanny Davenport, and John McCullough. Then on February 28, 1880, Frederick Bryton left the Murray-Cartland Company. To make matters worse, Mr. Murray had a falling out with Mr. Pence over the need for more remodeling of the theatre, but worst of all, he apparently also had a falling out with his staunchest supporter, the *Tribune*, which suddenly became silent,

simply ignoring the remainder of his season. Finally, after an unsuccessful attempt to raise funds for a new theatre, John Murray and Grace Cartland relinquished their control of the Pence, together with their dream of establishing
a permanent theatrical home in the Twin Cities.

With competition gone, business began to improve at the other theatres.
But any rejoicing that the rivals may have experienced was cut short towards
the end of August, 1880, when Frederick Bryton, the matinee idol himself,
reappeared at the Pence in a double role, as leading man and as manager of
his own company. There was an initial flurry of excitement, but it did not last.
Attendance soon became only average, and Bryton began to rely on Clausen's
scenery and spectacles like *Around the World in Eighty Days* to attract attention.
Finally on January 1, 1881, he called it quits. Newspapers were kind, but expressed the opinion that Bryton's attempt to serve as both leading man and
manager had simply been too much.

But if the managements of the Opera House and Academy of Music once
more rejoiced to find their road attractions free from local competition, their
joy was short-lived. On November 8, Bryton had employed an actress named
Phosa McAllister. He obviously knew that she could act, but what he probably did not know was that this plucky little lady also had the potential to become a fine manager. When Bryton departed, Phosa took over.

The two years that followed were a struggle to survive, quite as heroic
as Van Liew's struggle during the fifties. Phosa first upgraded the literary
quality of the plays being presented by including such classics as *Twelfth
Night*, *As You Like It* and *Othello*. Unfortunately she was up against over-
powering competition from road stars like Thomas Keene, Maggie Mitchell,
Charlotte Thompson and Joseph Jefferson. In spite of such competition, Phosa's final spectacle of her first season, *The Naiad Queen*, ran until June 18, and
was well attended. Woods, in summarizing the season, was able to point out,
that, although it had been a struggle, Phosa McAllister had, since taking over
the company, presented a total of 120 performances at the Pence, while her
chief competitor, the Academy of Music, had managed to offer only 28 performances.

By the beginning of the next season, 1881–1882, competition grew more
and more intense. To combat Peter Clausen's spectacular scenic successes at
the Pence, the Academy of Music purchased new scenery. It then booked the
Madison Square Company's presentation of *Hazel Kirke*, the hit of the decade.
Next came Lawrence Barrett in *Hamlet*, *Richelieu* and *The Merchant of Venice*.
Then in September another of America's great tragedians, John McCullough,
appeared in *Virginius*, *Othello*, *Richard III*, and *The Gladiator*. Other personalities included Buffalo Bill, Denman Thompson, Frank Mayo and Steele Mackaye. Moreover, Col. J. H. Wood opened a popular-priced stock company in
St. Paul. With so much competition it seems remarkable that Phosa McAl-

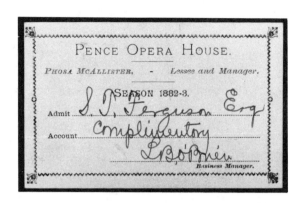

Complimentary pass for the
1882–1883 season of the
Pence Opera House.

Photo courtesy
of the Hennepin County
Historical Society.

lister's company was able to survive at all, but survive it did. In January, Phosa began to meet the competition head on. Her *Merchant of Venice* proved that she could still do an effective classic. Her *East Lynne* was pronounced superior to Ada Gray's road production of the same tear-jerker. But eventually road attractions like James A. Herne in *Hearts of Oak* and Rossi's *King Lear, Othello* and *Hamlet* convinced her that it would be wise to take her company on an extended tour as far west as Denver. She returned to town briefly from March 31 to April 8, then departed on another tour that included St. Cloud, Fargo and Winnipeg.

At the start of what proved to be her final season in 1882–1883, her company was back at the Pence, but although her season began bravely, she was obviously struggling. This time she avoided the classics, and, as managers are wont to do when in financial trouble, began to rely more and more upon the sensational and spectacular. Early in 1883 she tried another approach. She invited John Murray and Grace Cartland, who had started it all, to join her company for a week each as guest stars, but Murray's Rip Van Winkle was judged inferior to Joe Jefferson's, even though the *Spectator* congratulated Murray for having omitted Rip's drinking scene and Grace Cartland received only a "cordial" response. Phosa managed to carry on, but finally, with two lavish new Grand Opera Houses opening, one in Minneapolis on April 2 and the other in St. Paul on October 15, she called it quits. As a somewhat ironic consolation she was invited to recite the dedicatory ode for the opening of the Grand in Minneapolis. Her last performance was given at the Pence on April 30, 1883.

The theatre that Phosa was asked to help dedicate opened on April 2, 1883, under the management of J. F. Conklin. It was located at 60–62 South Sixth Street, Minneapolis, in the Syndicate Block. According to Randolph Edgar, the Grand was referred to many years later as an "ideal playhouse" by New York managers. Four years after its opening the leading interior decorator in Minneapolis, John Scott Bradstreet, was hired to redecorate the theatre

The Grand Opera House (1883–1897), 60–62 South Sixth Street, Minneapolis, about 1888.

Photo courtesy of the Minnesota Historical Society. Jacoby, photographer.

in the newly-fashionable Moorish style. Bradstreet introduced Moorish design to Minneapolis for both the decoration of theatres and of numerous private homes. In his treatment of the Grand, art historian Michael Conforti writes that Bradstreet never used any ornament a second time, doors became mihrabs (prayer niches) and a domed and curtained oriel set high in the wall at balcony level looked like the top of a minaret. Despite its elegance, the Grand Opera closed in 1895 and was demolished in 1897.

Wood's Stock Company

As already mentioned, Phosa McAllister had been facing not only the competition of first class drama from the great road companies, but her dominance over popular priced entertainment had been challenged by Wood's Stock Company in St. Paul. It was during the late summer of 1882 that Colonel Wood from Detroit rented an empty pork packing house from the McMillan Company and in a few weeks transformed it into a "cozy little theatre," seating approximately one thousand. Prices were set at $.25 for general admission and $.50 for reserved seats. Boxes ranged from $3.00 to $10.00.

Interior of the Grand
Opera House,
Minneapolis, as it
was redecorated by
John Scott Bradstreet
in 1887. The theatre
was wrecked in 1897.

Photo courtesy
of the Minnesota
Historical Society.

The theatre opened in September, and by the end of the second week the *Pioneer Press* was happy to report, "Col. Wood has given our citizens just what they have so long desired, a thoroughly first class entertainment at popular prices . . . "

That the Colonel's success continued through the autumn may be seen from the following open letter, published in the *Pioneer Press*:

> To the citizens of St. Paul . . . accept my grateful thanks for your good feeling
> and kindness in tendering me a complimentary benefit . . . but my business has
> been so surprisingly good . . . that I would prefer . . . to dedicate the receipts
> to any charitable institution or purpose selected by yourselves or the may-
> or . . . /s/ Col. J. H. Wood. [November 19, 1882.]

Whether Colonel Wood was really that generous, or simply a master of public relations is uncertain, but all indications are that business was "surprisingly good." As the season continued into 1883, he imported guest stars for almost every production. Today the names of these "stars" are unknown, yet they appear to have had one astonishing talent in common; they were playwrights as well as actors, being invariably listed as the authors of the plays in which they appeared. A hint as to how such an abundance of talent was possible came from the *Pioneer Press* [January 17, 1883] when it referred to *On The Brink*, by guest stars Frank Jones and Alice Montague, as *The Octoroon*, Dion Boucicault's well-known melodrama. Quite obviously, these plays were simply adaptations of well-known plays under new titles, thus escaping the payment of royalties, for the copyright law of 1856 protected the title rather than the play itself.

But whatever the reason, the success of Wood's Stock Company continued throughout the season, and when Phosa McAllister finally relinquished her lease of the Pence Opera House, the alert Col. Wood leapt into the breach with a brilliant modification of the old pattern of playing in both cities. He alternated his stock company between them on a weekly basis, but, instead of leaving one of the houses dark during the off-week, he filled it by booking a travelling variety show. Business appears to have boomed; then, only one week before his 1882–1883 season was scheduled to close, his Opera House in St. Paul burned to the ground. Its destruction appears to have been as dramatic as its melodramas had been. According to the *Pioneer Press* account:

> When the fire was discovered Col. Wood, who had been sitting in front, became frantic and tried to rush in but was held back, and as he acted as if insane, was carried by force to his room across the street where he was soon joined by the company. Fred Will, leader of the orchestra, ran in and was nearly suffocated by the smoke, and was struck on the head by the falling skylight. His hand was badly cut. He was dragged out by bystanders. [December 24, 1883.]

Although the building, with most of its stage equipment, musical instruments, and decorations, was a total loss, Col. Wood refused to give up. He continued operating at the Pence in Minneapolis and by October 22, 1883, a new and much finer "Opera House" had risen in St. Paul. The public responded to the new opening with enthusiasm, but the nature of Wood's enterprise had changed. Variety rather than legitimate stock was emphasized, especially after Ida Siddons and her female minstrels scored such a smashing success that crowds, unable to find seats, stood on tip-toe in the foyer to catch glimpses of the stage.

Just what happened during the following weeks is uncertain. Col. Wood seemed to have the popular priced stage entertainment of the Twin Cities in his grasp, yet towards the end of November he sold his interest in both Wood's Opera House and his lease of the Pence to the S. R. Grant Company of Fargo. Wood's Opera House was renamed The Seventh Street Opera House, but under the new management it soon failed. Then on February 11,

1884, it reopened, this time as The Olympic Theatre under the management of Pat Conley and Edwin Hilton. The Olympic then remained as St. Paul's leading variety theatre for years to come. Thus, the so-called "low-brow" theatre managed to survive along with dime museums, panoramas, and other inexpensive attractions, but all attempts to establish a legitimate resident theatre seemed doomed to failure.

4

Road Companies from the Late Sixties to the Early Eighties

AILURES of Macfarland, Plunkett and McAllister to sink permanent theatrical roots into the Twin Cities area would have been a greater disappointment had it not been for the growth of the road companies. Although today we may be primarily interested in theatrical companies that tried to establish a home in the area, it must be admitted that contemporary interest tended to center on the road companies. The road companies were numerous, usually able to achieve a comparatively high standard of performance, and most of them featured recognizable stars. In addition to the real merit of such stars, the innate snobbishness of people makes them eager to be able to say, "Joe Jefferson was my favorite," or "You should have seen Edwin Booth, as I did." Moreover, the difference between a resident company and road company was only a matter of degree. Permanent members of resident companies were often only temporarily permanent. In fact, troupers like Joseph Jefferson, who came year after year, undoubtedly spent more total time in the Twin Cities than did most of the so-called resident actors.

Real history, like nature itself, abhors classification, and this fragile quality of arbitrarily classifying theatre companies is well illustrated by one of the first road companies to come after the Civil War. This was the Alice Oates company which first appeared in the Twin Cities in the autumn of 1869. It is considered a road company, yet James Oates, the husband of Alice, had just taken a one year lease on the St. Paul Opera House which suggests that the company might have hoped to remain longer. Classification is further complicated by the fact that the company was billed as the "Mrs. James A. Oates Burlesque Opera Company," and both burlesque and opera are beyond the scope of this book. However, the major productions by the Alice Oates company were legitimate plays like *Rip Van Winkle*, *The Colleen Bawn*, and *Under the Gaslight*. In any event, a headline in the *Daily Pioneer* following the company's opening on August 2, 1869, proclaimed it "The Best Entertainment Ever Given in St. Paul, Audience Wild With Delight."

The company's success appears to have been another example of Minnesota's love affair with sprightly young women like Emilie Melville, Sallie St. Clair, and Azlene Allen. Audiences and critics in St. Paul were captivated by what the *Daily Pioneer*, on August 8, referred to as "the charming, piquant, petit, Mrs. Oates." The company's reception in Minneapolis was equally extravagant. When the troupe departed the *Minneapolis Tribune*, on August 24, 1869, proclaimed it "the most successful season . . . ever played in the city," and added the hope that James Oates would soon bring the company back again. For some reason he never did. In 1872, however, Alice Oates again came to town, not to perform but to visit friends. News of her arrival quickly spread and special arrangements were soon made for her to appear as a guest star with the McKee Rankin Comedy Company, which happened to be playing in St. Paul at the time. The result was not just one performance but an entire week of enthusiastic successes. Alice Oates returned with her "English Opera Company" in 1877 and again in 1883, but by then her popularity had begun to diminish, even though she was still a success. But as Beatrice Morosco observed, "In show business a beautiful woman dies twice — and the death of her beauty is far more tragic than that of her body." [Morosco, 1972: 11]. In any event, when Alice Oates returned to play at the Olympic in 1886, the critics turned downright hostile. Broken in body and spirit she disbanded her company. A brief note in the *Pioneer Press* provided a bitter contrast to the adulation that had been hers only eighteen years earlier: "Miss Alice Oates is said to be dying in great agony . . . Miss Oates is thirty-seven years old." [*Pioneer Press*, January 2, 1887.]

Alice Oates was not the only actress to captivate the area during these years. Laura Keene, America's "queen of comedy," visited the Twin Cities in 1870 with her repertory of comic classics, including *She Stoops to Conquer*, *The School for Scandal*, and, of course, *Our American Cousin*. She may have been past her prime in 1870, but her appearance set the standard by which classic comedy was to be judged for years to come. As one critic expressed it, "Last night *She Stoops to Conquer* went off with the vim and sparkle of good champagne." [*The Pioneer Press*, July 6, 1870.] And on the following day, "The gay wit who conceived *The Rivals*, never dreamed of a fairer Lydia than fair Laura." [*Pioneer*, July 7, 1870.]

But if Laura Keene set the standard for comedy it was Lawrence Barrett who set the standard for tragedy. Although Barrett was not America's most inspirational actor, he was probably its most conscientious one. Scenery, costumes, supporting players — everything about a Lawrence Barrett production was usually pronounced perfect by Twin Cities critics. Crowds of the elite usually greeted him in spite of his high prices ($1.50 for reserved seats.) Moreover, Lawrence Barrett deserves recognition because he came so often and because of an unusual curtain speech he made at the close of his first engagement. According to *The Pioneer*:

> At the conclusion of the performance Mr. Barrett appeared before the curtain and in a few gracefully turned sentences stated that the extraordinary circumstances in which he found himself placed impelled him to depart from the rule he had formed never to speak to an audience except in character. Being fifteen hundred miles from home in a region he had long been taught to consider the very confines of civilization, he had been amazed to find an audience as cultivated and appreciative as any he had met in the largest and oldest cities of the continent. [*The Pioneer*, April 26, 1874.]

St. Paul, always very sensitive about its reputation for culture, could not have been more pleased!

Although Lawrence Barrett might be described as the gentleman tragedian preferred by the elite, a more popular Minnesota favorite was John McCullough. His rugged style was especially fitted to roles like Richard III, Virginius, Othello and Spartacus. Just as the St. Paul audiences felt a special kinship towards Barrett because of his curtain speech, so they felt a special relationship towards McCullough because in 1881, following a triumphant summer as a guest star at the famous Drury Lane theatre in London, McCullough opened his American season in St. Paul during Minnesota State Fair Week. He again opened with great success during State Fair Week in 1882, but by the time he returned in 1883 something had gone wrong. His support was described as "wretched," and at times even McCullough could not remember his lines. The mystery was explained shortly afterward, when he suffered a complete mental and physical breakdown in Chicago. He died the following year, hopelessly insane.

Among the other tragedians (and there were many) who appeared prior to 1883, Thomas Keene deserves attention because he also came often, and because he was invariably good. L. N. Scott, Minnesota's outstanding theatre manager in the years to come, later expressed what appears to have been the prevailing impression:

> Thomas W. Keene was as fine an actor as I have seen, but he never got a real hearing in New York. I think that he was unexcelled as Richard III and next to that I should place his Richelieu. He had a tremendous fund of emotional power, and I always looked forward to his coming with great anticipation. [*Minneapolis Journal*, August 31, 1924.]

A list of important character actors who appeared during these years would have to include: Joseph K. Emmet, the German dialect comedian; John Dillon, the Irish comedian; Denman Thompson, the American Yankee; Frank

Mayo as Davy Crockett; and Joseph Jefferson as Rip Van Winkle. The last two are the most important.

Frank Mayo, before he had greatness thrust upon him as Davy Crockett, had entertained dreams of becoming a classic tragedian. In fact, he first arrived in the Twin Cities in the summer of 1871, not as an actor but as an elocutionist. He was persuaded to join the Joseph Wheelock Company, then at the Opera House, in an impressive array of classics. But the best that the *Pioneer* critic could say was that his Hamlet, "showed originality and study"; his Macbeth, "showed an enormous amount of study"; while his Othello, "sustained his well-earned reputation." [*Pioneer*, July 22, 1871.] Ten years later he made another attempt to play tragedy, but the review in the *Pioneer Press* on November 27, 1881, was headed, "Davy Crockett as Iago." The *Dispatch* critic on March 5, 1887, seemed to speak for all when he declared that Mayo's Davy Crockett stood on a par with Jefferson's Rip.

To be compared to Joseph Jefferson was the ultimate compliment that any character actor could hope to attain, and Minnesota had special reasons to love the old master. To begin with, he was one of the area's most constant visitors. It is hard to determine whether he was loved primarily because of his acting or because of his personality. L. N. Scott, who was well acquainted with the problem of dealing with temperamental stars, related the following about Jefferson:

> One night, Joseph Jefferson was playing "Rip Van Winkle." As he lay down in the center of the stage for his 20 years' sleep, a great big rat, with gray whiskers, appeared from the wings and deliberately walked across Jefferson's chest. The audience yelled with laughter, but the actor never moved. He said nothing that night, but the next day he appeared at my office at 10 A.M. "Mr. Scott," he said, "I'm afraid your theatre is troubled with rodents. I would suggest that you get some cats to catch them." He was as mild as if he had been asking for a couple of free seats. The ordinary star would have slammed into the office in a rage, although he must have been much upset to have a rat walk over him. He was a benign, kindly man whom you would never take for an actor on the street. [*Minneapolis Journal*, July 6, 1924.]

Few men have ever come closer than Jefferson to exemplifying the stereotype of the ideal American: self-reliant, generous, unpretentious, understanding, blessed with common sense plus a sense of humor. Acting was not his only accomplishment. He was a painter, a writer, and a lover of the great out-of-doors. In fact, he often tried to end his season in the Twin Cities so that he could spend the next few days fishing on Lake Minnetonka or elsewhere in the land of the sky blue waters.

Alice Oates and Laura Keene were not the only actresses to score success during the period from 1869 to 1883. Even though most of the great stars

Joseph Jefferson.
Photo Courtesy of George D.
Pyper Collection, Special Collections,
University of Utah Library.

such as Sarah Bernhardt and Ethel Barrymore came later, women still held their own in stage popularity. Actresses before 1883 included Charlotte Thompson, a representative of the so-called emotional school whose starring vehicles were *Jane Eyre*, *East Lynne*, and *The Hunchback*; Kate Claxton, whose chief claim to national fame rested upon her portrayal of the blind sister in *The Two Orphans*; and Rose Eytinge, a beautiful and uncontrolled actress of the emotional type whose repertory included *Led Astray*, *Miss Multon*, and *Camille*.

But the favorite, with the possible exception of Laura Keene, appears to have been Maggie Mitchell. She first appeared April 17, 1876 in her favorite role of Fanchon in *Fanchon the Cricket*. And although she played many other roles during her numerous visits in the years to come, the *Pioneer Press* critic appears to have been correct when he pointed out that, "The same character runs through all her plays . . . (an) ingenious, passionate, wild, but honest-hearted little hoyden." [*Pioneer Press*, October 19, 1884.]

Not only did women meet men on an equal footing in legitimate drama, but they held a decided edge in the semi-legitimate world of variety which was gaining rapidly in popularity among the masses. For example, on February 18, 1875, Mlle. Lameroux and her "Can Can Dancers from Paris" invaded the Opera House. The *Pioneer* reported that the legislature, which was in session at the time, instead of protesting, found it necessary to hold committee meetings that evening—at the Opera House. A year later a Madame Rentz attracted another large crowd with her "Great Original Female Minstrels," but she also disappointed them. There was not a touch of vulgarity during the entire evening. The show was reported to resemble a production of "*Hamlet* with the Hamlet left out". An even greater disappointment was experienced in 1877 when the New York Specialty Company presented an attraction entitled, "Living Art Statues." Apparently the statues were too far up-stage to be clearly seen by those who came to enjoy the show, but too close to escape the piercing eyes of those who came to censor it.

But the climax of misfortunes came during July, 1879. May Fisk's English Blondes had scarcely entered the area when two of her actors had writs served upon Miss Fisk for overdue salaries. The unfortunate lady was thrown into jail, her cell caught fire, and she had to be rescued by the jailer. For several days thereafter the papers featured her trial.

After the construction of Colonel Wood's second Opera House (later rechristened The Seventh Street Opera House and finally known as the Olympic), such variety shows achieved long-lasting popularity. The intimate house seemed to provide a more appropriate atmosphere for variety entertainment than had the "dignified" first class opera houses. In any event, variety, which eventually developed into vaudeville and burlesque, had come to stay. Its appeal and character during the early years can be seen from such titles as: "Madame Le Clair's Lovely Ladies in *The Deamon's Frolics*, a teasing, tasty, tantalizing Burlesque;" "Mlle. Sidona's Frisky French Favorites;" and "Lilly Clay's Colossal Gaiety Company in *An Adamless Eden.*"

The years from 1864 to 1883 not only marked the rebirth of theatre in the Twin Cities, they were also years of transition and development. Charles Plunkett (and there were many others) began touring to other cities of the region as soon as the railroads made such touring possible. There was a transition from the traveling family repertory companies who came up the river during the summer on open-ended schedules, to the great national road companies that travelled by rail, came mostly during the regular "winter" season and travelled according to fixed schedules. The period also saw at least four determined bids to establish a resident company in one or both of the Twin Cities. Moreover, while the old companies had been forced to improvise as best they could in whatever halls might be available, the construction of the Opera House in St. Paul, and the Pence Opera House and the Academy of Music in Minneapolis meant that "first class" playhouses were available to road companies, even though each of these "first class" theatres was located on either a second or third floor. Finally, as the period drew to a close, each city constructed a Grand Opera House with its auditorium on ground level, thus setting the stage for the big business of show business which was to follow.

PART TWO

The Big Business of Show Business
1883–1933

5

The Managers and their Theatres

IN almost every way the half century from the construction of the Grand Opera Houses in 1883 to the termination of the Bainbridge Stock Company in 1933 was the most important period of commercial theatrical activity in Minnesota history. In the number and elegance of its theatre buildings, the abundance of its live performances, the hundreds of famous stars who appeared, the size of its audiences, the attention awarded to the theatre by press and public, and especially in the sums of money involved, this period tended to outrank the decades before and immediately after. We could, of course, examine the theatre of this time from many angles, but its dominant feature was its commercial importance. This was the period when the theatre was not only regarded as business, but as big business.

As in all things, whether this commercial emphasis was an advantage or a disadvantage depends largely upon the prejudices of those examining it. Theatre of this period did not beg for grants or hand-outs; it was not only expected to be self-supporting but also profitable, and sometimes very profitable. According to Jerry Stagg, the three Shubert brothers, for example, are said to have "invaded New York City in 1900, armed with tireless energy, boundless confidence, a lust for money . . . and $15,000, most of it borrowed." A quarter of a century later their worth was estimated at half a billion dollars. [Stagg, 1968: 1.] No such fortunes are known to have been accumulated in the Twin Cities, and yet the theatre here as elsewhere was regarded by practical, hard-headed citizens as a business—that should either show a profit or be discarded.

The theatre of Minnesota during this major period of its history was not an artistic expression of the life in its area; it showed no interest in Minnesota's actors, playwrights, directors or technical artists. What Minnesotans saw, or did not see, depended almost entirely upon what its business managers and the owners of its theatre buildings could book into the Twin Cities, usually from New York, just as the motion pictures that Minnesotans saw in later years depended upon what managers booked from Hollywood.

Minnesota's dominant theatrical personality during this period was a giant, Louis Napoleon Scott. Scott was one of the most important theatrical managers between Chicago and San Francisco, and his active life in the theatre (1883–1929) coincided almost exactly with the span of years under discussion. But anyone inclined to see Scott as a big business tycoon, or a domineering ogre, is in for a shock. L. N. Scott was unquestionably a man of deep integrity who devoted most of his life to the theatre in a way that few artists have done, and yet he always thought of himself, and others thought of him, not as a theatre artist but as a business man. It may be symbolic that the major newspaper articles about his distinguished career appeared, not in the art or entertainment pages of local newspapers but in the financial or the business-editorial sections. Of course, L. N. Scott, like most of his contemporaries, would have seen nothing unusual about this. To him, as to them, there was no conflict between the artistic and the commercial. To them good art, or more properly good entertainment, meant good business and vice versa. Nor would it be fair to picture Scott as concerned with money alone. He loved and believed in the product he sold. In his later years, he clung tenaciously to the living theatre, even after it must have been clear to him, as it was to most other theatre managers, that profits now lay in the movies rather than in the legitimate theatre.

Scott's devotion to the living theatre is all the more remarkable when one considers his background. He came to St. Paul in 1876 at the age of seventeen to work in the riverboat business, not in the theatre. William F. Davidson, who owned the steamboat line where Scott was employed, also owned the old St. Paul Opera House, and so one day Scott was sent to deliver the steamboat tickets to a theatrical company. We can pick up the story in Scott's own words:

> I had not been inside a playhouse more than five or six times . . . But in those days theatrical companies would take the boat down the river to the next destination, and it so happened that I was sent to see William H. Crane . . . I'll never forget his greeting of "Come right in, my boy," welcoming me as if I had been a visiting prince. [*Minneapolis Journal*, June 22, 1924.]

The influence of the comedian's warmth on the young steamboat agent was obviously something Scott never forgot. In 1883, when two of the Opera House managers (Charles Haines and J. R. Hatcher) died within a few months of each other, Davidson turned to his young shipping agent and said, "Scott, you go up to that theater and see what you can do with it." A few weeks later, Davidson arrived to inspect the Grand Opera House, which was being built directly behind the old Opera House:

Opera House, located on Wabasha between 3rd and 4th Streets, St. Paul, about 1870.

Photo courtesy of the Minnesota Historical Society. Whitney's Gallery, St. Paul, photographer.

"Scott," he said, "do you know who is going to manage this theater?" "I haven't an idea," I replied. "Me and you," he said. The double managership meant me, of course. And I have remained in show business ever since. [*Minneapolis Journal,* June 22, 1924.]

The Grand was an attractive playhouse resplendent in the elegance and gingerbread so typical of its day. Its exterior was impressive and so were the standard scenic settings created for its stage. According to one report:

The Scenery. — There will be in all twenty-five sets of scenes when completed, but thus far the scene painters have finished those only which will be required in the production of the operas this week, and such scenes as are necessary in the ordinary play. A wood scene, mountain scene, rocky pass, landscape, garden, modern street, ancient street, rustic kitchen, plain kitchen, Gothic chamber, and a prison. [*The Pioneer,* October 14, 1883.]

The dedication, of course, was a gala event. *Il Trovatore* was the opening production with Emma Abbott as the prima donna. For the leaders of St. Paul society it was an opera not to be missed. As one reporter described it:

The richest and loveliest of St. Paul's womanhood, the first among her scores of merchant princes, came in great crowds; and long before the curtain went up every seat was filled; and the boxes, with Gov. Hubbard and family, Brig. Gen. Terry and staff, and Mayor O'Brien and family on the left of the stage, and on the right Ansel Oppenheim and family, J. Little and family on the lower tier, and Hon. Edmund Rice and family in the upper boxes, reflected back an added brilliance to the scene. And what a flash of diamonds there was everywhere. . . . Mrs. Lorenzo Brooks was charming in bronzed silk with white lace, and dia-

Interior view of the Grand Opera House, St. Paul, about 1885.
From *The Northwest* Magazine, March 1885, p. 20.

Photo courtesy of the Minnesota Historical Society.

mond adornments, Mrs. Harbaugh in black brocade velvet . . . [*The Pioneer*,
October 16, 1883.]

Earlier Twin Cities theatres such as the Opera House in St. Paul and the
Pence Opera House in Minneapolis had been located on upper floors, illumi-
nated by gas and considered to be fire traps, yet both theatres lived to an old
age. (Only the Academy, on December 25, 1884, a year after it was no longer
used as a theatre, met with a fiery death.) The Grand, on the other hand,
boasted of having "an abundant water supply with special pipes in case of
fire." On February 19, 1884 electric lights, the ultimate in safety, were added
at the Grand. But on January 21, 1889, five and one half years after its dedication, the Grand Opera House burned to the ground. The cause was believed
to have been a short circuit in the electrical system!

The fire did not stop the theatre's young manager, L. N. Scott. He first
made an attempt to move his already scheduled season to the St. Paul High

School auditorium. Seven members of the School Board approved of the idea, but one member, Mr. B. F. Wright, objected so strenuously that Scott, after one performance in the high school, quietly moved his productions to the old Market Hall theatre which he remodeled and renamed The Newmarket Theatre. In the meantime some progressive business men set about the task of constructing the finest nineteenth century theatre that the upper midwest was ever to have. This was the Metropolitan Opera House, dedicated in 1890. It was a well-conceived proscenium theatre that cost approximately half a million dollars, a considerable sum in that day. It included such back stage features as an excellent paint frame, ample wing and fly space, electricity from its own power plant, six traps in the stage floor, and twelve well-equipped dressing rooms. Seating capacity of the auditorium was held down to a modest 1,576 seats (288 in the parquet, 346 in the parquet circle, 402 in the balcony, 90 in the boxes, and 450 in the gallery). This meant that the audience, massed horizontally and vertically close to the stage, could see and hear. This simple fundamental was soon to be forgotten as cavernous auditoriums were later constructed in the Twin Cities and elsewhere with such foolish pride. A final added feature of the Metropolitan was its primitive air-conditioning system which functioned by forcing incoming air across huge cakes of ice, a not very successful idea which increased the humidity but did little to lower the temperature. But the wisest decision made by the owners of the new building was their decision to appoint young L. N. Scott as its manager.

Although Scott's relationship to the Metropolitan was first simply as a hired manager, his alert business sense was indicated when he quickly began to acquire stock. By the end of 1897 Scott held 103 shares and was elected chairman of the board of directors; by 1919 he had acquired 2031 out of the total 2987 shares. His wife, who ran the Metropolitan from Scott's death in 1929 until the theatre was wrecked in 1937, came to own all except 5 of the shares available. Although his chief source of income appears to have come from the plays that he booked, there were other sources: for example, he rented office space, sold electricity, and sold program ads. Nor did his alert mind limit itself to the theatre. His other business interests included an outdoor advertising agency, a steamboat excursion project, and a penny arcade. He founded the St. Paul Elks lodge in 1886 and became its exalted ruler in 1898.

The St. Paul Metropolitan Opera House was not the only theatre to fall under Scott's control. In 1894 he acquired control of the Lyceum in Duluth and the Grand in Superior. It was also in 1894 that Lac Stanford built the New People's Theatre in Minneapolis. Theodore Hays became its first manager, and the theatre was renamed "The Minneapolis Metropolitan Opera House." By 1895, however, Scott had also gained control of this theatre, although Hays seems to have stayed on as "manager." L. N. Scott thus controlled the

Caricature of L. N. Scott, theater manager.

Photo courtesy of the
Minnesota Historical Society.

big three: the two Metropolitans in the Twin Cities and the Lyceum in
Duluth, which was an enormous advantage when booking attractions. In addition, he had great influence on other theatres in the area for he obviously
had a gift for working harmoniously with other managers such as Theodore
Hays, J. F. Conklin, Jacob Litt, Dick Ferris, and Buzz Bainbridge.

L. N. Scott's importance in the history of the commercial theatre is not
limited to Minnesota. For better or worse he had a hand in the organization
of the Theatrical Syndicate which transformed theatrical booking from a
haphazard, chaotic, small business to a huge, tightly-organized big business.
According to Scott, the old practice had been for theatre managers from
across the country to meet in a New York hotel with actors, managers, and
agents—a wilderness of confusion as they attempted to book attractions for
the coming year. In 1883, Scott and ten other managers gave a Mr. H. S. Taylor $100 each in the hope he could bring some order into the chaos by estab-
lishing a booking agency. Five years later, Scott met with Marc Klaw and Abe
Erlanger in his St. Paul office to consider the problem. The result was that
Klaw and Erlanger bought Taylor's agency and established the Theatrical
Syndicate, the booking agency that was soon to monopolize most theatrical
booking in America.

This movement toward centralized control, first established by the Syndicate but later challenged by the Shubert Brothers, simplified the theatrical
booking process, but whether it helped or hindered the American theatre is
an issue that has been debated long and bitterly. The theatre has usually been

a follower rather than a leader. In scenic styles it followed the lead of the painters; in literary styles (since Shakespeare) it followed the lead of the novelists and poets, but in the transition from little business to big business, from thousands of independent (usually family) theatrical troupes to huge, centralized, booking chains, the theatre was one of the leaders.

We should quickly add, however, that the Theatrical Syndicate was never entirely successful. Theatre people more than most tend to be independent. Some of the greatest artists, including David Belasco, Minnie Maddern Fiske, and Sarah Bernhardt, refused to yield to the Syndicate even though this meant playing in circus tents, high school auditoriums, and miscellaneous halls. The real challenge to the Syndicate, however, came from another equally aggressive and equally commercial chain, the Shubert Brothers.

Even though centralized booking may have eased the burden on local managers like L. N. Scott, it certainly did not solve all of their problems. Enough of Scott's correspondence has been preserved to indicate the endless bickering that went on concerning dates, advertising, and percentages of the gross receipts.

Although L. N. Scott was primarily a business man and therefore dedicated to the belief that good theatre could be measured in terms of the dollars brought in, he was shrewd and idealistic enough to realize that financial success must oftimes be approached indirectly. Accordingly, he showed great skill in dealing with others: other managers, the public, temperamental actors, and employees, including the stagehands union. Germain Quinn, long-time head of that union, speaks highly of Scott because of his "frank, firm, honest approach with those who labored backstage." The same frank, firm, honest approach may be seen in his dealings with actors. James O'Neill, father of Eugene, once refused to play a Wednesday matinee of *The Count of Monte Cristo* and then flew into a rage because Scott presented the matinee anyway, using O'Neill's understudy in the role of Edmond Dantes. A few firm words from Scott quickly quelled O'Neill's temperamental outburst. The great star began to smile as he said, "You're all right, Scott . . . Come out and have a drink." On another occasion, Scott had to cancel a Fanny Davenport performance and refund the money because her leading man was too drunk to go on. Instead of scolding Miss Davenport, who was in tears, Scott consoled her, "It isn't your fault. You can't help it." Another incident involved Clara Morris, the great emotional actress, who had an unpleasant habit of delaying the curtain "because she was ill." On one such occasion after the orchestra had begun its "overture," Clara sent word that the music had upset her frightfully and unless the orchestra was withdrawn from the pit she would not go on. Scott's reply was:

I will not take the orchestra out of the pit. I will have them play for 10 or 15 minutes more, but if Miss Morris is not ready then, we'll make an announcement and dismiss the audience. [*Minneapolis Journal*, July 6, 1924.]

According to Scott, there was no more trouble.

And so it seems safe to conclude that L. N. Scott, as an individual, was a business manager in the best sense; he loved the product he sold and worked skillfully with the artists and craftsmen he employed. Yet the fact remains that by the time of Scott's death in 1929, the commercial theatre was very ill indeed. T. O. Andrus, after examining most of the declining years of the theatre in his dissertation, laments the role played by the managers who in their frantic desire to give the public what they thought it wanted turned more and more towards trashy, sexy entertainment such as *Up in Mabel's Room*, *Getting Gertie's Garter*, and *Ladies Night in a Turkish Bath*. The managers, he concluded, failed to assume any leadership because their primary objective was purely commercial. The theatre of the period "was content to live as a parasite feeding on what money it could devour and contributing nothing except entertainment for the few." [Andrus, 1961: 122.] L. N. Scott agreed that the theatre had been commercialized. He also felt that "in lighting and in setting we have improved tremendously, in acting I do not think we equal the so-called palmy days." [*Minneapolis Journal*, August 31, 1924.] The Andrus view that the commercialism of the commercial theatre was one of the major factors in its decline is supported by the fact that three major Minnesota examples of theatres that most successfully survived the decline of the nineteen twenties and thirties were the Bainbridge Players, the college-university theatres, and the New York Theatre Guild, all of which tended to present a comparatively high quality of dramatic literature.

Labor unions and artists have tended to argue that the chief villain in the death of America's commercial theatre was commercialism itself—primarily in the commercialism of its owners and managers. While there is some truth in this view, it is certainly not the whole truth. From our present perspective the death of the commercial theatre was caused by factors outside the theatre. Chief among these factors was competition from movies, especially after 1927 when *The Jazz Singer* with Al Jolson gave films a voice. To a lesser extent, there was competition from vaudeville, burlesque, sports, radio and all other forms of entertainment. The final coup de grace, of course, came from the Great Depression. It could be argued that wise enough management would have discovered a way out. The legitimate stage survived in New York because it discovered that a much smaller, yet substantial, audience would support a more serious literary theatre featuring such playwrights as Eugene O'Neill, Maxwell Anderson, Tennessee Williams, and Arthur Miller. It might also have been possible for theatres to retrench, cut expenses, and survive. But

Americans have always found it difficult to go downhill. In times of stress, cooperative retrenchment seems impossible to achieve. Instead, each segment of the whole tends to fight for its own survival, and so it was in the theatre. Actor's Equity fought to protect the actors, the stagehands union fought to protect the craftsmen, playwrights organized to protect their plays, and owners struggled to save their playhouses, until finally the warring parts destroyed the whole.

But, except during its final years, the decline of the commercial theatre was not nearly as depressing as most people have painted it. John K. Sherman, one of Minnesota's outstanding drama critics who lived through the last portion of the period, may give us a more accurate picture. After glancing at the battle between the Syndicate and the Shuberts for control of the great booking chains, he observes:

> But the public was no loser in the innumerable plays and players that came to the Metropolitan Opera Houses of the Twin Cities during Scott's long tenure. These and other downtown theatres rarely had a "dark" night. [Sherman, 1958:48.]

An article in the *Minneapolis Journal* confirms the city's reputation as a "good show town." In 1906 Minneapolis had seven theatres whose annual attendance was given as 2 million. Chicago's 29 theatres drew 12 million patrons while New York's 50 theatres counted 18 million customers. Clearly, Minneapolis theatres in 1906 were not doing badly. [*Minneapolis Journal*, February 4, 1906.]

Obviously, then, the half century of commercial theatre in the Twin Cities under Scott's dominance was, taken as a whole, the greatest. Whether Scott and other business managers made it so, or were, on the other hand, responsible for its demise, seems impossible to determine. We know what happened. Why it happened and whether a less commercial approach would have prevented it from happening remains an insoluble question.

The Other Managers

Although L. N. Scott was clearly the outstanding theatrical manager of the period he was not alone. Ignoring for the moment such brilliant stock company managers as Dick Ferris, Frank Priest, and Buzz Bainbridge who will be considered in the next chapter, there were several other excellent men, who, like Scott, were primarily concerned with the road show business.

Theodore Hays

Scott's closest rival in importance would have to be Theodore Hays, who
began his career at the age of nineteen, when, in 1886, his father built the People's Theatre in Minneapolis and placed his son in charge. The theatre burned
on December 28, 1890, but was quickly rebuilt and renamed the Bijou. By
the time the Bijou opened, young Hays had assumed control of an even more
impressive playhouse, the Jacob Litt Grand Opera House in St. Paul. Although L. N. Scott soon maneuvered the agreement that relegated the Grand
to "second class" status, Hays was able to prosper with his less expensive
offerings, which tended to stress the melodramatic and the sensational. His
productions included realistic and thrilling fire scenes, boats on the river, actors plunging into real tanks of water, a 200 foot train, a sawmill in operation,
and the wrecking of a handcar. When plays with such sensational effects began to lose their ability to pack the house, Hays turned to give-aways, prizes,
and games, in an effort to attract audiences. When even these devices began
to fail, he turned more and more towards variety. By 1913 the Grand was
playing vaudeville and burlesque. Finally in 1917 it became a movie house.
By then Theodore Hays was general manager of the Finkelstein and Ruben
Company, which eventually became the powerful Minnesota Amusement
Company that was destined to control most of the motion picture business
in the area. Hays is usually given credit for having shown the first motion picture in Minnesota—at least the first one to tell a story; bits of news may have
been seen earlier. This event occurred in 1898 when he presented *The Great
Train Robbery* at the Bijou. Unlike Scott who refused to yield to the movies,
Hays rode with the tide and embraced them.

His greatest achievement, however, may have been his leadership in developing The Twin City Scenic Studio. The effectiveness of Peter Clausen's
scenery at the Pence has already been stressed. The alert Theodore Hays
quickly saw great possibilities for such scenic embellishment. He not only
employed Clausen to paint scenery for the Bijou, but also established a studio
for scene painting on the top floor of the building. By 1906 this studio has
become so successful that it was moved into a building of its own on Nicollet
Avenue just north of Lake Street. The Studio supplied scenery for opera
houses, theatres, halls, schools and Scottish Rite temples across the nation,
and especially throughout the upper northwest.

By the late nineteen twenties the art of scene painting (realistic perspectives on back drops and wings) was falling out of fashion. Hays, as he had
done when the movies arrived, adjusted, shifting his emphasis to stage
draperies and curtains, and auditorium decorating for the educational market.
But in spite of Hays' efforts the scenery business gradually declined. A Detroit
branch of the Twin City Scenic Studio closed in 1937. The Minneapolis plant

Jacob Litt, owner of the Grand
and Bijou Opera Houses.
From *The Book of Minnesota* (1903).

Photo courtesy
of the Minnesota Historical Society.

produced its very last drop curtain in 1979 and in 1980 the building housing the company burned. In its day, the Twin City Scenic Studio had been one of the proud theatrical success stories of the area.

Hays died at his home in Minneapolis on May 5, 1945.

Jacob Litt

Although he was not a Minnesotan, Minnesota was always proud to claim Jacob Litt as a part-time resident, for Litt was a powerful figure in the region as a theatre–builder, producer and manager. His career began in Milwaukee in 1883 when he conducted a summer season for opera. A few years later he acquired the rights to a number of big-time road productions, including *A Sea of Ice* and *The Lights of London*, spectacles which packed theatres across the nation. In 1890 he built the Jacob Litt Grand Opera House in St. Paul. Located on the corner of Sixth and St. Peter Streets, the house was dedicated on September 1, 1890. The cost was said to be $150,000 and the seating capacity 2,192. By the time the theatre was dedicated, Litt had also gained control of the Bijou on Washington Avenue in Minneapolis, and of another Bijou in Milwaukee. He next acquired a ten year lease on the New People's Theatre in Minneapolis, which he promptly renamed the Metropolitan. By

1899 Jacob Litt had acquired a circuit of theatres with units in at least sixteen other cities. One of the most successful productions Litt ever offered was the world premiere of Charles T. Dazey's *In Old Kentucky*. It premiered at the Bijou during State Fair week of 1892 and returned every year at the same time for the next eighteen seasons. It appears that Jacob Litt with his spectacular, popular-priced melodramas was developing a chain that might have rivaled the Syndicate and the Shuberts had not his career been cut short at the age of forty-five. Even so he is believed to have left behind a fortune of some two and a half million dollars.

Charles A. Parker

Another important manager during these years was Charles A. Parker. A native of Minneapolis, his first contact with the theatre began as an usher at the Minneapolis Grand Opera House. According to Parker, Minneapolis never had another theatre that could compare with the Grand for comfort, elegance, and good management. The ushers were selected from the "best families" and wore formal evening clothes. "Star" of the Grand staff, however, was the doorman, Dick Jackson. His great coat came almost to his ankles which were encased in patent leather boots. A tall silk hat with pompoms and spotless white gloves completed the effect. He would meet a carriage and "throw a cape over the evening dress of the ladies, if the weather was cold or rainy." The driver was given a numbered check; then, as patrons were ready to leave, Jackson would go to the curb and call the carriage. According to Parker, Jackson never lost his beautiful black dignity or his popularity. At times the Grand presented red roses to the ladies, and at other times satin programs were used. Such courtesies, Parker maintained, were not for profit but for elegance and civic pride.

After the Grand closed, Parker went to New York for about three years, then to Chicago for another three. He next managed a stock company on its tour across the country. Finally, he returned to Minneapolis where he managed theatres until his retirement. He left a manuscript which contains much valuable, and sometimes amusing information. In one anecdote mentioned by Parker, the state legislature once introduced a bill to ban the wearing of tights. Manager Wilbur of the Wilbur Opera Company, which was playing at the Lyceum in Minneapolis at the time, advertised that he would present a performance in strict conformity with the law. Accordingly, not only the chorus girls but all the Shakespearean males appeared in ample bloomers, as did the chair legs, table legs, and even a little dog. The proposed bill to ban tights did not even come to the legislative floor for a vote.

There were, of course, numerous other managers, but Scott, Hays, Litt and Parker were clearly the ones during this period about whom we know the most.

6

Regional Stock Companies

LTHOUGH money may have been the driving force behind the commercial theatre during the half century between 1883 and 1933 there were exceptions, the most obvious being the stock companies. True, stock companies were expected to be self-supporting or perish, but only a fool hardy optimist could have expected a stock company to make much of a profit. To begin with, a stock theatre was always expected to be a "popular priced" theatre which means that tickets usually sold from $.25 to $.75 apiece. Good houses were therefore a necessity even to pay expenses, which fortunately were modest, largely because the actors were willing to work for modest salaries. This, in turn, was possible because, as Francis Drake concluded after a thorough study of actors' personalities, one of the reasonably reliable characteristics that seem to distinguish actors from the normal run of Americans is that they tend to be impractical about money. It may be true that star actors today, under the influence of movies and television, and encouraged by their agents and their unions, have come to expect exorbitant salaries, but this is because being impractical about money can work both ways. Actors may work for little or nothing or they may squander fortunes—both extremes are good examples of impracticality in regard to money.

It should be remembered that, even in the "good old days," employment in the theatre was seasonal, uncertain, and intermittent. Stock companies usually began with the avowed intention of becoming permanent, but most of them closed within a few weeks or months. Moreover, actors were expected to supply their own make-up, wearing apparel (except for period costumes), and incidentals. Most of them lived in hotels and ate at restaurants, since their work schedules allowed little time for cooking or housekeeping. And by modern standards their work schedules were unbelievable.

The standard practice was to produce a new show beginning on Sunday of each week. Following this Sunday opening, players received their sides (scripts containing only their own speeches plus cues) for the next play; they would then study these until 2:00 or 3:00 a.m. On Monday the first rehearsal would take place during which basic blocking (positions, entrances and exits) would be established. Then, of course, they performed the "old play" that evening. Tuesday saw a second long rehearsal of the new play and another performance of the old one. Wednesday, in theory, was a day off, but, of course, they performed the old play that evening, and memorized lines under pressure during the day because by Thursday they were required to be "line perfect." Thursday was also the day for costume fittings, and for two performances of the old play, matinee and evening. Friday was usually a grueling technical rehearsal with lights, props, sound, etc., plus another evening performance, while Saturday usually consisted of a morning rehearsal followed by another matinee and evening performance of the old play. Then on Sunday the new play opened and the cycle was repeated.

Marie Gale Bainbridge, probably the most beloved of Minnesota's stock company stars, outlined a similar routine when George Grim interviewed her:

> Home after the (Sunday) show, Marie and Buzz hoped that Buzz Jr. would stay asleep—it was time to learn lines for the next show . . . Up at 7, Marie would attend to Buzz Jr., do some household puttering. At 10, she was back in the theater rehearsing the next show. On Wednesday afternoon (matinees were Sunday, Thursday, Saturday, performances every night) there was wardrobe worry . . . Friday, dress rehearsal. Sunday, the new play's first performance, at the matinee. [*Minneapolis Tribune*, August 22, 1965.]

Obviously, few rational human beings would work such hours, under such pressure and with such dedication for money alone, and yet Marie Gale Bainbridge concluded her long interview with, "Could there ever be a better way to earn a living?" But, although an actor's financial rewards in a stock company may have been limited, his or her rewards in other ways were not. No other form of theatre offered quite such an abundant variety of opportunities for an actor to develop as an artist. It is no accident that so many of America's greatest actors grew up under the system. Nor were actors the only ones to benefit from a good stock company. The community itself experienced a sense of pride by identifying with such a group. Moreover, a stock company provided the chance for the community to see good, unpretentious plays at popular prices, and, finally, local talent was sometimes given a chance to break into the profession.

The People's Stock Company, 1888–1889

From 1883 to 1933 some forty stock companies are known to have appeared in the Twin Cities. Not all of them, however, were resident companies. Many had headquarters elsewhere and simply visited Minnesota, usually during the summer season. Our concern is only with stock companies who maintained a home base in one or both of the Twin Cities and who managed to stay for an extended period of time.

After Phosa McAllister's courageous attempt failed in 1883, and after Colonel Wood transferred his interest from stock to variety, five years went by before yet another attempt was made to establish a stock company in either of the Twin Cities. In many ways this attempt by The People's Stock Company commands respect. It was a genuine though modest success both financially and artistically, and it achieved most of the things a good resident theatre should achieve: it provided a steady supply of quality entertainment at popular prices; it provided steady employment for a group of actors; it gave several local actors a chance to be seen; and it presented the work of at least one local playwright. The unanswered question is, why did it fail?

The Company was the brainchild of four Minneapolis men, who, for unexplained reasons, decided to establish a stock company in St. Paul. Frank Whitmore and Eugene Trask put up the money; they then employed Charles Wilson as manager and Lewis Walker as business manager. Early in May, 1888, they remodeled old Turner Hall into a very attractive intimate theatre. Meanwhile Lewis Walker managed to assemble an unusually talented company. *The Daily Globe* [May 27, 1888] marveled that "so many actors of the reputation these people bear could be induced to accept service." While the *Globe*'s comment was obviously influenced by a tendency of the press to encourage new projects, it contained more than a grain of truth. Linda Dietz, the company's first leading lady, was especially popular. The *Pioneer Press* critic, in reviewing her opening night, mentioned "her frank beautiful face . . . . expressive eyes, and rare personal magnetism" and added that "she plays naturally and easily." [June 12, 1888.] A. S. Lipman, the first leading man, was a professional with an impressive list of accomplishments, including favorable reviews of his former Twin Cities appearances as a supporting player with such stars as Robson and Crane, C. W. Couldock, and Rose Coghlan. His outstanding success at the People's Theatre was his portrayal of Dr. Jekyll and Mr. Hyde. A third company member, Harold Russell, claims special interest because he was a Twin Cities actor, having made his debut a few years before at the Pence in Minneapolis. In the People's Stock Company he served as second lead and character actor. He was noted for his youth and his handsome face.

But of all who contributed to the company's success, the most important appears to have been Barton Hill, who was the stage manager (director) and sometimes an actor. Hill's effectiveness should be no surprise. He had served as stage manager of the Bidwell Stock Company in New Orleans, associate manager of the John McCullough company in California, and as manager and chief comedian with the travelling companies of both Edwin Forrest and Edwin Booth. His greatest triumph in St. Paul came towards the end of the season when he appeared as Othello, a role he had played opposite America's greatest: Lawrence Barrett, Thomas Keene, and Edwin Booth. "Every seat in the house was occupied" and that although the performance lasted until after midnight, the audience was "lavish in approval." [*The Pioneer*, May 7, 1889.]

Nor were the major players the only noteworthy feature about the company. At least five local amateurs managed to break in during the year, and two of them, Ada Hawkins and Ben Johnson, continued in the profession. Also of local interest was the company's heavy (or villain), F. C. Huebner, who married a local girl and settled down to a career of directing amateur plays and teaching elocution in Minnesota. Villains were traditionally the most stable and reliable members of a stock company.

Nor were the actors the only ones to benefit from the presence of the People's Stock Company. Two original plays were produced. The first of these new scripts, *Forsake Me Not*, was the work of two company members, Charles Coote and R. L. Cotton. Other than the play's originality there appears to have been little to recommend it. The second original, *Our Foreign Correspondent*, by Will O. Bates, former *Pioneer Press* drama critic, was a more successful effort, although it, too, failed to achieve further recognition. It is interesting, however, to muse about how many new playwrights and young actors might have been discovered and developed had the People's Stock Company continued to the present day. Unfortunately it came to an abrupt end on August 6, 1889, one year, one month, and 26 days after it had opened. The only reason appears to have been that, as in the case of Col. Wood's company, there was a change of management—a new management that preferred to book traveling troupes.

The Ferris Stock Company, 1902–1905

According to John K. Sherman, the most interesting theatrical personality during the first decade of the twentieth century was Dick Ferris. He was said to be a flamboyant man about town with a gift for promotion. With his wife, Grace Hayward, Ferris started in 1902 to lease the Lyceum theatre, and kept it running with plays of middling merit. Ferris was both manager and director, and frequently he took part in the plays, but he was considered more of a showman than an artist. [Sherman, 1958: 52–3.]

Audley Grossman echoes Sherman's opinion and adds that although Ferris was supposed to be 38 years old in 1905, vanity required that he remain 38 (a year younger than comedian Jack Benny's perennial age) until his death in 1933. [Grossman, 1957: 165.] The major reason for Ferris' questionable

Florence Stone and Dick Ferris, who appeared at the Lyceum Theater on Hennepin Avenue in Minneapolis in 1905.

Photo courtesy of the Minnesota Historical Society.

reputation, however, appears to lie in the fact that he married his first leading lady, Grace Hayward, and probably used her money, plus his own skill as a promoter, to establish the Ferris Stock Company. Then, once the company had been established, he deserted her for his next leading lady, Florence Stone, a union which also ended in divorce. These actresses were highly regarded, both as human beings and as artists, which seems to account for the fact that Ferris was sometimes hissed when he made an entrance. [*Minneapolis Tribune*, April 2, 1933.]

But in spite of his questionable reputation the fact remains that Dick Ferris was more active and lasted longer in the Twin Cities than any other theatre artist prior to Buzz Bainbridge. Although, as Sherman indicates, he fancied himself to be an actor and a director, he was primarily a promoter. The Ferris Stock Company opened at the (Hennepin Avenue) Lyceum, on August 31, 1902. The first season, relying primarily on melodramas, was apparently a great popular success. Ferris was reported to have netted a profit of $52,000, an astonishing sum (if correct) inasmuch as the top of his price scale was only fifty cents.

After the first season the enthusiasm apparently subsided since, at the end of his three year lease of the Lyceum, Ferris seems to have made no effort to extend his tenure. In the years to come, his company made a number of summer appearances at the Metropolitan, and in 1925 he appeared briefly as an actor with the Bainbridge Players, where his wife, Florence Stone, had become one of the featured players. Beatrice Morosco calls Florence Stone "the most adored woman in Minneapolis" and maintained that, "the beautiful lemon-haired woman . . . was one of the greatest actresses of her day. Her interpretation of Sardou's 'Cleopatra' caused even the astute David Belasco to acclaim it as one of the greatest performances he had ever witnessed." [Morosco, 1972: 11.] It seems clear that, although Dick Ferris may have had limitations as an actor and as a director, his eye for women was superb, as was his "tempestuous and flaring imagination" which was reported to be capable of promoting "almost anything." After leaving Minnesota he invested in oil wells and then began promoting Jim Jeffries, the world's heavyweight champion prize fighter—but not as a fighter for Jeffries had turned to religion. At the time of Ferris' death, he and Jeffries were planning a grandiose, religious "Disneyland" called the "New Jerusalem," designed to bring the faithful from around the world to a reconstructed Holy Land in California. [*Minneapolis Journal*, March 13, 1933.]

The Wright Huntington, Ernest Fisher and Shubert Players

The Wright Huntington Players first appeared during the summer of 1913 at the Metropolitan (May 11th to August 23). The most noteworthy achievement of this group may have been that it gave a young Minnesotan, Richard Dix, his start in show business. Dix eventually became a handsome, rugged All-American type of movie star who was featured in such films as *The Vanishing American* and *The Quarterback*. After this first summer at the Metropolitan, the company moved to the Minneapolis Shubert where they remained until May 1, 1915. The company's tenure in St. Paul was well summarized by the *Pioneer Press*:

> . . . When two seasons ago, the Shubert was leased by Mr. Huntington the venture was looked doubtfully upon by many who had seen similar institutions rise and wane there before them. To the surprise of everybody the clientele was gradually established that by degrees began to fill the house to capacity. [April 25, 1915.]

Although Huntington and many of his players departed, others did not. They remained in St. Paul under the umbrella of Ernest Fisher, a Minneapolis hotel man, and survived for another year at the Shubert as "The Ernest Fisher Players." The season closed and Fisher, like Huntington before him, departed, but once again the company did not die. The business manager at the Shubert was Frank C. Priest, who had come up through the ranks: first as a young actor on the "kerosene circuit" (a name applied to companies who toured small towns that still used kerosene lamps for stage illumination), then as the manager of the Lyric Theatre in Minneapolis, then later, manager of the Princess, and finally, in 1911, manager of the St. Paul Shubert, where he not only booked traveling attractions but was also on hand to observe the trials and triumphs of the local stock efforts by both Huntington and Fisher. And so after Fisher threw in the towel, Priest made his own bid. He picked a talented stage director, Guy Durrell, whom he had known as a member of the Huntington Players, and sent him to New York to select a company. With the aid of the Shuberts, Durrell did an excellent job, and the new company, under Durrell's direction, soon began to win praise from the critics and crowds for the Shubert Theatre. Charles Flandrau in reviewing the company's second production, *A Pair of Sixes*, concluded that "St. Paul should not only congratulate itself on having so talented a company in its midst, it should endeavor to retain them." [*The Pioneer*, September 18, 1916.]

Flandrau's review of *A Pair of Sixes* was the first among the many excellent notices that the company was to receive. It seems clear, both from the praise of the critics and from steady support of the public, that this Shubert Stock Company was one of the best resident companies that St. Paul had ever seen. The plays themselves were not especially noteworthy: *The Cowboy and the Lady*, *Jack of Diamonds*, *Captain Rocket*, etc., nor were most of the players recognizable stars. Generally speaking, it appears to have been a solidly competent company rather than an outstanding one. The one exception to this prevailing competence was a young man with a smiling face who had appeared briefly with the Wright Huntington Players. His name was Edward Arnold, and the *Pioneer* was able to announce:

> The girls will be glad to know that Edward Arnold is back. Followers of matinee idols will thrill with the announcement that the former member of the Shubert Stock Company here has been re-engaged and that he will join for second lead parts some time this week. Since leaving St. Paul Mr. Arnold has been prominent in a number of film masterpieces. [May 20, 1917.]

By December Arnold had been promoted to leading man and his popularity with both the critics and the public continued until the end of the season, when he returned to Hollywood where later his film gangsters, together with his "Mr. President" series on radio, made him one of the most popular actors in America.

Durrell, the director, who had done so much to establish the Shubert Company, left at about the same time as Arnold did, but the company refused to die. It continued its strong reputation for good productions until November 8, 1918, when it closed abruptly together with all movies, churches, soda fountains, and other places where crowds might assemble. The great influenza epidemic had struck St. Paul.

The Arthur Casey Players, 1926–1929

By early 1919 theatres and other places where crowds might congregate were permitted to reopen, but by then the Shubert Stock Company had disbanded. On January 26 another group, the Otis Oliver Company, opened and played until June 1. Then on August 21, 1919, the Bainbridge Players from Minneapolis began a full season. With his companies in both cities, Bainbridge often exchanged personnel and sometimes alternated productions. The project appears to have been quite successful, but it was not successful enough to survive. The St. Paul season closed on May 1, 1920 and did not reopen in 1921–1922.

In 1922 James Gray, who later became a well-known drama critic and novelist, tried unsuccessfully to establish a stock company composed mostly of students from the University of Minnesota. Then in 1925 L. N. Scott persuaded Bainbridge to try another season in St. Paul, but it closed after four productions. Finally, however, beginning on September 15, 1926, Arthur Casey opened what proved to be a very successful run of stock in the Orpheum Theatre, which had been redecorated and rechristened as the President.

Arthur Casey appears to have been the kind of leader who in more favorable times would have given St. Paul the permanent resident theatre it was always seeking just as Bainbridge was doing for Minneapolis. He came with an extensive background of stock experience in Duluth, Boston, and Kansas City. As a good promoter he managed to stir up considerable interest before his St. Paul season even opened. He released information about the remodeling of the Orpheum; he and his entire company were guests at a Rotary Club luncheon; on the opening night the mayor and one of the St. Paul city commissioners welcomed the company to St. Paul. This stress on good community relations continued throughout the year. Members of the company were frequent guests and speakers at local clubs; a University of Minnesota male quartet was included in Casey's October production of *Buddies*. On November 7 Grace Troy, a junior at the University, made her debut as actress and soon became a leading member of the group. Verna Steele, Lillian Nelson, and Virginia Safford were among other local talents who gained a hearing.

The plays produced were the popular pieces of the day, such as *Rain, Is Zat So*, and *Getting Gertie's Garter*. Most of the players' names are no longer recognized. Mary Hart (Mrs. Casey), Eugene Shakespeare, and Grace Troy were among the favorites. Probably the major ingredient in the company's ar-

tistic success was Arthur Holman, who did most of the directing and sometimes appeared as an actor. During the 1928–1929 season more and more use
was made of guest stars, but for the most part, their names are also no longer
remembered.

As the 1929–1930 season began, signs of trouble emerged. Apparently St.
Paul was beginning to feel the stress of the Great Depression. The mayor ap-
pealed to the city for support, Mary Hart campaigned, the St. Paul Gavel
Club pledged its backing, critics praised the productions, but, in spite of these
and other efforts, the Arthur Casey Players closed on November 23, for lack
of patronage.

Stock in St. Paul, however, did not die immediately. Arthur Holman,
director of the Casey Players, assembled a company and tried again in the next
season, 1930–1931. He is reported to have spent $25,000 redecorating the
Shubert, where the company opened on October 4. The season that followed
was probably about as good as Casey's seasons had been, but Holman was
battling the Depression and indications are that this season at the Shubert
barely managed to survive. Nonetheless, Holman announced another 32
week season for the next year, 1931–1932, and, with glowing promises of
support from groups like the Chamber of Commerce and the Women's City
Club, opened with great fanfare on October 10. But the enthusiasm was
short-lived; a bit over a month later Holman and his leading man resigned.
Other members of the company managed to struggle on until February 20,
when the Shubert, like so many other playhouses before it, was transformed
into a movie house. Still the company kept on trying. It first moved to the
St. Paul Auditorium and finally to Central High School. But even with the
help of Minnesota favorites like Grace Troy and Eugene Shakespeare the odds
against a resident professional theatre proved to be insurmountable, and the
last stock performance in St. Paul took place on March 20, 1932 at Central
High School.

The Bainbridge Players, 1911–1933

During most of these years while Huntington, Priest, Casey and others
were struggling with only partial success to establish a high quality resident
stock company in St. Paul, Minneapolis was able to look on with smug complacency. It already had a permanent stock company. Minneapolis, of course,
also managed to attract its share of other, more temporary stock companies,
but these fade in importance by comparison to The Bainbridge Players. By
1930 the Bainbridge company was in its twentieth season and claimed the distinction of being "America's Oldest Stock Company." Whether or not this

Robert Hyman, Blanche Yurka,
and John Dilson in
The Bainbridge Players production
of G. B. Shaw's *Candida* at the
Shubert Theatre, May 16, 1926.

Photo courtesy of the
Minnesota Historical Society.

claim was fully justified matters little, for longevity, as we shall see, was not
the major reason for the company's importance.

A. G. (Buzz) Bainbridge was born in Pittsburgh on September 4, 1885.
He came to Minneapolis while a small boy and attended Jefferson school. His
career as a showman was launched while still in his teens when he became a
circus bill poster and later an advance man. He also gained experience with
a wild west show. One day in 1909, while out of a job in Chicago, he met
L. N. Scott. Scott told Bainbridge that he was trying to find a stock company
that could play at the Metropolitan, which would otherwise be dark for six
weeks during the coming summer. Bainbridge had no company at the time,
but the brash young man agreed to supply one. Within a week he had succeeded in assembling a group of players and thus the theatrical career of Buzz
Bainbridge was launched. [*Minneapolis Sunday Tribune*, December 12, 1915.]
After his summer at the Metropolitan, Bainbridge disappeared to Duluth and
Winnipeg for two years, but by 1911 he was back in Minneapolis. According
to his obituary, "He was a genial and warm-hearted man whose friends were
numbered in the thousands—a man long prominent in the theatre and in
Shrine circles . . . His fondness for people and good fellowship prevented
him from accumulating a great deal of material wealth, and so long as he had
a dollar a friend could have it for the asking." [*Hennepin County History*, Winter, 1967.] And, according to John K. Sherman, Bainbridge knew how to pick
his stars and casts. The gifted Florence Stone could in one week, for example,

give verisimilitude and conviction to Rebecca (of Sunnybrook Farm) and in the next week, to a sultry Cleopatra.

Sherman mentions other stars but his list is far from complete. During the late twenties and early thirties both the quality of the plays and the quality of the performers set a new standard for stock companies across America. During 1925–1926 Blanche Yurka, a native of St. Paul who had become a Broadway star, appeared in *A Doll's House, Hedda Gabler, The Wild Duck,* and *Candida.* The 1926–1927 season included Marie Gale in *Seventh Heaven, Smilin' Through, John Ferguson, The Little Minister,* and *Anna Christie.* Other important plays that year included *What Price Glory, The Great Gatsby, The Vortex,* and *Romeo and Juliet,* as well as popular thrillers such as *The Gorilla* and *The Creaking Chair. Craig's Wife,* in 1927, was the eighth Pulitzer Prize winner that Bainbridge produced, the others being *Beyond the Horizon, Why Marry?, Miss Lulu Bett, Anna Christie, Icebound, Hell Bent for Heaven,* and *They Knew What They Wanted.* This was a marked contrast to the stock companies in St. Paul where Andrus, studying nine stock companies which operated between 1918 and 1939, found not a single production of a play by Shakespeare, Shaw, O'Neill, or by any of the Greek playwrights, and only a handful of plays by American playwrights of literary significance. After Victor Jory joined the Bainbridge Company during the 1928–1929 season the literary quality of the plays became even more impressive. The production of *An American Tragedy* had to be held over for an extra week, while *The Shanghai Gesture,* starring Florence Reed, played for three weeks.

Victor Jory deserves special attention not only because of his later successes on Broadway and in Hollywood, but also because of his achievements while in Minneapolis. *The Journal* described him as "a leading man, a character man, a singer, a clever boxer, a wrestler, and a poet." [January 5, 1930.] He also made numerous appearances as a public speaker and even tried his hand as a critic. By 1930, he claimed to have appeared in more plays by Eugene O'Neill than any other American actor. A special clause in his contract allowed him to pick two plays each season; the choices in 1930 were *All God's Chillun Got Wings* and *The Racket.* The Bainbridge Players production of O'Neill's *Strange Interlude* in 1930 was a mammoth challenge for any stock company, especially for the actors. Jory memorized 175 sides (typed pages with cues and speeches) and by the usual Wednesday deadline was "word perfect." Jory boasted that he now held the record for memorizing the longest role in the shortest time, and challenged other actors to deny his claim [*Minneapolis Star,* February 15, 1930.] He and the other leads, including Gladys Hurlbut who played Nina, had four complete changes of make-up, and Jory changed suits of clothing seven times.

It was probably Jory's influence that lured another outstanding actor to Minneapolis, Gladys George. Jory and George had worked together in stock

Victor Jory, who starred in many productions of The Bainbridge Players in the 1920's.

Photo courtesy of Jean Jory Anderson.

in Salt Lake City. The beautiful blonde quickly became one of the most popular of the Bainbridge leading ladies, starring in plays like *Mary the Third, The Brat,* and *The Three Bears,* before she moved on to success on Broadway.

But of all the performers discovered or imported by Bainbridge, the most intriguing, both personally and artistically, was Marie Gale. Her family had moved from Mason City, Iowa, and, according to her own story:

> . . . I went right down to the Shubert and asked if they had a job. That was in 1914 and I was a teen-ager. Buzz Bainbridge didn't even have that usual apprentice set of roles for me—a dead body or off-stage scream. So I just sat and watched Florence Reed, the visiting star, at rehearsals. That flattered her, so that she started telling Buzz to let me play this or that tiny part. [*Minneapolis Sunday Tribune,* August 22, 1965.]

Within a few years Marie Gale became the darling of the Shubert clientele and played an immense number and variety of parts from cheerful moppets like Pollyanna to sinful ladies like Sadie Thompson. She also became the darling of the boss. She and Buzz were married in 1917 and she retired from the stage long enough to bear him two sons. But she always came back, and even after the Bainbridge Players closed in order that she and Buzz might become mayor and first lady of Minneapolis, her career did not end. Following the death of her husband in 1936, she did some radio work and then finally made her way to Broadway in the New York production of *I Remember Mama.* A much later generation of Minnesota theatregoers had a chance to discover her charm and talent when she appeared in a superb production of *I Remember Mama* at the Old Log Theater in 1950.

Marie Gale Bainbridge as she appeared in The Bainbridge Players production of *Saturday's Children* at the Shubert Theatre, May 28, 1929.

Photo courtesy of the Minneapolis Collection, Minneapolis Public Library.

A list of other well-known players who made appearances for Bainbridge at the Shubert would have to include Mrs. Leslie Carter, Edith Taliaferro, Clara Kimball Young, Majorie Rambeau, Alice Brady, Florence Reed, Jacob Ben Ami, Bert Lytell, and Ben Erway. Minnesota's Lenore Ulric and Grace Troy also made featured appearances.

There can be little doubt that Buzz Bainbridge had an unusual gift for selecting plays, handling players, and charming audiences. He also seemed able to meet the innumerable miscellaneous problems that accompany the running of any theatre. According to a story in *The New York Telegram*, when the stagehands in his theatre went on strike he promptly filled their places with women and maintained that they did the work as well as men. Although the *Tribune* asserted that the *Telegram*'s report was not quite true, it does admit that Buzz Bainbridge could resort to novel and creative methods of solving problems.

That the Bainbridge Players fulfilled one of the major functions of a true resident company by becoming part of the community is emphatically indicated by the fact that Buzz Bainbridge was elected Mayor of Minneapolis in 1933. Whether because he came into office at a difficult time during the depths of the Depression, whether because ill health struck him down at this critical time, or whether he simply was not well cast for a role in politics seems uncertain, but in any case his political life was not remembered as a successful one. He died at the Veteran's Hospital on March 14, 1936, but as one of his obituaries concluded, "who can forget the smiling happy 'Buzz' who stood outside the little office in the Shubert Theatre and greeted the throngs passing into the world of make-believe." Many so-called resident theatres in the history of Minnesota began with a promise to do great things for the communities in which they were located, but then quietly faded away. The Bainbridge Players, on the other hand actually delivered. They represented the American stock company system at its very best.

7

The Great Road Companies, the Great Stars, and Others

As already indicated, theatrical touring companies were scarcely more indigenous to life in Minnesota than was their offspring, the movies. Both were imports, one came in Pullman cars from New York, the other in tin cans from Hollywood, yet, in spite of the fact that these road shows were intruders, they deserve attention, for they were the dominant form of theatrical entertainment which Minnesotans attended during the period from the Civil War through the Great Depression.

The slight human relationship that at first existed between road companies and the communities in which they appeared tended to diminish as the half century progressed. As we have seen, early traveling companies were usually family companies under the leadership of an actor-manager, like Charles Plunkett. Since such companies were self contained repertory units, adjustments could be made; engagements often lasted for a week or more and could be extended indefinitely or curtailed as the attendance warranted. Accordingly, an informal relationship between community and touring players was always possible, but by the end of the period this system had altered. The actor-manager had been replaced by a producer and a director, who remained in New York but still maintained an iron-clad control over the show; schedules had been condensed and rigidly limited. In most cases the repertory system had given way to the specialized production of a single play. A Broadway hit might spawn four or five road companies, each striving to be a carbon copy of the original. As someone once said, "When New York took snuff, cities sneezed all across America."

Augustin Daly, author of melodramas like *Under the Gaslight*, is usually credited with having originated the new system when his Fifth Avenue Company began sending out "combination companies" as early as the eighteen seventies. These "combinations" placed the emphasis upon the play rather than the players. Stars were avoided, at first, and type-casting began to be emphasized. From an audience's point of view this was an improvement, and from the producer's standpoint such specialized shows saved money. The actors were the ones who suffered. There was no longer a chance to develop as artists by playing a variety of roles, and any creative additions to the one role to which an actor had been assigned were quickly eliminated. George M. Cohan, for example, had a habit of calling his companies back to New York "to remove the improvements." In summary, rigid schedules prohibited companies from establishing friendly, informal relationships with the communities in which they appeared, while rigid directors prohibited actors from becoming creative artists.

A major exception to the above may be found in the case of the great stars who performed in the classics. *Hamlet,* for example, was presented in St. Paul nine times during the five years between May, 1884 and December, 1889, but judging from the reviews and the advertising it seems obvious that few people really came to see the play. They came instead to see Thomas Keene, Lawrence Barrett, Louis James, or Edwin Booth perform in the role of Hamlet. Edwin Booth could probably have attracted an audience had he been scheduled to read selections from one of the daily newspapers. This appeal of a star has, of course, never entirely disappeared, yet by the end of the period there was a noticeable change. Even the production of a classic found critics and audiences once more concerned with the play itself.

This shift of interest from the player to the play was only partially due to a weakening of the "combination" system. A more important balancing influence may be found in the quality of the playwriting. The old repertory of familiar classics and brainless melodramas naturally threw the emphasis upon the performers, but as these plays began to be replaced by the works of playwrights like Steele MacKaye, Augustan Thomas, Bronson Howard, and Clyde Fitch, the characters and their problems became more important, complex, and challenging; then finally, by the nineteen twenties, as MacKaye and the others were succeeded by playwrights like Eugene O'Neill, Maxwell Anderson, George Kelly, Elmer Rice and Sidney Howard, there was much more in the plays themselves to interest both critics and audiences.

So many plays, players and events are scrambled into these years that an examination of the whole would prove to be confusing and tedious. Moreover, other books are available on the subject. It seems advisable, therefore, to concern ourselves with only some of the road-show highlights of the period.

Shakespeare and the Great Actors

During the half century under consideration, Shakespeare remained a relatively constant and reliable pillar of strength. Most of the great actors, especially the men, felt obliged to prove their skill by performing Shakespeare.

Edwin Booth and actors of his troupe at Minnehaha Falls, Minneapolis, in 1886.
Photo courtesy of the Minnesota Historical Society.

The most famous actor of all was, of course, Edwin Booth. Booth visited the
Twin Cities in 1886, 1887 and 1888. His 1887 visit was perhaps the most
notable, for Booth had joined forces with his friend Lawrence Barrett to form
what was considered to be, and may well have been, the greatest repertoire
of classic Shakespearean tragedy that America has ever seen. As soon as the
company was announced, anticipation began to run high, but so did the cost
of booking it—so high in fact that both L. N. Scott, manager of the St. Paul
Grand, and J. F. Conklin, manager of the Minneapolis Grand, rebelled. The
result was that Booth and Barrett appeared at neither of the "first class" houses
but were seen instead as the opening attraction at a new Minneapolis theatre,
the Hennepin Avenue Theatre (later renamed the Harris, then the Lyceum,
and finally the Lyric). St. Paul was mortified. Critics and public vented their
scorn, disappointment, and anger upon Scott—the only time he is known to
have aroused general disfavor. *The Pioneer Press* began its scathing evaluation
of the situation as follows:

A FIRST CLASS THEATRE NEEDED. The necessity of a first-class theatre in
St. Paul, which has long been seriously felt, has never been more forcibly brought

> home to its people than this week, when, in consequence of the policy of the
> third-class manager of the second-class opera house in this city, they are subject-
> ed to the mortification and inconvenience of having to go to Minneapolis
> . . . [September 24, 1887.]

In the following year Scott and Conklin relented and brought the Booth-
Barrett combination to both cities after which all appears to have been
forgiven.

Booth was in his fifties when he made these visits to the area; critics noted
his advancing years and were also impressed by his quiet melancholy, which
added such depth and power to his performances—especially to the role of
Hamlet. Some of the greatness may have been supplied by the audience itself.
After all, the performance that counts is the one that takes place in the hearts
and minds of the auditors; members of Twin Cities audiences in the 1880's
were keenly aware of Booth's tragic life. Who knows, therefore, what
thoughts and half-formed images may have skimmed through their minds as
they filled the dramatic pauses; for example, the record-breaking sixty second
pause Booth sometimes took between the two halves of "to be—or not to be."

Booth's melancholy followed him off-stage as well as on. Charles Parker,
a Minneapolis manager, was never able to forget how returning home late one
night, long after the show, he saw Edwin Booth standing alone, gazing into
the window of a harness shop across the street from Schiek's cafe.

Hamlet was Booth's outstanding role but Twin Cities critics were equally
ecstatic about his Richelieu and his Shylock. *The Daily Globe*'s review of
Richelieu mentioned that there were "thunders of applause, and the great artist was compelled, as the curtain fell upon each act, to come forward and bow
his thanks." [October 1, 1886.] And another review marveled at his Shylock:

> His wolflike revenge, his joyless solitary life, his tenacity of passion and resolve,
> each of these varying emotions was so faithfully and withall so naturally brought
> out, that it seemed as if Mr. Shylock himself were there and not Mr. Booth. [*Pi-
> oneer Press*, September 23, 1888.]

Twin Cities audiences during these years saw not only performances by
American stars; international stars made frequent appearances, among them
Tommaso Salvini, whom John Rankin Towse, the New York critic, called
"the greatest actor and artist I have ever seen." Salvini was also the actor
whom Konstantin Stanislavsky, father of a creative approach to acting commonly known as "The Method," seems to have admired above all others. Attendance at Salvini's appearances in the Twin Cities seemed invariably to have
been disappointing—not surprising since he spoke only Italian while his supporting players answered in English. The high price of tickets, $2.00, may
also have had a limiting effect, but small houses did not dampen the ardor of

Julia Marlowe. About 1893.

Photo courtesy of the
Minnesota Historical Society.

at least one St. Paul critic, "It is doubtful whether the stage of any past epoch has furnished a match for this extraordinary man." [*Pioneer Press*, January 21, 1890.]

Shakespeare's popularity did not diminish as the half-century drew to a close. Walter Hampden, Sothern and Marlowe, Fritz Lieber, David Warfield, Robert Mantell, George Arliss, Otis Skinner, Maude Adams and others kept Shakespeare alive. E. H. Sothern and Julia Marlowe appear to have been Minnesota's favorites during these years. Long after repertory had been generally replaced by single specialized productions, Sothern and Marlowe continued to offer well-rounded programs which usually included *The Merchant of Venice, Romeo and Juliet, Twelfth Night* and *Hamlet*. Sothern, more clearly than most stars of the day, foresaw the future. He recognized the growing importance of the college, community and resident professional theatres of the present day when he expressed the opinion that what America needed was a municipal theatre devoted primarily to the production of the great literary classics [*Daily News*, February 1, 1920], a dream that Tyrone Guthrie finally began to realize in 1963.

The Winthrop Ames production of *The Merchant of Venice*, which played the two cities in 1928, featuring George Arliss as Shylock, deserved special notice. Not only was it a beautifully mounted production with supporting players like Peggy Wood, who of course played Portia, but it went a step further than even David Warfield had done in transforming Shylock into a tragic character rather than a comic or villainous one. For example, the old Jew, as he tried to leave the courtroom after having been stripped of everything except his life, suddenly collapsed. Antonio and Portia, the two most understanding of his tormentors, made a move to help him, but he brushed them off, struggled to his feet, and made his long exit with a quiet dignity that never failed to rock the house with applause.

Although the total number of Shakespearean productions remained surprisingly constant over the years, the popularity of the individual plays varied. *Richard III* and *Othello*, both very near the top in popularity during the early years, were seldom presented by 1920, while *The Merchant of Venice*, infrequently seen during the early years, finally exceeded even *Hamlet* in the frequency of its performances.

Other Stars and Other Classics

Although Daly's "combination" system deliberately tried to down-play the importance of the actors, it was never entirely successful. A star's name simply had too much publicity value, especially if the play was a well-known classic. During the period under consideration, great actresses were as effective as great actors in attracting an audience. Most of them, however, did not share the male drive to excel in Shakespeare. They were content to shine in the more sentimental and sensational pieces of the day, such as *Camille*, *Hazel Kirke*, and *East Lynne*, or in a few comedy classics such as *The School for Scandal*. A number of the most famous stars were foreign: Helena Modjeska (Poland), Fanny Janauschek (Bohemia), Rhea (Belgium), Adelaid Ristori (Italy) and Sarah Bernhardt (France).

Sarah Bernhardt, "the Divine Sarah," was undoubtedly the most colorful and the most famous, even though, like Salvini, high ticket prices plus a foreign language barrier presented problems. When she first appeared in 1887, her entire company spoke French, a disappointment to many who had assumed that English would be spoken. Although she read her lines in French, the *Pioneer Press* critic maintained that she "spoke unmistakably to the heart in a language that needs no interpreter." [May 3, 1887.] At the close of the second act of *Camille*, one St. Paul reviewer, writing a day later, maintained that "The very voice of the great actress was as if full of falling tears." [May 4, 1887]. When she returned in 1891, *The Minneapolis Journal* expressed concern about her language. "If she cares so little for that public as to remain ignorant to the national tongue, the public should and will care too little for her to patronize her performances." [October 4, 1891.] But when she returned once more in February, 1892, the *Journal* capitulated. "What a foolish waste of time and brain matter it would be for her to learn English. She might as

Helena Modjeska, appearing
at the Grand Opera House,
Minneapolis, during the 1880's.

Photo courtesy of the
Minnesota Historical Society.

well study Choctaw or Chinese." Bernhardt's last successful visit was in 1911. Her final appearance in 1918 can only be described as pathetic. She performed the last act of *Camille* during a patriotic World War I vaudeville program at the Orpheum. According to one reporter, "Burt Earle, a banjoist, and three young ladies were better received than she by the jazz enthusiasts in the audience." [*Daily News*, September 10, 1918.]

Among America's "emotional actresses" of the nineteenth century, Clara Morris was the most outstanding, even though her first appearance in 1884 was reported to have been marred by an unfortunate combination of temperament, ill health, and a disagreeable husband. *Camille*, *Article 47*, and *The New Magdalen* were among her favorites.

Not all plays favored by actresses were of the emotional type. Richard Brinsley Sheridan's plays maintained a steady following. In 1925 Minnie Maddern Fiske appeared in *The Rivals* with an all-star cast that included the extremely popular Chauncey Olcott. For several days preceding this presentation, Clayton Hamilton, the well-known author and critic, gave a series of lectures on Sheridan. As late as 1931–1932, Ethel Barrymore opened the touring season with an excellent production of *She Stoops to Conquer*.

During the nineteenth century portion of the period, Minnesota's favorite actress appears to have been another of those sprightly, musical young women, like Azlene Allen, Emilie Melville and Alice Oates. This time it was Lotta Crabtree, "100 pounds of sheer delight." She very nearly achieved Twin Cities importance in quite another way when, in 1888, the St. Paul newspapers announced that she had purchased the Grand Opera House. Then, just before the deal was legally closed, the Grand burned to the ground (January, 1889). At first there was some question as to where the loss would fall, but eventually the Opera House Company composed of L. N. Scott, Frank Clark, Andrew Delany, E. E. Davidson and William Davidson shouldered the loss estimated at $100,000, of which $60,000 was covered by insurance.

The abundance of noteworthy plays and players during the period is impressive. John Drew, uncle of the Barrymore clan, appeared in the Twin Cities several times between 1907 and 1917. He played in an easy "natural" style that never failed to impress the critics. Twin Cities audiences preferred Ethel among the Barrymores, partly because her visits continued into the nineteen thirties and forties when plays from New York were seldom seen.

Opinions were always mixed concerning Richard Mansfield who made a number of Twin Cities appearances between 1894 and 1906. Andrus described him as a "demon of temperament and conceit . . . who had to be the star of every situation." But in spite of his temperament, Minnesotans owed him a debt for bringing them three important examples of modern dramatic literature: *The Devil's Disciple* by Shaw, *Cyrano de Bergerac* by Rostand, and *Peer Gynt* by Ibsen.

Maude Adams made her first appearance in Minnesota in 1893 in *The Masked Ball*. In 1912 she returned in Edmond Rostand's *Chantecler*, which was deplored by St. Paul critics. Any disappointment, however, that the Twin Cities might have experienced in regard to her performance as Chantecler, the conceited rooster, was quickly forgotten the following year when she appeared as Peter Pan.

Among the stars who came primarily during the twentieth century was Helen Hayes who was seen in Kaufman and Connelly's *To the Ladies* in 1922, for which she received unusually high critical acclaim. Her later performances in *Victoria Regina* and *Harriet* were also lauded. Katharine Cornell, with Basil Rathbone as her leading man, made an impressive appearance in December, 1933, with productions of *Romeo and Juliet* and *The Barretts of Wimpole Street*. A list of the hundreds of other stars seen during these abundant years would have to include: Sir Henry Irving, Walker Whiteside, Billie Burke, May Robson, Mrs. Leslie Carter and Alla Nazimova. Several old standbys from former years like Joseph Jefferson and Frank Mayo also continued to visit the Twin Cities.

Modern Drama

In 1879, the same year in which Thomas A. Edison invented the electric light, Henrik Ibsen rocked the theatrical world with *A Doll's House*. This, of course, was not really the sudden birth of the drama of ideas that it has sometimes been pictured. Earlier writers on both sides of the Atlantic, including Ibsen himself, had already begun to write plays dealing with human problems, but *A Doll's House* still provides a convenient landmark for the beginning of "Modern Drama," under which title most of the better plays from Ibsen to Arthur Miller were to be studied in college English departments for decades to come. The following from the *Pioneer Press* is an interesting example of one of Ibsen's first critical receptions in Minnesota:

> Mr. Ibsen's drama, "The Doll's House" is a good representative of the whole group of Ibsen pieces — "The Pillars of Society", "An Enemy of Society", "Ghosts", etc. They are neither good for the stage nor good for the general reader. It is presumed that most people know, by this time, that Ibsen deals with the marriage question in this play, and treats it in a manner that is considered unconventional, that is, he gives the impression that marriage, in cases where the husband and wife do not thoroughly understand, trust in and love each other in all desirable ways, is a sort of slavery. Several years ago the play was produced in this country under the name of "Thora" by Mme. Modjeska, but although the brilliant talents of that fine actress were then at their meridian, it was a complete failure. The most shocking feature of the play is the desertion by the woman of her children. One does not pity the husband, who has hitherto treated her as a doll, and is awakened from his dream of superiority and petty providence by her decision to leave him, but it is just the question of the future of the innocent children, to whom a mother owes a special duty. The piece is not in any sense a play; it is an essay. [*Pioneer Press*, January 26, 1890.]

The conservative nature of St. Paul and its critics may also be seen in its reaction to Oscar Wilde, who lectured at the Grand Opera House in 1882. At least one critic was gratified by the fact that only a handful of people bothered to attend. Other examples of the conservatism of St. Paul audiences will be seen in the resistance to Sunday performances, in the ban against *Tobacco Road* in 1935 which forced its company to play two weeks in Minneapolis instead of the intended one week in each city, and in the outrage over "bedroom farces" which will be considered later. By the end of the period, according to Grossman, Twin Cities "morality" had begun to soften. Ibsen had become respectable, particularly in Minneapolis where a sizeable Scandinavian population was beginning to take pride in the achievements of the Norwegian master. An important breakthrough, as already mentioned, had been scored by the appearance of Richard Mansfield in *Peer Gynt* in 1907, even though the enthusiasm generated by this appearance may have been due to the popularity of Mansfield rather than to the international reputation of Ibsen or to the inherent values of the play. Of greater significance was Alla Nazimova's appearance in *Little Eyolf* and *A Doll's House*. Otherwise, Ibsen's plays were performed only by The Bainbridge Players and by various performances by Twin Cities amateur groups.

Even more noticeable than the commercial theatre's failure to present many of Ibsen's dramas was its failure to recognize the second great pillar of "modern drama," George Bernard Shaw. This failure of Shaw's wit, skill, and humanism to attract a following is puzzling, since he is one of the most entertaining playwrights who have ever lived. Moreover, he is not morally objectionable; his plays are devoid of profanity and lewd situations, which should have pleased even St. Paul. It may be instead that his humanism was politically and religiously objectionable. It is always more dangerous to upset people politically and religiously than it is to upset them morally. In any event, only four of Shaw's plays are known to have been booked into the Twin Cities between 1883 and 1933. These were *The Devil's Disciple* (1907), *Pygmalion* (1915), *Saint Joan* (1925), and *The Apple Cart* (1930).

The works of the great "modern" playwrights of Europe seemed to have had slight exposure in the Twin Cities prior to 1933. No commercial productions whatsoever by New York road companies have been found of any plays by August Strindberg, Ferenc Molnar, Arthur Schnitzler, John Galsworthy, John Millington Synge, Nicolai Gogol, or Maxim Gorky.

During the final years of the period, America's playwrights of literary importance fared somewhat better. In fact, during the 1920's they finally began to win world recognition. Earlier playwrights like William Vaughn Moody and Clyde Fitch had gained considerable attention nationally, but it was not until 1920 when Eugene O'Neill's *Beyond the Horizon* won O'Neill his first Pulitzer Prize that the literary world beyond America began to notice. A number of O'Neill's plays were soon to be seen in Minnesota. *The Emperor Jones*, with Charles Gilpin playing the Emperor as he had done in New York, arrived in 1922; *Desire Under The Elms* came in December, 1925; *Strange Interlude* was seen during September, 1929; and *Mourning Becomes Electra*, with Minnesotans Florence Reed and Walter Abel, played in April, 1932. Maxwell Anderson's *Elizabeth the Queen*, starring Alfred Lunt and Lynn Fontanne made a noteworthy appearance in 1931. On the whole, however, the American playwrights who dominated the road show business were the popular, semiliterary writers like David Belasco and George M. Cohan, together with others of lesser fame.

Popular Plays and Players:
The Money-Makers

In the twenties, when plays by writers like O'Neill and Anderson began to become available, the commercial theatre and especially the road companies, were under enormous stress simply trying to survive. Like shipwrecked sailors they grabbed for whatever might keep them afloat; long range problems had little meaning. "What will show a profit this week?" took precedence over "What might be the most profitable over a period of years?" Andrus and others feel that managers such as L. N. Scott made a mistake when they failed to take the long range view, for this tended to produce a theatre stressing entertainment only. In other words, as long as the legitimate theatre clung to the drama of words and ideas, to plays by Shakespeare, Molière, Sheridan, Ibsen, Shaw and O'Neill, it enjoyed a stage monopoly on the artistic expression of ideas, but, as soon as the legitimate theatre began to rely more and more upon sights and sounds, upon instinctive and emotional entertaiment values, it was thrown into deadly competition with other theatrical forms including opera, ballet, and, especially during the early twentieth century, into competition with movies, and vaudeville and radio. What did the popular stage play have to offer as "entertainment" that was not offered as well or better and cheaper by movies or vaudeville? What could it offer in the realm of visual and auditory arts that could equal the lavish scenery and beautiful sounds and sights of ballet and opera? But whether or not the theatre could have been saved had it embraced the more literary, intellectually challenging plays is difficult to judge. We only know that it did not do this, and that it did not survive. Those who still insist that better plays would have saved the theatre must admit that the big money-makers, measured in terms of their temporary but tangible income, were seldom plays with a high rating as dramatic literature. A few classics like *Hamlet*, *The Merchant of Venice*, and *The School for Scandal* might seem to be the exceptions, since they normally drew near the top in gross nightly income. It must be admitted, however, that their popularity may have depended more upon the great stars who performed in them rather than upon the literary appeal of the plays themselves. Moreover, from the standpoint of local managers, like Scott, such classics were not money-makers. Classic road company managers sometimes demanded and received 70% or more of the gross, while most companies were satisfied with the standard 60/40 split or even were content with 50/50.

In the early years of the period the big money-maker was still *Uncle Tom's Cabin*, but by the end of the period that had lost its appeal. Scott tried booking it in 1921, but the results were dismal. It fared even worse when he tried it again in 1928. Another of the big money-makers around the turn of the century has already been mentioned. This was Jacob Litt's *A Sea of Ice*, a melodramatic spectacle concerning the rescue of stranded survivors in the Arctic. It featured a steamship crashing through the arctic ice against a flaming background of northern lights, the Aurora Borealis.

Later the popular money-makers tended to shift away from rugged melodramas and spectacles toward the more gentle, sentimental comedy-dramas such as *Peg O' My Heart* by J. Hartley Manners. Laurette Taylor created the role of Peg in the New York production which incidentally also featured an old Minnesota favorite, Emilie Melville, as Mrs. Chichester. By the time *Peg O' My Heart* arrived in the Twin Cities the role of Peg had been taken over by a young Irish girl, "straight from the old sod," by the name of Peggy O'Neill. Twin Cities critics were ecstatic about her performance. All this was much to the joy of L. N. Scott whose gross for the week exceeded $2,000.

But the greatest money-maker of them all appears to have been *A Bird of Paradise*. Written, directed and produced by Richard Walton Tully, *A Bird of Paradise* was not only a smashing success when it first appeared in the area, it continued to succeed during its numerous return engagements and also whenever it was presented by a local stock company. Perhaps the most important road company productions were the ones with Lenore Ulric, who had been born in New Ulm, as the beautiful, ill-fated native girl, Launa. The romantic nature of the play is obvious from its title. That it is not great literature is not surprising, yet it was a comparative step in that direction. Arthur Hobson Quinn includes it in *A History of American Drama, from the Civil War to the Present Day* because in spite of all its color, romance, native dances, and mystic ceremonies it does attempt to explore a serious problem, a clash of two cultures. Moreover, it avoids the inevitable happy ending that characterized popular plays of its day. The great climax that so impressed its audiences came when Launa hurled herself into the flaming mouth of a Hawaiian volcano — invariably a scenic masterpiece of sound, smoke and flames!

A Bird of Paradise certainly made money. Andrus reports the following receipts for one week engagements in St. Paul from 1919 to 1922:

February 1919	$11,104.00
April 1920	11,211.00
February 1921	10,647.00
March 1922	6,402.00

Another very popular play, that, like *A Bird of Paradise*, treated a serious problem gently was *Abie's Irish Rose*. It tried to bring some common sense into the no-man's land of religious prejudice as a Jewish boy falls madly in love with a Catholic girl. But the play is loaded with so many lines intended for laughs that those who took its problem seriously were offended. Still it played for five consecutive weeks at the Metropolitan in St. Paul, thus continuing its ability, already seen in New York and Chicago, to set long-run records.

Among other romantic plays is one with local significance. *A Prince There Was* was adapted by George M. Cohan from a novel by Darragh Aldrich, a writer for the *Minneapolis Tribune*. Minneapolis naturally liked it, but when it played in St. Paul in January, 1920, Frances Bordman of the *Daily News* found its situations improbable and "sickeningly sweet," but concluded, "You'll enjoy *A Prince There Was* . . . So will your mother and the children." [January 12, 1920.]

Some plays and their players made no apology for being romantic and sentimental. Walker Whiteside who played the area with *The Master of Ballantrae* in 1920, stoutly defended such productions. As he told the *Daily News* reporter, "People do not want to go to the theatre to see a reproduction of life now. They don't want realism. They want a play. They want life heightened, stressed, contrasted. They want costumes, perfume, romance." [*Daily News*, March 16, 1920.]

Lagging not far behind the "perfume and romance" plays were some sentimental Irish musical plays. The names of the plays no longer matter, but the names of their star performers, Chauncey Olcott and Fiske O'Hara, were once almost as familiar to Minnesotans as the names of Paul Bunyan or Governor Ramsey. Chauncey Olcott was the star with the greater national reputation. He appeared in the Twin Cities seventeen times, playing at least 136 performances, more than any other actor (male or female) who was not a member of a resident company. He was typed as a "sympathetic, humorous, children-kissing, song-singing Irishman," his plays as "pure and sweet as breath from the new mown hay." But if Chancey Olcott had the greater reputation, Fiske O'Hara (obviously another Irishman) was the better singer. A *Pioneer Press* critic in 1913 expressed the opinion that trained ears listening to his Irish tenor might well be intrigued by "what could be done with it." From 1908 to 1924 O'Hara appeared frequently in St. Paul, usually opening the theatrical season for L. N. Scott with performances during Fair Week. His popularity both with Minnesota's rural State Fair visitors and with St. Paul's Irish inhabitants appears to have been almost indestructible. Songs like "My Wild Irish Rose," "Where the River Shannon Flows," and "When Irish Eyes are Smiling" retained their magic even when O'Hara appeared years later as a guest star with the Bainbridge Players during November, 1931. As the period moved towards its close another type of play became popular, the mystery thriller or "who done it?" One of the first and best was *The Bat* by Mary Roberts Rinehart and Avery Hopwood which played very successfully in 1922 and again in 1923.

There was yet another group of popular plays that delighted some and disgusted others. These were bedroom farces. These farces appeared, significantly it seems, shortly after the men began returning from France following World War I. *Parlour, Bedroom and Bath* arrived at the Metropolitan in February, 1919; *Twin Beds* in September, 1919; and *Up in Mabel's Room* in October of the same year. Public protests began to mount, but did not stop *Sleeping Partners* from being seen in September, 1920, nor *Ladies Night in a Turkish Bath* from playing a full week in October, 1921. Moreover, most of these farces appeared for repeat engagements. From February, 1919 to November, 1921 Andrus found ten weeks of "bedroom comedies" booked into the Metropolitan. Although these farces now seem innocuous and rather dull, St. Paul's club women complained, the mayor and city council objected, especially to the advertising — but the shows continued. They were popular, but not popular enough to save the commercial theatre from financial ruin.

The above account only scratches the surface. The abundance of live theatre during these years is indicated by Sherman:

> To pick a normally busy month at random, October of 1906, we find ten plays at the Metropolitan in 38 performances, five at the Lyceum in 40 performances, and another five at at the Bijou in 40 performances — a total of twenty plays in 188 performances in thirty-one days. [Sherman, 1958: 51.]

These figures covered Minneapolis only, yet by the time Buzz Bainbridge closed his theatre in 1933 to become mayor of Minneapolis the legitimate theatre was essentially dead — both its stock theatres and its road companies. The glowing exceptions were (1) a few high quality productions that continued to be toured into the Twin Cities via The New York Theatre Guild's subscription series, and (2), some courageous accomplishments on the grass roots level by Minnesota amateurs.

Generally speaking, audiences in the Twin Cities, like those in most of the nation during the period of the great commercial road companies, showed little interest in plays that tried to examine human life or its problems. Such things were left to theologians and philosophers. The stage was a place for amusement — with an occasional dash of Shakespeare added for cultural respectability.

Minnesota's Theatre Beyond the Twin Cities

Minnesota's theatrical activity was not limited to the Twin Cities (or, to a slightly lesser extent, to Duluth.) Lest anyone get such an impression a brief glance at the rest of the state seems necessary. The difficulty is that there is so much activity and that most of the record has been lost or not yet uncovered.

The development of theatre is, of course, closely related to transportation. Rivers obviously provided the only ready-made highways which meant that during the 1850's and 1860's settlements on the Mississippi River like Winona and Red Wing, or settlements on a tributary, like Stillwater, had essentially the same access to visiting theatrical troupes that St. Paul and St. Anthony did. Pioneers also followed the Minnesota River to establish settlements like St. Peter, Mankato, and New Ulm where German language drama blossomed almost as soon as it did in St. Paul. A bit later as railroads penetrated the woods and prairies in all directions, many troupes that played the Twin Cities, including the Plunkett and Macfarland companies, made excursions into the outlying centers of the region. Transportation, of course, was never rigidly limited to rivers and railroads; there were also horse drawn sleighs, wagons, and buggies that could carry smaller, mostly local units to neighboring towns.

My own theatrical career began with such a small semi-professional unit when I was about 15, not in Minnesota but in Utah. If I now conjure up a memory of these days it would include a large bob-sleigh drawn by thoroughbred horses plentifully arrayed with jingle bells. Inside the deep box of the sleigh went first a layer of hay, then a layer of hot rocks, then another layer of hay, then a layer of well padded quilts, then a layer of actors, and finally a plentiful layer of blankets. And there were other memories: the sandwiches, pickles and snacks before performances, the oyster stew suppers after the performances, the roaring fires in the huge pot-bellied stoves that heated the little auditoriums; the smell of grease paint; but above all, the bond of trust and good fellowship not only between members of the company but also between members of the company and members of the audience, for we knew most of them personally. I now realize what happened on those magic evenings was something much deeper than the theatre alone. It was a reunion of friends, a journey together into the land of make-believe. We were not important enough to be recorded in newspapers as most of the towns in which we played were too small to publish a newspaper. Maybe somewhere beside the grave of an unknown soldier there should also be a grave for an unknown theatrical trouper.

The larger professional companies usually travelled by rail and played in settlements that did have a newspaper as well as one or two restaurants, a grocery store, a general merchandise store, a bank, a livery stable, a church or two, a train station, and an opera house — an opera house not because a real opera company was ever expected to play there but because "Opera House" sounded so much more aristocratic and respectable than "Theatre." Until the time of the first World War the companies that played such communities were usually repertory or "rep. companies." Obviously a rep. company able to play three or four different plays could stay in a community three or four nights,

while one night stands were a drain on both money and energy. The Trousdale company, one of the best known companies that regularly included
southern Minnesota in its tours, finally developed a variation of the rep. system that was soon widely copied by others and became known as "circle
stock." The idea was to present the same play or plays in a circle of towns on
a regular basis. In addition to regularity there was an additional psychological
value; the entire circle of communities where the company played could each
feel that the Trousdale company was "our company."

   Such companies were preceded by an "advance man," usually a friendly,
fast talking salesman who not only distributed posters and handbills but also
secured licenses, reserved hotel rooms, booked the "opera house," and tried
to con the local newspaper editor and other key citizens into supporting the
project. The problem was that the most obvious way to encourage support
was to offer free passes; a common practice which often resulted in an audience of "dead heads," for people who get something for nothing are notori-
ously ungrateful.

   The history of at least one city in Minnesota has been studied carefully by
Evelyn Anderson, who wrote a master's thesis on St. Peter, Minnesota. She
found much that was interesting but little that was surprising. Theatrically the
history of St. Peter resembled that of St. Paul but on a smaller scale and at a
later date. Charles Plunkett, Billy Marble and John Dillon were the favorites
in St. Peter. Theatrical activity increased when the attractive 700 seat Ludke
theatre opened in 1905. It was torn down in 1944. As far as local contributions were concerned there was again the theatrical activity of St. Peter's German inhabitants; there were also a number of community plays and church
plays directed by Mrs. C. T. Weibezahn; and there was some outstanding
work done at Gustavus Adolphus College.

   Silent movies, shortly before and after World War I, naturally began to
provide stiff competition for medium and small sized theatrical companies,
but surprisingly as the 1920's advanced, the rep. shows with live actors tended to gain the upper hand; this was true not only in Minnesota but throughout
the Central States. This came about partly because the novelty of silent films
wore off, partly because most of the 1920's were comparatively prosperous,
partly because many of the companies learned to carry their theatres with
them in large "circus tents," but mainly because live actors could adjust to the
tastes and traditional values of their audiences. As Jere Mickel points out in
his excellent study, *Footlights on the Prairie*, the essentially rural audiences of
the whole central region were very different from the audiences in the
cities—or, at least, they thought they were. The emphasis still centered on
"entertainment" meaning that legitimate theatre, vaudeville, bands, county
fairs and carnivals were closely related. To true rural minds, however, this
was not "city entertainment," it must instead be "wholesome entertainment."

Above all such entertainment was expected to reinforce rural values. Plays by writers like Ibsen, Shaw, or O'Neill that questioned or challenged these values were ignored or stoutly resisted. Even as late as 1952 a University of Minnesota tour of Eugene O'Neill's *Ah, Wilderness!* resulted in a storm of angry letters from the prominent citizens in Sleepy Eye, Minnesota. As a result of this extreme sensitivity about morals, most companies tried to pose as family companies. Their reputations off-stage as well as on were important. They paid their bills, and, if able, gave free band concerts in the park, and again, if able, tried to field a baseball team that could hopefully defeat the local team, thus proving that actors were real people not sissies.

Out of all this emphasis on rural values, a favorite character developed in the plays of the rep. companies. His name was Toby. He was a freckle-faced, red-headed, farm boy who in the beginning of a play invariably seemed to be a comic oaf in comparison to his polished city slicker rival, but Toby's common-sense and rural integrity invariably outwitted the aims of his polished rival before the last act was over.

Mickel maintains that the leading lady (or in some companies the ingenue) was often blessed by something less than an hour-glass figure and with something less than abundant histrionic talent, but she usually had one indispensible qualification. She was the wife of the manager!

During the 1930's tent rep. shows became fewer and fewer as talking pictures gained the upper hand. Novels like *Main Street* by Sinclair Lewis gradually eroded the myth of rural moral superiority; moreover, the automobile, the airplane, and the mass media gradually turned America into one large cultural omelette. By the 1940's tent rep. shows were largely a memory. Incidentally, one of the last tent shows to end its tours and one of the best was the Aulger Brothers Players Company which was based in Mankato, Minnesota.

We may smile at the old nineteenth century theatre of thrills, spectacle, laughter, and tears, but it had its rewards. John Steinbeck's words at the funeral of one of these old actors may apply, "He was an actor, a member of that incorrigible band to which belonged gypsies and vagabonds and against whom laws were passed lest they cause living to be attractive, fear unthinkable, and death dignified."

PART THREE

Professional Interlude: The Amateurs Come of Age 1933–1963

8

From Little Theatres to Community Theatres

HE three decades from the demise of The Bainbridge Players in 1933 to the opening of The Guthrie Theater in 1963 took the nation through the Great Depression, World War II, the Korean War, and the Cold War. In the theatre, musical comedy emerged as the dominant form on Broadway; "The Method" become the dominant form in serious acting; there was a drastic decline in the number of road companies; and the amateur theatre achieved a respectible level of maturity. In fact, as far as Minnesota was concerned, amateur achievements provided the primary interest of the period.

The Professionals of the Period

As far as the professional theatre in Minnesota was concerned, a general impression seems to be that it dropped dead as soon as The Bainbridge Players departed from the Minneapolis Shubert in 1933. This, as already indicated, is far from the case. True, the number of New York road shows dropped from 36 in 1932–1933 to 9 in 1933–1934, but the quality of the 1933–1934 season largely compensated for the drastic drop in quantity, and this was also true during the years that followed. For example, not many, but a few very impressive productions of Shakespeare continued to be presented; *The Taming of The Shrew* with Alfred Lunt and Lynn Fontanne (1939); Maurice Evans in his uncut version of *Hamlet* (1940); Margaret Webster's *Macbeth* with Evans and Judith Anderson (1942); Paul Robeson in *Othello* (1944); and an unforgettable Katharine Hepburn as Rosalind in *As You Like It* (1951). Shaw also managed to attract a few bookings which included *Man and Superman* (1949) and *Don Juan in Hell* (1950). Ibsen was represented by Eva La Gallienne and her Civic Repertory Company in *Hedda Gabler* and *A Doll's House* (1934) and by Ruth Gordon and Paul Lukas in *A Doll's House* a few years later. Greek and Roman classics even made their appearance: *Medea*, starring Judith Anderson

(1949); *Amphitryon 38*, the Giraudoux adaptation of the Amphitryon story, with Lunt and Fontanne (1939). Nor were these established classics the only important examples of dramatic literature that road companies brought to the Twin Cities. An impressive array of modern plays and players appeared on local stages: *Elizabeth The Queen* again starring Lunt and Fontanne; *Victoria Regina* starring Helen Hayes; *Whiteoaks* and *The Corn is Green* starring Ethel Barrymore; *The Little Foxes* starring Tallulah Bankhead; and *The Fourposter* with Hume Cronyn and Jessica Tandy. There was also *Mister Roberts*, written by Minnesota's Tom Heggan, and *The Tender Trap* written by another young Minnesotan, Max Shulman, in collaboration with Robert P. Smith. Shulman, from St. Paul, may be best known for his '50's television hit, *The Many Lives of Dobie Gillis*.

From the above it is obvious that the professional road company business between 1933 and 1963 did not completely wither away. Approximately half a dozen plays were trouped into the area annually, practically all of them produced by the New York Theatre Guild, which therefore deserves primary credit for keeping the professional theatre alive. There were, however, a few others who also kept it breathing. At least five groups, as we shall see in Chapter 10, tried to establish local professional theatres in the area, and two of them, The Old Log Theater and the Paul Bunyan Playhouse, succeeded. Nevertheless the fact remains that most of the significant contributions to Minnesota's theatrical history during these decades came primarily from dedicated amateurs.

Amateurs of the Late Nineteenth Century

Any suggestion that the amateur theatre was limited to the years between 1933 and 1963 would be an unfortunate distortion. A discussion of the amateur theatre belongs in this period primarily because these were the years during which it reached comparative maturity, even though amateurs had been active in Minnesota as early as the 1820's at Fort Snelling. Old newspapers and other sources produce hints, bits, and pieces of evidence concerning their work, especially during the last quarter of the nineteenth century, but most of the activity appears to have been on a very shallow social-recreational level. As an example, there is the following report from the *St. Paul Pioneer Press*:

> Parlor Theatricals. A most delightful entertainment of this character took place on Friday evening, at the residence of Mrs. Dr. Brisbine on Pleasant Avenue. The principal feature of the evening was the presentation of the sparkling little comedy entitled "Smashington Goit" . . . Following the farce a Shakesperian (sic) charade introduced Mr. Strickland in a soliloquy, Miss Newington recited a

poetical selection, and a pleasant dance and elegant supper concluded the evening's pastime . . . Two brilliant little farces will be rendered at the splendid
residence of William Pettit, Esq., on Summit Avenue to-morrow evening. The
pieces are entitled, "A Cup of Tea" and "Done on Both Sides", and will be represented by Miss Pettit and Messrs. White, Fogarty and Hanson. Quite an elegant
miniature theatre has been prepared in the spacious drawing rooms with all of
the conventional theatrical accessories. [*Pioneer Press*, November 21, 1875.]

During the early years of the twentieth century the amateur activity seems
to have improved, especially some of the ethnic activity. We know, for example, that shortly after World War I a strong Yiddish theatre was organized.
It usually performed in the Labor Lyceum which had a proscenium stage and
an auditorium equipped with about 200 folding chairs. Among the plays
produced was a Yiddish version of *King Lear*. They even toured one play as
far as Duluth, over unpaved roads.

We also know that Scandinavian performers were very active. Anne
Charlotte Harvey and Richard Hulan published an interesting account concerning Swedish-American road shows in the *Swedish-American Historical
Quarterly*. Another source informs us that in 1910 a Swedish Dramatic Club
presented Ibsen's *Ghosts* at the Metropolitan, and that a famous Swedish actor,
Elis Olson-Ellis visited Minneapolis to perform the title role in *Sten Stenson
Steen fran Eslof*. The performance was later repeated in Duluth. The activities
of the amateur German language theatre in St. Paul, New Ulm, and elsewhere
has already been described. In other words, we know enough about such amateur activity to realize that we know very little. Yet clearly the interest in amateur theatre helped support the establishment of a chapter of the Better Drama League of America in Duluth in 1912.

The Little Theatre Movement

The Little Theatre movement started some two decades before our ar-
bitrary date of 1933; it, in turn, was related to an earlier and much larger
movement, the age of science, already in full bloom during the last half of the
nineteenth century. This age of science was the result of a new way of
thinking—a willingness to rely on rational and experimental evidence—on
"natural" explanations, no matter how complicated or unpleasant, in prefer-
ence to supernatural interpretations, no matter how simple or comforting.
This scientific attitude soon began to produce wonders in the physical
sciences, resulting in machines, inventions and medical miracles. Idealists and
intellectuals quite naturally began to hope for a break-through in the humanities and social sciences that would give human beings the same understanding

of and control over human nature that the physical sciences were providing in control over the environment.

In the world of the theatre, for example, a French playwright, Emile Zola, proclaimed that the stage should become a laboratory; a place where bleeding slices of life could be presented, examined, analyzed and hopefully understood. In Scandinavia Henrik Ibsen and August Strindberg began probing relentlessly into the nature of human behavior; in Russia Anton Chekhov and Nikolai Gogol began doing much of the same thing; in Germany and Austria the crusade was headed by playwrights like Arthur Schnitzler and Gerhart Hauptmann; and in England there was that master of wit and intelligence, George Bernard Shaw. Nor was this spirit of theatrical revolt and innovation confined to playwriting. In acting, Konstantin Stanislavsky originated a new "creative approach," while Gordon Craig and Adolphe Appia revolutionized methods of lighting and staging. In directing, Andre Antoine in France and Otto Brahm in Germany created small non-professional theatres where simplicity, honesty, ideas and naturalism could be emphasized.

In America one of the early results of this new spirit was a high-minded intellectual revolt against old ways of doing things; a revolt that became known as the Little Theatre Movement. It was spearheaded by professional artists like Percy MacKaye, Sheldon Cheney, Robert Edmund Jones, and Kenneth Macgowan. The movement towards smaller, more intimate theatres and better dramatic literature acquired power, respectability and strong support from American colleges and universities through the efforts of pioneers like George Pierce Baker at Yale, Alexander Drummond at Cornell, Maud May Babcock at Utah, Thomas H. Dickinson at Wisconsin and Richard Burton at Minnesota.

On March 22, 1910, The Better Drama League of America was organized in Chicago with Mrs. A. Starr Best as president, Mrs. Henry L. Frank as first vice-president, and Dr. Richard Burton as second vice-president. A major aim of this drama league was to establish a chapter in every important American city. Each chapter would be dedicated to the encouragement of good drama and the discouragement of bad, by the refusal of its members to attend plays of which they disapproved. The organization also issued a quarterly magazine, *The Drama*, which had a profound influence, even though it was replaced in 1916 by an even more potent periodical entitled *Theatre Arts*.

With the University of Minnesota's Richard Burton as one of the Drama League's founding officers, it might have been expected that a strong chapter would immediately be established in one or both of the Twin Cities, but this was not the case. A Minneapolis chapter led by Mrs. George Palmer lasted only from 1930 to 1938. Perhaps the fact that the Bainbridge Players were already producing a surprising amount of good dramatic literature as well as the fact that both the University of Minnesota and the St. Paul colleges were frequently mounting impressive literary productions, relieved the pressure for such a chapter.

The Duluth Playhouse (1912 to Date)

In any case, the historic campaign for better drama in Minnesota took place not in the Twin Cities but 160 miles north, in Duluth, where on February 12, 1912, Mrs. S. R. Holden assembled a small group for the purpose of organizing a chapter of the Better Drama League. The crusade they initiated was not so much against the trivial nature of amateur dramatics, as exemplified by the nineteenth century "Parlor Theatricals" mentioned earlier, as it was a crusade against the commercial theatre and its commercialism. It was a high-minded crusade, deadly serious, determined to replace both the recreational amateur theatre and the commercial professional theatre with an "art theatre," a theatre that would present dramatic literature rather than entertaining trash. Accordingly, during its first two years, members of the Duluth chapter of the Drama League tried to persuade commercial managers to present better plays, but their success was minimal. Frustrated in their efforts, they finally decided to produce their own plays. Defying contrary advice from the national headquarters in Chicago, the Duluth Chapter of the League remodeled an old Christian Science church into a small, very intimate playhouse which they christened "The Duluth Little Theatre." They opened on November 17, 1914, with a world premiere of George Bernard Shaw's *The Dark Lady of The Sonnets.* This opening attracted attention far beyond Duluth. *Harper's Weekly* even noted the event with an editorial.

In the years to come the Duluth Little Theatre not only produced plays of literary importance it also presented an impressive array of speakers, including Percy MacKaye, father of the Drama League idea, Lady Gregory, grand old lady of the Irish theatre, Granville-Barker, the great English dramatist-critic-writer, as well as such regional celebrities as Thomas H. Dickinson from the University of Wisconsin. World War I closed the theatre temporarily, but it soon reopened and by 1924 decided to hire Maurice Gnesin as its first full-time director. Gnesin immediately began producing such Russian classics as *He Who Gets Slapped* and *The Lower Depths.* Gnesin was followed by a number of other notable directors including John Wray Young (1933–1936). Young was not only a skillful play director; he and his wife, Margaret Mary, were high quality human beings who greatly increased respect for the theatre through community participation and interest. Another of Duluth's full-time, affectionately remembered directors was Ultmont Healy (1943–1952). Under such leadership the Duluth Little Theatre gained a national reputation. In 1941 it changed its name to The Duluth Playhouse,

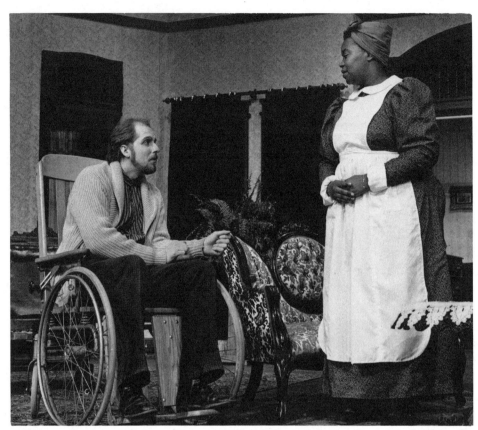

The Little Foxes (1941), directed by Gregory Foley. Jenita James and Jack Starr. Photo courtesy of Duluth Playhouse.

a name which was thought to be less high brow and elitist. The Playhouse now lays claim to being the oldest community theatre in the nation. Today, though it no longer employs a full-time director, it does find itself comfortably housed in the St. Louis County Heritage and Art Center (the city's former Union Depot) as one of the living art treasures of the area. In common with other such theatres it is able to supplement its ticket (earned) income with modest grants from the State Arts Board and other sources. Incidentally, the 1988–1989 season will mark the seventy-fifth anniversary of this historic group.

Community Theatres in the Twin Cities

The Little Theatre movement, while never as strong in the Twin Cities as it was in Duluth and many other cities, still exerted an influence which

A Man for All Seasons (1965), directed by Donald Durand. James Kish, Steve Friedman and A. D. Ludden.

Photo courtesy of Duluth Playhouse.

resulted in a laudable and honest effort to improve the quality of the theatre. The movement's early leaders, both locally and nationally, were men and women with talent, intelligence and integrity. But all good movements soon attract fools and phonies. This was especially true in the Little Theatre movement whose social dilettantes and aesthetic freaks became more and more numerous until they were finally unmercifully and quite justifiably satirized by George Kelly in his comedy, *The Torch Bearers.* Consequently, by the middle of the century the words "Art Theatre" and "Little Theatre" had joined the trash heap together with other terms like "Elocution" and "Oral Expression." "Community Theatre" finally emerged as the acceptable name for such amateur groups, but in spite of different names, amateur groups, like professional groups, continue to rise or fall primarily on the basis of how well and how convincingly they produce plays. Theories and names are only a matter of style and decoration. The things that count are the quality of the play and its production.

Douglas P. Hatfield, in his study of the amateur theatres of the Twin Cities area from 1929 to 1963, found 35 community theatres that merited attention. Only a few of the most representative will be considered here.

The Studio Players (1916 to 1929)

One of the earliest community groups, related in spirit if not in name to the ideals of the Better Drama League of America, was founded in 1916 by Charles and Louise Holt, who taught at the Minneapolis School of Music, Oratory, and Dramatic Art. The Holts also frequently directed plays at the University of Minnesota. The Studio Players began as a closed group, active participation being limited to their own current or former students. Performances were at first given at the school's recital studio, hence the group's name, but by 1925 the activity was transferred to the Woman's Club, located at 16th Street and Harmon Place in Minneapolis.

Although the Studio Players apparently never became an official chapter of the Better Drama League of America, they obviously staunchly supported its ideals. The plays they produced were invariably of literary importance, often those being studied in college English courses under the title of "modern drama". Entire seasons were sometimes based on a theme such as "Woman as Man Thinks She Is", chosen for 1926–1927. Moreover, the plays were often accompanied by lectures. The plays which followed that theme were *Man and Superman* by Shaw (woman pursues man); *The Tragedy of Man* by Masefield (woman betrayed by man); *Chains* by Goodman (woman breaks with conventions); and *Man and The Masses* by Toller (woman as a leader). Charles Holt stopped directing in 1926, but Mrs. Holt carried on until 1928 when advancing age and hearing problems also forced her to retire. With their Studio Players the Holts had made a distinguished contribution to the quality of the theatre in the Twin Cities.

The Portal Players and the Assembly
Players (1922 to 1937)

The Portal Players, who began producing in 1922, tried to avoid the usual classics such as Shakespeare, Ibsen and Shaw, preferring instead to produce the unusual modern classics seldom seen in America—plays such as *Six Characters in Search of an Author* (Pirandello), *He Who Gets Slapped* (Andreyev), *The Brothers Karamazov* (Dostoevsky) and *The Adding Machine* (Rice). Programs indicate that the plays were directed by a mysterious James Monteblas, but Hatfield discovered that no such director existed. The plays instead were directed by Dean Jensen, a free-lance writer, and Helen R. Fish, the outstanding drama director at Minneapolis' South High School.

The community efforts of Ms. Fish were not limited to the Portal Players. She had an equal, if not greater influence on the Assembly Players at the Unitarian Center in Minneapolis. During the early years of these Assembly Players (when Ms. Fish was doing most of the directing) the group concentrated on classics such as those by Ibsen and Shakespeare. As the Depression deepened, however, the group turned more and more towards modern plays with social and political significance. On April 28, 1934, a production of *Precedent* created such excitement that the Minneapolis Central Labor Union sponsored it for production at the Shubert Theatre. Eventually the Assembly Players veered so far to the political left that some members, including Tom Russell, the technician and one of the directors, resigned. By 1937 the Assembly Players had faded away.

The Group Theatre (1930 to 1955)

Most community theatres of the twenties and thirties began with high hopes and noteworthy literary, social or political ideals. This was especially true in St. Paul where an impressive beginning was made by St. Paul Community Theatre, Inc., in 1928. Unfortunately it did not last, but another St. Paul unit, The Group Theatre, fared better. It began at the Jewish Center on Holly and Grotto Streets and was first known as the Grotto Players until it later transferred most of its activities to the downtown YWCA. Religiously oriented in a very humanistic way, the Group Theatre, under strong leadership from Ethel and Sylvan Pasternak, Jack Gelber, and Donald Singerman, developed a dedicated following. It selected plays with "artistic integrity"— preferably, also, plays with an abundance of social significance—plays like *Awake and Sing* by Odets, and *The Dybbuk* by Ansky.

In acting, the Group stressed the creative "Stanislavsky" approach and encouraged the idea that almost anyone can act. Jack Simos' book, *Social Growth Through Play Production*, was inspired by The Group's social and artistic values. The Group Theatre possessed an idealism and a dream of a better world that was so lacking in the commercial theatre. Its active life unfortunately came to an end in 1955 when Donald Singerman suffered a serious illness.

The Edyth Bush Little Theatre
(1940 to 1965)

The most unusual and promising of all the Twin Cities community theatres, perhaps even in the entire nation, was the Edyth Bush Little Theatre. The building itself was a birthday gift—a present to Edyth Bush from her husband, Archibald Granville Bush, one of the founders of 3M, the Minnesota Mining and Manufacturing Company. Before she married, Mrs. Bush had been an actress-dancer, and a theatre building was therefore a generous and appropriate birthday gift. Moreover, it was a superb little theatre, well designed and intimate, seating just under 300. It was located at 690 South Cleveland Avenue, in St. Paul. Mrs. Bush announced that her theatre was open to Minneapolis as well as to St Paul, as "a home for any who wished to participate in good drama." Unfortunately, most people assumed that the Bush family fortune would provide a firm financial foundation for the theatre's operation. Mr. and Mrs. Bush, on the other hand, had accumulated their fortune via hard work and skillful management and felt, understandably so, that the theatre should be basically self-supporting.

Largely because of such a misunderstanding, the Edyth Bush Little Theatre never really managed to live up to its great potential. Much of the problem was undoubtedly the overly sensitive ego of Mrs. Bush herself, but, after all, it *was* her theatre—a fact that actors and especially directors seemed constantly to forget. But she cannot be entirely absolved from blame. She pretended to be democratic, yet when directors tried to make decisions regarding plays, casting, or other matters, she sometimes stepped in with a veto. Moreover, unlike most of the early community theatres which were dedicated to liberal, humanitarian ideals, Mrs. Bush tended to be equally dedicated to very conservative ideals. The choice of plays was largely limited to those that were morally and politically inoffensive, plays stressing entertainment and conservative morals rather than ideas. Directors found it difficult to work with her and most of them soon resigned or were fired. Perhaps the most successful was James Grunke. At the end of his term he was not fired but was promoted to a position at 3M.

In 1965 Mrs. Bush became too ill to continue the management of her theatre so its ownership was transferred to Hamline University. Hamline, in turn, transferred the building to the Chimera Theatre in 1976. Finally, in 1981, building inspectors decreed that new rest rooms and a wheel-chair ramp would have to be added to bring the structure "up to code." Chimera, unable to assume such an expense, decided to sell it, but the deal was blocked. In the meantime water pipes had frozen making the theatre unusable, so the Edyth Bush Little Theatre is primarily a rather sad story of what might have been.

Theatre In The Round Players
(1951 to Date)

The most successful community theatre in Minnesota and perhaps the most successful in the entire nation—a community theatre that has survived and deserved to survive—is most commonly known simply as TRP.

The immediate ancestor of TRP was the Circle Theatre Players, which, under the direction of Frederick Hilgendorf, presented a series of four plays in a small arena at Minneapolis' Calhoun Beach Club during the 1951–1952 season. Unpaid bills caught up with the group early in its second season, and it was officially terminated on October 22, 1952. But seven members of the group refused to let the idea die. During 1952 they reincorporated, this time under the present name, and began selling memberships. They next set up a small theatre in the Minneapolis YWCA's Benton Hall and employed Hilgendorf to direct the plays on a show–by–show basis. This was distinctly contrary to the widely accepted belief that the first thing a community theatre must do is to employ a regular full-time director. But in the case of TRP, the policy of using numerous directors has proved to be so successful that, as Mike Steele wrote in 1977, "Theatre in the Round has served as a national and regional model."

In 1963 TRP moved to the old Wesley Temple Annex on Stevens Avenue in Minneapolis. It then lost its lease and again was threatened with extinction. TRP had always prided itself on being self-supporting, but faced with the problem of survival, it launched a fundraising drive in the community which netted some $32,000, enough to remodel an old burned-out pizza parlor into a humble but extremely effective arena theatre in the West Bank Entertainment District of Minneapolis. Proximity to the University of Minnesota proved to be advantageous, both through an increase in its potential audience and through an increase in the availability of talent. Moreover in 1983 the area acquired a 16 story hotel, a 772 car municipal parking ramp, restaurants, and saw continued expansion of the West Bank Campus of the University of Minnesota.

As early as 1972, Dan Sullivan in an article for the *Los Angeles Times* entitled "Off-Guthrie Theatre Thrives," singled out a few theatres in the Twin Cities that were doing outstanding work before Guthrie arrived, and his chief praise went to TRP. The play he had just witnessed there was *The Chalk Garden*, directed by Charles Nolte. He concluded his article with "The amateurs at TRP meet the dictionary definition of that word. They love theater, they give it their best, and their best seems to get better every season." [*Los Angeles Times*, February 19, 1972.] And "their best" has been recognized. In 1973 *The Unknown Soldier*, written and directed by Warren Frost, was selected via na-

The Unknown Soldier (1973),
directed by Warren Frost.
Virginia Harris and Mac Harris.

Photo courtesy of
Theatre in the Round Players,
Mike Paul/Act Two, photographer.

tional competition to represent America at the International Festival of Community Theatres held in Monaco. In 1983 TRP took first place in competition with other Minnesota community theatres for Christopher Durang's *The Actor's Nightmare*, and yet another first was won in 1985 for *Tennessee.*

TRP is amateur in the best sense of the word. Only two positions are funded: the salary of an administrator responsible for holding everything together, and a small stipend paid to each director. Approximately 40,000 volunteer hours are contributed annually in producing an ambitious, usually ten play season. Some 1,500 actors and actresses are included in TRP's audition list, most of them thoroughly trained and experienced. A major reason that so much talent is available is a conviction, based on past history, that any new show at TRP will be a good one—in which all connected with the production can take pride. This is partly because the list of directors over the years has been impressive. The list would have to include Stephen Kanee, Claude Woolman, Douglas Hatfield, Al Rossi, James Wallace, Charles Nolte, Lee Adey, Robert Snook, Jean Congdon, Scott McCoy, Karen Osborne, Gordon Howard, Gary Gisselman, Warren Frost, Mac Harris, and Dr. Richard Fliehr.

Dr. Fliehr, an M.D., who also holds a degree in Theatre Arts, has been a mainstay of the group almost from its beginning, as has Paul McCormick (Mac) Harris, president of the Twin Cities American Federation of Television and Radio Artists (AFTRA). Dr. Fliehr and his wife, Kay, have both served nationally as presidents of the American Community Theatre Association (ACTA).

The Great White Hope (1975), directed by Michael Arndt. Earnest L. Hudson and Willis Burks.

Photo courtesy of Theatre in the Round Players, Mike Paul/ Act Two, photographer.

In vivid contrast to the bedroom farces, the spectacles, and the popular entertainment with which commercial managers tried to save their theatres during the 1920's, TRP has come to depend more and more upon "the academic, the serious, and the classical." Big attractions have been plays by Tennessee Williams, Arthur Miller, Eugene O'Neill, Shaw, Shakespeare, Chekhov, and Molière. Shaw, in fact, is jokingly referred to as "our playwright in residence." Nor have new scripts been neglected. Local playwrights are frequently given high quality productions. Charles Nolte, for example, has had seven of his plays produced by TRP.

Not only does TRP select high quality plays, it also performs them with skill. Although comparisons, as Shakespeare's Dogberry maintains, can be "odorous," they can also be illuminating as the following from a 1983 review indicates: "The differences between a horrible professional production, and a terrific amateur one are sometimes alarming. While the Guthrie lumbers through *Hedda Gabler*, Theatre in the Round is breezing through an utterly delightful production of *Once In A Lifetime*." Even allowing for the usual prejudice in favor of local talent, such a comment indicates that TRP productions can and do achieve remarkable levels of excellence. In September, 1983, *Theatre Crafts* devoted its issue to Twin Cities theatres. Of the area's 106 theatre groups at the time, only three were considered in depth: The Guthrie, The Children's Theatre, and TRP.

One other reason for TRP's enviable success is to be found in the physical form of the theatre itself—an irregular arena designed by Ralph Rapson where no auditor is seated more than 30 feet from the acting area. In such a theatre an audience can see and hear, and plays dealing with ideas have a chance to be understood. Moreover, the arena form makes it practically impossible to present big musicals or spectacles. The result is a surprising advantage, both from a financial and a literary standpoint.

Finally it can be said that TRP has never been narrowly confined within its own walls. It has toured extensively throughout the state and has been generous about lending props and equipment to neighboring groups. Good management, modest aims, hard work, and good productions have paid off. After some thirty-seven years of continuous operation, The Theatre in the Round Players now enjoy a reputation as one of the most highly respected and dependable community theatres in the nation.

The Lakeshore Players (1953 to Date)

A number of other community theatres were born in the Twin Cities area during the thirties, forties and fifties, but most of them soon passed away. One that has survived is The Lakeshore Players, which was formed in 1953 when a notice was placed in the White Bear Lake newspaper inviting "theatrically minded persons" to attend a meeting at the city hall. Six weeks later the newly organized Players, with Laurie Peterson as their president, presented *Ah, Wilderness!* by Eugene O'Neill at the White Bear Lake High School auditorium. After several years of producing plays in school auditoriums, the Players in 1959 purchased a former Presbyterian church, and remodeled it into a 175 seat theatre. In 1969 this first playhouse was destroyed by fire. Lost as well were props, costumes, equipment and many records of the theatre's past, but by 1971 the Players were able to buy another former church, at Sixth and Stewart Streets, and this building (seating 200) remains as their home.

Now in their 35th season (just barely younger than TRP), the Lakeshore Players present six shows during a season which lasts from September to May. The budget is $75,000; there are four part-time employees. Directors and set designers are paid for each production. Funding is obtained from ticket sales and contributions from businesses and patrons, not from grants. Actors and staff fill the traditional community theatre roles of "one minute a star, the next making coffee." Productions have ranged from heavyweights like *Desire Under The Elms* to such lightweights as *Under The Yum Yum Tree*. An exception to this diet occurred in 1958 when Lakeshore mounted one of its

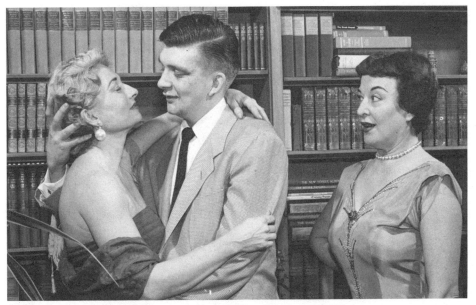

Hay Fever (1955), directed by Ebba Nelson and Art Heckler. Helen Peters, Roger Erickson, and Ebba Nelson.

Photo courtesy of Lakeshore Players.

largest productions ever. *Lakeshore Legend* was written for the town's centennial by Truly Latchaw. Ebba Nelson and Helen Peterson directed the cast of over 400.

The Bloomington Civic Theater
(1955 to 1979)

Organized primarily through the efforts of Donna Utecht, the Bloomington Civic Theater began with audiences totalling 500 per year and a budget of $1,700. By the 1960's its productions were viewed by 12,000 persons each year and the budget totalled $40,000. BCT was one of the first local groups to produce musicals with full orchestras. At first a different director was hired for each show, but in 1963 Gary Schulz became BCT's first full-time director. BCT's budget was based on ticket sales and memberships; its activities were supported by a large group of volunteers. In the late 1970's finding enough volunteers to continue its programs had become very difficult so BCT closed. During its long history BCT had presented musicals, dramas, and comedies. Like TRP and Lakeshore it was one of the important contributors to the theatrical base that existed in the Twin Cities before Tyrone Guthrie came.

The Fantasticks (1963), directed by Chris Ringham. Bill Murray and Jan Ellen Anderson appearing in Bloomington Civic Theater.

Photo courtesy of Mike Paul/Act Two.

Theatre St. Paul (1956 to 1966)

In 1950 the Junior League of St. Paul conducted a survey of the cultural resources of the capital city and concluded that an arts center was needed. Six years later the Arts and Science Council suggested that the League study local interest in community theatres. Accordingly, a theatre organization was formed in 1956 and a director, Louis Marcuson, selected. After only one reasonably successful season, Marcuson resigned, which could have proved fatal to the new organization had not Marcuson's successor, Rex Henriot, turned out to be such an excellent choice. Henriot not only came with an excellent background including experience, and solid training at the University of Washington, he was also accompanied by an attractive and talented wife, Zoaunne. Locating suitable physical facilities was a problem, but a grant from the Hill Foundation enabled the Henriots to transform an old Synagogue at 675 Holly Street into an intimate thrust-stage theatre seating 180. Rex was soon directing a regular season of seven to ten plays while Zoaunne was directing at least three plays for children. In 1960 the Henriots formed a small, semi-professional summer stock company and produced a summer season of six plays. These Theatre St. Paul seasons provided high quality plays with

The Lady's Not For Burning
(1965), directed by Rex
Henriot. Larry Linville and
Kate Geer appearing in
Theatre St. Paul.

Photo courtesy of
Mike Paul/Act Two.

Waiting for Godot, The Taming of The Shrew, The Threepenny Opera, and *Hamlet*
being among the more memorable productions. Finally, in 1964, Theatre St.
Paul turned professional and moved into the beautiful new Crawford Livingston theatre at the St. Paul Arts and Science Center at 10th and Cedar Streets.
Unfortunately, professional theatres are not only more expensive to operate
than community theatres, but audiences arrive with greater expectations.
Productions that had seemed outstanding in cramped, humble surroundings
were unable to measure up to the new space, and so Theatre St. Paul was disbanded.

The Eastside Theatre (1963 to 1969)

The failure of Theatre St. Paul would have been a much greater loss to
the area had not another non-professional group, The Eastside Theatre, already demonstrated its ability to do outstanding work. The Eastside began
in 1963 when Macalester College was forced to raze its temporary theatre in
a World War II army barracks in order to begin the construction of a first-
class theatre plant in the Janet Wallace Fine Arts Center. Left with no place
to perform, three Macalester students, Craig Scherfenberg, David Hobart,

The Taming of the Shrew (1967),
directed by Scott McCoy.
Mike Sevareid and Brooke Meyers
appearing in Eastside Theatre.

Photo courtesy of
Performing Arts Archives,
University of Minnesota Libraries,
Mike Paul/Act Two, Photographer.

Marat-Sade (1968), directed by
Scott McCoy. Dick Jackson, Cynthia
Wells, and Tamara Anderson
appearing in Eastside Theatre.

Photo courtesy of
Mike Paul/Act Two.

and Jack Westin, organized a theatre of their own in the basement of a restaurant belonging to Westin's father. They named it The Eastside Theatre. It was a surprising success, especially after it moved into the old German Presbyterian church designed by Cass Gilbert, and located at the base of Ramsey Hill. The old church (built in 1890) had been used as a clubhouse and then as a mortuary. Thus, the Eastside was able to boast that they and The Guthrie had the only power stage lifts in the Twin Cities, but that only Eastside's had been designed to raise coffins.

The seasons, mostly directed by Westin, covered a wide range from *Ten Nights in A Bar Room* to plays by Tennessee Williams and Molière. With the help of some very talented actors including Cynthia Wells, Rosemary Hartup and Bill Driver, the group gained and maintained a strong reputation. This was especially true after Scott McCoy, the University of Minnesota's first M.F.A. candidate in directing, began staging plays for them in the 1967–1968 season. His modern dress *The Taming of The Shrew* set in a sleepy town on the Mexican border with Eric Sevareid's son, Michael, as Petruchio and Brooke Meyers as Kate was outstanding, as was his *Cat on a Hot Tin Roof* which followed.

The following year Eastside presented *Marat-Sade* and the play with the endless title became the theatre's greatest hit. John Harvey wrote that tackling such a play "required courage, confidence and tremendous work." The result was "a free swinging, punchy job which can leave nobody untouched." [*St. Paul Pioneer Press*, March 16, 1968.] *Marat-Sade* played to 105% capacity as the theatre brought in extra chairs to supplement the 190 regular seats. *Marat-Sade*'s very success vividly illustrated Eastside's predicament. It had successfully attracted an audience and had outgrown its theatre.

In 1967 the Eastside produced *Macbird*, a savage satire on President Johnson and our involvement in Vietnam. It was extremely popular with young people and liberals, but its negative effect on the Establishment was reinforced by other avant-garde productions that finally earned The Eastside a reputation sometimes described as "radical and immature," a reputation which may have contributed to the theatre's downfall. In any case, the demise of Eastside was not due to the usual problems: loss of audience, poor productions, or internal strife. The demise of Eastside was caused by the threatened destruction of the theatre.

Its home in the old church on Pleasant street was first condemned as a "fire hazard." Then, when this problem (mostly electrical) was corrected, "somebody" decided to run a new highway through the building. All this, of course, may have had nothing to do with the fact that Eastside produced plays like *Macbird*, but the young people at Eastside who were losing their theatrical home were naturally suspicious. That their suspicions were justified became apparent when as soon as the Eastside players were safely eliminated, it was decided that the old church could remain standing.

Centre Stage (1968 to 1984)

This community theatre began even before the Jewish Community Center at 4330 South Cedar Lake Road in Minneapolis was completed. The original goal of the Centre Stage was to sponsor a theatre in the western suburbs which could present plays that had a feeling of Jewishness in them. Support came from the Jewish Community Center and from ticket sales. Among the founders were Irv Fink and Bernie Singer.

The first director was Aaron Foxman. Later directors included Kendrick Wilson who was active with other Twin Cities theatres and served previously as the director of the Omaha Community Playhouse, Steve Barnhart, and Bob May. Centre Stage was known for its musicals and for a number of directors and actors who have continued active careers in the theatre. Names on such an alumni roster would include David Ira Goldstein, Buffy Sedlachek, Jim Hartman, Mike Levin, Dwight Larson, Bob Davis and Russell Curry.

Centre Stage took first place in the Minnesota Association of Community Theatres competition twice, in 1977 and 1979, and, both times, with original scripts by Michael Kassin.

In 1984 a dispute over budgetary considerations led the board of directors of Centre Stage to resign en masse. There is no longer a theatre by that name, although the Jewish Community Center has subsequently sponsored a new theatrical group called Genesis.

Chimera Theatre (1970 to 1987)

From the ashes of the Eastside rose the Chimera, as a story in the *St. Paul Dispatch* reported [September 8, 1969]. Artistic director Scott McCoy sought to continue the group's activities in a new site. McCoy and businessman Jim Borland led the effort to find a new location. Their attempt to raise funds for the purchase and remodeling of another old church failed, perhaps because the church fathers feared that the theatre's name meant "devil" and was most inappropriate. Their application to move into the now unused Crawford Livingston theatre was finally given consideration—provided that the St. Paul Arts and Science Council could see examples of their work. How to present these examples without a theatre was a problem, but it was solved when Dr. Thomas Read, headmaster of the St. Paul Academy, arranged for the group to produce a summer season of four plays at Summit School. Plays like *The Lark*, dressed in costumes graciously "rented" to the group by The Guthrie Theater, finally convinced the Council that The Chimera Theatre, was made of "the right stuff." Unfortunately, the strain had been too much for McCoy. He, like Scherfenberg before him, resigned, leaving it to Borland to establish Chimera at the Crawford Livingston.

Under Borland's leadership, Chimera opened at its new home in December, 1970 and succeeded in giving the Crawford Livingston a successful theatre where others, including Theatre St. Paul and Guthrie II failed. In typical business-like fashion Borland resolved to "build an audience first and concentrate on artistry later," and he succeeded. The 84 performance season in 1970–1971 grew to 278 performances by 1978–1979; attendance rose from 36,609 to 128,171; fixed assets grew from zero to $229,615; and the governing board grew from 5 members to 20.

Although building an audience may have been Borland's primary objective, artistry was not entirely neglected. Seasons contained a respectable proportion of classics, and new plays were not avoided. The 1972–1973 season, for example, included an impressive production of Richard Hilger's *The Steeple*. In 1973–1974 Tomas MacAnna, from the Abbey Theatre in Dublin, was imported to direct his prize-winning *Borstal Boy*, and in 1975–1976

Meredith Willson was appointed "guest artist in residence" for the production of Willson's own Broadway success, *The Music Man*.

Most of Chimera's plays were staged by some of the best directors in the local area including Warren Frost, Roger Hendricks, and Larry Whitely. The theatre also profited from the reliable talent of technical director Dick Borgen, who enjoyed the luxury of working in a far better than average theatre.

In 1976, as previously mentioned, Chimera acquired the Edyth Bush Theatre for its educational program and its ambitious achievements continued to expand. Theatrical celebrities like Allen Whitehead, Hal Prince, Henry Hewes and Edward Albee were imported for short visits and/or seminars; theatre tours throughout the region were sponsored; an actor's scholarship fund was established; community theatre festivals were hosted, and Christine Stewart was employed to conduct a lively children's training program.

Borland resigned in 1979, but was replaced by Dale Huffington from the Extension Service of the University of Minnesota. Huffington had already distinguished himself not only at the University but also nationally, having served a term as president of the American Theatre Association. Under his leadership, Chimera continued to make progress, and exhibited an increasing tendency to become a theatrical service center for the area. Its 1979–1980 season of 278 performances played to an impressive 84.1% of capacity; between 1979 and 1983 its educational programs tripled. It became a theatrical center with a full time professional staff and a budget of over a million dollars. Huffington was succeeded by Curt Wollan whose production of *1940's Radio Hour* was a popular success for Chimera. Consequently, for all of these reasons, it came as a shock to many people when in October, 1987, Chimera declared bankruptcy and closed. Explanations as to why it failed were, of course, numerous. Perhaps it had become too democratic, too service oriented, and finally, too big and expensive. David Hawley pointed out that its operating budget was only exceeded by those of The Guthrie and Children's Theatre. It had become professionally expensive in every way except that it did not pay professional salaries to its actors. Salaries for actors may not have been a problem when Chimera was founded. At that time there were many good actors willing to work for nothing, but not so by 1987. With the abundance of professional theatres in the area, talented actors could expect to be paid. Or, maybe the Crawford Livingston Theatre itself, apparently one of the finest in the state, is the jinx. Ironically, Theatre St. Paul was thought to have failed when it moved into the Crawford Livingston because it tried to become professional; Chimera, according to Hawley, probably failed because it did not become professional [*St. Paul Pioneer Press Dispatch*, October 14, 1987.]

The Rochester Civic Theatre
(1951 to Date)

A number of Minnesota's most important community theatres are quite naturally located outside of the Twin Cities, in areas that provide a strong cultural-educational base but little or no competition from professional theatres. The Rochester Civic Theatre is a good example. With a population of about fifty thousand, Rochester can be rated as a "small urban center," but since it is also the home of the world famous Mayo Clinic it has a highly sophisticated populace, quite capable of supporting an intelligent theatre.

Rochester's community theatre was launched in 1951. The driving personality who organized, directed and spearheaded the project was Marilyn Monsour who was said to have discovered a way of extracting 72 energy hours out of every 24 clock hours. Her first production was *Light Up The Sky* by Moss Hart. Its scenery came mostly from corrugated cardboard mattress boxes, scrap lumber, egg cartons, some scene paint, endless love, and free labor. The play was finally presented in a log cabin belonging to the Isaac Walton League on September 13, 1951.

One or two years later the Rochester Civic Theatre moved into a home of its own at North Broadway and 7th Street. The building had been a dirty old storage space without heat, but volunteer labor transformed it into a fairly adequate playhouse which served as the Civic Theatre's home for some 12 years. But the most important thing about the Rochester Civic Theatre was that it continued to produce plays, mostly Broadway hits like *Brigadoon*, and produce them very well. This was especially true after the Theatre employed a full-time director, Jim Cavanaugh. Cavanaugh was not only a gifted stage director, he was a natural-born leader, effective on radio, and on a speaker's platform—effective anywhere. He not only directed and promoted the individual plays, he also promoted the importance of theatre as an art, and finally convinced the community that Rochester should have a theatre building in which it could take pride. On December 6, 1964 the dream was realized. The Rochester Civic Theatre's production of *South Pacific* opened in a new $250,000 theatre that is still one of the finest community theatre plants in the nation—not just a stage house and auditorium, but also a building which contains shops, offices, air conditioning, and storage facilities. All this had been accomplished with no expense to the taxpayers. The city's only contribution had been the lease of the ground on which the building rests, at a rental figure of $1.00 per year.

Cavanaugh left in 1967, but the theatre has continued under other able directors. It sponsors productions and classes for young people. It has varied the usual diet of Broadway hits by securing foundation grants for the production of original scripts. Today (1988) the theatre has a staff of five full-time members: administrative director, technical director, office manager, and two artistic directors. Almost from the first it has conducted a Rosco (Rochester Oscar) Award Ceremony for outstanding achievements. In fact, the Theatre itself received such an award from the Minnesota Association of Community Theatres in 1978, an award for distinguished service.

Some Final Thoughts About The Amateurs

One need only glance at the Minnesota State Art Board's directory of theatres to realize that live theatre is indeed alive in Minnesota. Of course, many of the over two hundred theatres listed are amateur, some probably as inadequate as "professionals" naturally believe that amateurs are, but if the truth were known a number of these groups do excellent work. They just have no mass media to spread the word about their accomplishments. Some of the best probably do not realize how good they actually are. Talent can (and does) bloom in unexpected places.

9

Educational Theatres

ELATIONSHIPS between schools and the theatre are both ancient and interesting. We know, for example, that during the middle ages certain scholarly nuns discovered and translated several old Roman comedies; we know that the creative explosion of great playwriting during Shakespeare's day was largely fueled by young "university wits"; we know that the first English speaking production of a play in America was *Ye Bare and Ye Cub*, written and performed by college students in Virginia in 1665; and, although we do not know when plays were first performed in the schools of Minnesota, we do know that as early as the 1880's, impressive productions were being presented at the old St. Paul High School.

Any discussion of the relationship between the theatre and education is complicated by the very nature of the theatre. As an imitation of life, theatre reflects much of life's chaos and confusion. To oversimplify the matter we can observe that:

(1) Prior to World War I the theatre in most American educational institutions was simply regarded as a form of entertainment — as a reasonably harmless extracurricular recreation.

(2) Between the two World Wars, many American college theatres began to gain limited acceptance as one of the liberal arts alongside such traditional subjects as philosophy, history, and literature — subjects concerned with things of the mind: human ideas, problems, and the meaning of human existence. Dramatic literature naturally became the central ingredient of such college theatres; plays by realistic writers like Ibsen, Chekhov, and Shaw which examined ideas and problems seemed about to help launch a new age of understanding and wisdom.

(3) Following World War II and especially after Vietnam the theatre in America (as it had done in Europe much earlier) seemed to despair about reforming or enlightening society. Perhaps the avant-garde was right; the meaning of hu-

man existence was that there was no meaning. In any case, many theatres in American universities quietly shifted from a Liberal Arts College to a Fine Arts College where they could seek companionship with subjects like music and painting. No longer was a script with its intellectual ideas the primary concern; the aim instead was to provide an "aesthetic experience" — a complex amalgamation of all the arts.

In practice, of course, few theatre artists worry about such philosophical foundations. Each just tries to produce the best play possible not realizing that other people may have vastly different ideas concerning what constitutes "best." All this makes evaluation hazardous. As the Old Arab in William Saroyan's *The Time of Your Life* keeps repeating, "no foundation, all the way down the line."

On a less philosophic and more practical level the development of college-university theatre was greatly accelerated during the thirties by the collapse of the professional commercial theatre. Not only were college and community theatres able to capture audiences that had formerly supported the professionals, they were also able to capture and transform into teachers or directors some very talented theatre artists who would normally have been absorbed by the professionals. With this general background we are in position to consider what actually happened as the theatre developed at the University of Minnesota, in selected Minnesota colleges, and in a few Minnesota high schools.

The University of Minnesota

Dramatic productions at the University began in 1881 when the freshman class presented *The Last Loaf*. The most theatrical event, however, during the nineteenth century, was the destruction of Old Main, the University's only building of contemporary importance, which burned during a production of *A Box of Monkeys* on April 30, 1892. Fortunately the fire occurred after the performance and no one was injured. But just as numerous fires had not dampened the theatrical enthusiasm of the professionals, so the burning of Old Main did not dampen the theatrical enthusiasm of the students. This enthusiasm continued to grow and flourish until by 1919 six extracurricular theatrical groups were competing, sometimes hotly, for attention. Most of this activity appears to have been on a very amateur level, but some of the productions were obviously more important than has been generally supposed. Many of them were, as already mentioned, directed by Mr. and Mrs. Charles M. Holt from the Minneapolis School of Music, Oratory, and Dramatic Arts. Moreover, such outstanding University of Minnesota faculty members as Dr. Richard Burton and Anna Von Helmholtz Phelan actively supported some of these dramatic activities. The plays produced were usually of literary merit—plays by Shakespeare, Sheridan, Shaw, Ibsen and Pinero made up the bulk of these seasons. Performances not only played on campus but were frequently seen in downtown professional theatres and were sometimes toured to communities throughout the state.

There were, of course, exceptions to this emphasis on the classics. For example, in 1913, Merline Shumway, a young student from the School of Agriculture wrote a play entitled *Back on The Farm*. It was apparently a propaganda piece illustrating how an agricultural education could improve rural life. It played 50 performances in 36 communities and Governor Eberhart saw it twice.

In 1922 the construction of a new music building on campus provided dramatics with its first reasonably adequate home. It was emphatically a "Music Building," however. Dramatic activities were confined to the southern half of the basement, except for the excellent stage and auditorium, later known as Scott Hall, which could be rented by the theatre in the evenings for its major productions. Even this improved home on campus did not eliminate the theatre's tendency to sprawl in all directions.

Partly to diminish the chaos caused by the numerous competing groups, Lester Raines was appointed director of dramatics in 1925, but, as things turned out, Raines approached his job with such energy and enthusiasm that he appears to have increased the chaos. In 1927–1928 Professor Frank M. Rarig established a Department of Public Speaking on campus, and dramatics was included under its umbrella. Rarig's staff was impressive; it included Bryng Bryngelson who later became a national leader in speech pathology; Wayne Morse, debate coach, who later became an outstanding United States Senator from Oregon; and Edward Staadt, director of dramatics. Staadt was a graduate of Northwestern University and a playwright as well as a director. He faced a formidable task, but during his five years at the helm, he made considerable progress: he unified production on campus under the banner of the Minnesota Masquers; he employed Tom Russell as a scenic technician; and he employed L. Clement (Tim) Ramsland, an M.A. from the University of Washington and a very gifted director, as his associate director. Staadt's tenure was not an easy one, as student groups continued to battle for control. *The Minnesota Daily* printed hints of friction between Staadt and Ramsland, but the most difficult blow apparently came from somewhere in the University's administration. Staadt's predecessor, Lester Raines, was invited back to the campus to conduct a highly publicized "Dramatic Arts Roundtable" from July 15 to July 25, 1931, in the great new Northrop Auditorium. Professionals were imported to play the leading roles in Eugene O'Neill's *Marco Millions*, Rudolph Friml's *The Vagabond King*, and Edmond Rostand's *L'Aiglon*. There is no evi-

Scott Hall Auditorium on the East Bank Campus of the University of Minnesota, built in 1922, which for many years was the home of the University Theatre.

Photo courtesy of the University Theatre, University of Minnesota.

dence that Staadt was even consulted about all of this. But on the night of June 25, 1931, Edward Staadt simply swam out into the cool, clear waters of Lake Minnetonka. There was no way to determine whether he suffered a cramp or just made no effort to return. The coroner's death certificate simply reads, "Accident, Drowning while swimming."

A. Dale Riley, a former director at the University of Iowa, replaced Staadt in 1931. His first achievement may have been his most important. He placed dramatic activity on a solid academic and financially responsible footing and gave it a new name, The University Theatre. Students could finally major in Speech with a clear emphasis on the arts and crafts of the theatre. Working with a small but talented staff which included Ramsland and Warren Lee (Lee eventually became Dean of Fine Arts at the University of South Dakota), Riley began to achieve some of the professional quality that the theatre needed. Students like Gale Sondergaard, Richard Carlson, Arthur Peterson, Roman Bohnen and William Newgard were later to carve places for themselves in Hollywood and/or New York. But the strain once more took its toll. On July 1, 1936, Riley suffered a stroke. Three weeks later he was dead, at the age of 49.

In the fall of 1937 C. Lowell Lees, a man from Utah with a Ph.D from Wisconsin, assumed control of the University Theatre. Although sometimes disorganized, Lees was a dynamo of talent and ambition. Few people could be as charming as Lees at his best, and in 1937–1938 he was definitely at his best. Although a pall of financial depression hung over the nation, and although memories of trouble and tragedy still haunted the air of Scott Hall, the University Theatre under Lowell Lees simply exploded with promise and excitement. In reviewing Lees' first production, *High Tor*, Merle Potter, the *Minneapolis Journal* critic wrote:

> . . . before the curtain had been up many minutes, a highly gratified audience knew that it was in for an evening of grand entertainment. It realized that there was some new magic behind campus dramatics, that the theatre there had been revitalized on a most surprising fashion. [*Minneapolis Journal*, October 20, 1937.]

Nor was *High Tor* the only play of the Lees era to gain a rave review. *Life of Man*, with Kevin McCarthy in the lead, scored an equal success; *Johnny Johnson* with David Thompson; *Peter Pan* with Elsie Kelley; *Lilliom* with Allen Joseph; and *Romeo and Juliet* with Kenneth Graham, Holly Irving, Richard Fliehr, and David Thompson, were among the other outstanding productions during the four years of the Lees regime which followed. In addition to all this production activity, Lees managéd to publish a text book, *A Primer of Acting*. He also established a solid academic program leading all the way to the Ph.D.

But perhaps the Lees era began at such a high pitch that it could not last. Following Pearl Harbor, students and audiences faded away and in 1943 Lees left Minnesota to return to his native soil where he became chairman of the theatre department at the University of Utah. But the University Theatre at Minnesota, somewhat to the surprise of everyone concerned, managed to carry on. In fact, the two decades which followed saw the University Theatre enter into a period of great accomplishment.

These decades were the time when I had the good fortune to serve as director, but any credit for noteworthy accomplishments belongs to the University Theatre as a whole, to the staff and students, rather than to any one individual. It should, however, be mentioned that we gained strength through our close ties to some very outstanding artist-scholars in other departments: Norman DeWitt (Classics), Alrik Gustafson (Scandinavian Department), James Aliferis and Roy Schuessler (Music), and Robert Penn Warren and Eric Bentley (English).

As already noted, theatres, both amateur and professional, have a tendency to rely heavily upon high-sounding ideals plus publicity and public relations, but the thing they so often forget is that real, long-range success lies in their ability to turn out excellent productions. And it was down in the trenches of production that the University Theatre from 1943 to 1963 excelled. In reviewing *Junior Miss* James Gray began: "It is cheering to realize how high a level of competence the non-professional theater can achieve." [*St. Paul Dispatch*, January 12, 1945.] A month later Del Dusenbury's production of *Candida* played to equally ecstatic reviews. According to Robert Stevenson, "I would like to go on record as giving top-ranking honors (professional and non-professional) to 'Candida', produced by University Theatre . . . " [*Minneapolis Morning Tribune*, February 15, 1945.] The following year Robert Smith began his review of *Blithe Spirit* with:

> Once in every two or three blue theatrical moons, the stage or movies come up with rare treats such as "Life with Father" or "Here Comes Mr. Jordan." The University Theatre's current production of Noel Coward's Blithe Spirit is one such delightful occasion and may rank among the all time bests. [*Minneapolis Star Journal*, January 16, 1946.]

And concerning the production of *King Lear* later that season, Randall Hobart began:

> Shakespeare's great but seldom enacted tragedy "King Lear" came awesomely alive Tuesday night as the University Theatre players scored what can only be described as a dramatic triumph. [*Minneapolis Morning Tribune*, February 27, 1946.]

Nor were local critics the only ones impressed. Alice Griffin, associate editor and critic for *Theatre Arts*, pronounced the University Theatre's *King Lear* superior to anything she had seen in New York, and one year later, 1947, George Freedley, noted historian and drama critic for the *New York World Telegram*, wrote an excellent review of the University Theatre's *Lysistrata*.

Some twenty years later Sir Tyrone Guthrie, glancing back at this period in the University Theatre's history remarked, "You were not behaving like a theatre school, but like a young repertory company." The only reply to this sage insight was, "Perhaps a talented young repertory company provides the best kind of theatre school." At least out of the activity of those years came future New York actresses like Shirley Jac Wagner, Marilyn McCrudden (Lynn Mason), Joan Eastman, and Arlene Frank; Hollywood stars like Peter Graves, Jack Schmidt and Robert Vaughn; leaders in educational radio like Ruth Swanson, Marian English and Shel Goldstein; heads of outstanding university-college theatre departments like Keith Engar, Harold Oaks, John Elzey, Douglas Hatfield, Jed Davis, William McGraw and Donald Borchardt; and radio and television performers like Charlie Boone, Dave Moore and Roger Erickson.

The dedication, energy, and enthusiasm of staff and students during those years was perhaps a bit impractical, at times almost insane, but it was also inspiring. Through the efforts of Kenneth Graham and others, thousands of elementary school children in the Twin Cities were attending at least one play per year, and attending during school hours. Arthur Ballet organized a summer workshop for outstanding high school students, and a high school one act play festival was conducted each spring. A Drama Advisory Service was established through the University's Extension Division and was charged with assisting and coordinating dramatic activities on all levels throughout the state. And, finally, the University Theatre began sending out two semi-professional touring companies annually: a small group, usually three students, presenting a forty-five minute program of one act plays, skits, and scenes from plays, to hundreds of high school assemblies; a larger touring company, usually with eleven to thirteen students, presented full length plays for communities in Minnesota and the surrounding states.

On campus the Theatre cooperated with the Department of Music in the production of musicals and operas, among them a 1954 production of *Amahl and The Night Visitors* with the Minneapolis Symphony. The Theatre also cooperated with language departments in the production of French, German, and Spanish plays, all of them performed in their original language and some of them classics such as Goethe's *Faust, Part I*, Molière's *Don Juan*, and Lorca's *Yerma*.

During these same years the University Theatre made a few waves nationally, and even internationally; for example, in 1956 I was elected president of the American Educational Theatre Association and Kenneth Graham became its Executive Secretary, the first and only time that the Association's two most important offices had been held on the same campus. In 1957 the University Theatre's *A Midsummer Night's Dream* was selected to tour France and Germany for the Department of Defense. Later, in that same summer, *Midsummer*, with the addition of *Our Town*, was selected to visit Brazil on a good will tour for the Department of State. The following year, with the help of the Minnesota Centennial Commission, the University Theatre managed to secure a Mississippi stern wheeler which was remodeled into The Minnesota Centennial Showboat, a project to be considered in Chapter 10. And finally, at about this same time, the University Theatre initiated the drive that brought Tyrone Guthrie to the area.

Nor was teaching neglected. Enrollment in Arthur Ballet's "An Introduction to the Theatre" course was limited only by the size of the auditorium in which it could be taught, and Robert Moulton's skill as a choreographer was indicated when he was selected to choreograph "The Grassland Suite" for Queen Elizabeth's visit to Canada.

Innovations in staging were also seen in Scott Hall, long before they became common elsewhere. For example, the University Theatre's production of *The Taming of The Shrew*, in 1944, shocked traditionalists by omitting the

Dream Play (1948),
directed by Frank M Whiting.
Peter Aurness Graves and
Irma Rae Schroeder.

Photo courtesy of the University
Theatre, University of Minnesota.

use of a front curtain, at a time when front curtains were regarded as absolutely indispensable. In 1948, *The Dream Play* by August Strindberg used projected scenery as a background. The dreamlike quality, as one fragment of human suffering melted into another, was captured successfully. A tape recording of that performance was played on Swedish national radio and the copy was eventually deposited in the Strindberg archives in Stockholm. A set of photographs was later included in an international exhibit of theatre photography in Switzerland.

Although the University Theatre relies primarily on the classics by writers like Shaw and Shakespeare, new playwrights were not neglected. Fourteen full-length originals were presented between 1943 and 1963 and several later made it to New York or Hollywood, among them *A Cry of Players* (William Gibson) and *All The King's Men* (Robert Penn Warren). Literally hundreds of original one-act plays were written, directed, and acted by students.

The next decade, 1963–1973, of the University Theatre's history may be seen as the period in which it finally burst into full bloom, or it may be viewed with a sense of disappointment. Student enrollment skyrocketed as did financial support from the University. Perhaps the brightest feature was the quality of its students. Whereas in 1943 students seriously interested in theatre tried to enroll at such universities as Yale, Carnegie Tech or Iowa, by 1973 they clamored to come to Minnesota. The McKnight Fellowships program (discussed further in Chapter 11) was, of course, one of the reasons, but, even without this, Minnesota had gained recognition as one of the top theatre schools in the nation.

But there were problems. In trite terms, "bigger is not necessarily better." This was the period when the "we generation" was replaced by the "me generation" nationally, and the transition was especially noticeable at the University Theatre. Students and staff members, who had once worked together with totally impractical abandon, for the good of the show now became concerned about "Will this experience further my personal development as an artist?" Staff meetings, at one time informal get-togethers, bogged down into committees and parliamentary procedures. Student committees were formed to "aid" in the choice of seasons and to present grievances. The "me" spirit was also seen in relationship to other departments. The foreign language series had to be abandoned; cooperation with the Department of Music disappeared; everyone was totally occupied with "his or her own thing." Unfortunately the abundance of talent and money did not even result in better productions for the audiences. A typical audience comment in the 1940's would have been "What a superb play," whereas by the 1970's the comment would have been "What superb actors!" In other words, actors in the 1940's assumed that their function was to make the play look great. Those of the 1970's tended to be more concerned about making themselves look great.

There were striking exceptions, of course. Charles Nolte, after starring on Broadway as Billy Budd and in other plays, rejoined us and directed some outstanding productions including a superb production of one of his own original scripts, *A Night at The Black Pig*. Two other productions scored successes that produced vibrations far beyond the campus. Maxine Klein's production of *Comings and Goings* by Megan Terry was a delight. The production was so successful on campus and in the region that Ellen Stewart invited the group to appear at Cafe LaMama in New York City. A different but equally enthusiastic reaction greeted Wesley Balk's *365 Days* which was selected as one of the ten college productions for representation at the 1972 American College Festival in the Kennedy Center, Washington, D. C.

There were other obvious achievements during the decade from 1963 to 1973. At the beginning of the period theatre was one of the four divisions under the Department of Speech. By the end of the period it had gained full-fledged independent status as The Department of Theatre Arts. By 1986 it had acquired the title of Department of Theatre Arts and Dance. At the beginning of the decade the theatre had been scattered in seven different locations — one of these an old lawn-mower shed that had been abandoned by the department of Buildings and Grounds. At the end of the period the theatre found itself housed in the multimillion dollar Rarig Center on the West Bank campus, with shops, offices, and not one but four excellent theatres.

In 1987, Barbara Reid became head of the department, and the University of Minnesota now has a golden opportunity to build a strong working relationship with The Guthrie and other professional theatres of the area. Ms. Reid herself, among other impressive qualifications, has been a successful actress at The Guthrie, and other staff members have also served there: Robert Moulton as choreographer, Art Ballet (now retired) as dramaturg, and Wendell Josal and Charles Nolte as members of the board. Perhaps the most important of all, Steve Kanee, one of The Guthrie's most successful directors, has now become a full-time member of the University Theatre's teaching staff. And at least one foundation is seriously considering the funding of a special program for actors. True, the old days when the University Theatre served as a major producing unit for the region are gone forever, but an equally exciting and more appropriate goal now beckons. The department is becoming one of the nation's truly outstanding centers for theatre education.

Dramatic activity at the University of Minnesota has by no means been limited to the main Minneapolis campus. During the mid-years of the century the Duluth campus, especially while under the leadership of Harold Hayes, conducted a stimulating program. In 1960 another branch of the University was established in Morris, and in 1962 Raymond J. Lammers joined the faculty there to begin the development of a theatre program. Performances were at first presented in a miscellaneous assortment of areas, but by 1974 the University had constructed an excellent facility (with Ralph Rapson as architect) which contained two theatres plus control rooms, shops and rehearsal space. The curriculum had developed from a few courses to a full major, with productions that served the needs of the local community as well as the University.

In addition to its excellent physical facilities for theatre, Morris offers the students a chance to participate in a spring festival production for children as well as a chance to be included in summer theatre tours to either London or New York. Finally, the University's St. Paul campus theatre must not be overlooked. Its Punchinello Players in fact is probably the oldest producing group in the state; 1988 marks its 75th anniversary. Punchinello is the only survivor among the numerous extracurricular groups that once dotted the Twin Cities campuses.

Macalester College

From its beginning in 1905 until well into the 1930's dramatic activity at Macalester was primarily an extracurricular activity thought to be beneficial in giving students experience before an audience. During the late twenties and thirties Macalester placed its emphasis on rather formal "art productions." Grace Whitridge stressed eurythmics and Grecian tableaux. Mary Gwen Owen, the other teacher in the department, developed the art of choral reading for public presentation.

After World War II a surplus army barracks was transformed into a theatre seating 298. Jed Davis joined the staff as technical director and director of children's theatre. Davis later became director of theatre at the University of Kansas, and also served as president of the American Educational Theatre Association. In 1948 Mary Gwen Owen instigated the St. Paul Drama Festival, which was intended to pool the efforts of the major St. Paul colleges. During its first year Hamline presented *The Taming of The Shrew*, the colleges of St. Catherine and St. Thomas combined forces to present *Twelfth Night*, and Macalester presented *Henry IV, Part I*. The festival continued for the next three years, moving to a different campus each season.

In 1955 Owen appointed Douglas Hatfield as director of theatre. This was a wise choice. Hatfield, a conscientious and talented all-round man of the theatre with extensive experience in many of the community theatres of the area, led Macalester to consistently high quality in its major productions. In addition, he and his talented wife, Naomi Strang Hatfield, continued their work in the community. One of their noteworthy projects was the establishment, in 1961, of the Town and Gown Players, a small group which presented summer plays featuring both students and alumni. In 1963 Macalester theatre moved into a beautiful new theatre building in the Janet Wallace Fine Arts Center. The building actually contains two theatres: the main auditorium seats approximately 300 and a laboratory theatre seats 100. It was the first really modern theatre facility to be built on a Minnesota campus, and was designed by the famous theatre consultant, George C. Izenour. It is capable of push button modification to accommodate proscenium, thrust or arena staging.

Hatfield suffered a severe stroke in 1984 and Glen Wilson temporarily assumed control of theatre activities. With Wilson's retirement in the spring of 1986, Dramatic Arts and Speech Communication were separated into two different departments. Sears A. Eldredge was appointed to chair the newly created Dramatic Arts Department and a year later Cynthia Goatley was hired to complete the three-person program (Dan Keyser, the Designer/Technical Director was the one continuing member from the previous joint department). The Dance Program was moved from Physical Education to Dramatic Arts in the spring of 1987 so that the department is now known as the Dramatic Arts and Dance Department. An expanded and revised curriculum has been approved and will go into effect in the 1988–1989 school year.

Hamline University

As early as 1910 Hamline presented a play at the Metropolitan Theatre in St. Paul. Touring activities began in 1917 and during the late 1920's Elizabeth Evanson produced at least 21 performances during her two years as director of dramatics. She was followed by Alvina Krause in 1929-1930. Krause's production of *Pierre Patelin* won first place at the Northwestern University play festival and was probably influential in causing Krause to move to that institution where she eventually gained a reputation as one of America's outstanding teachers of acting.

But it was under the direction of another woman, Anne Simley, that theatre at Hamline was solidly established. Simley arrived at Hamline in 1930 with a degree in mathematics from Carleton College. Working as a one woman staff on an infinitesimal budget she made up with vision, energy, persistence and leadership for whatever she lacked in material goods and money. She and her students soon established a Little Theatre in the attic of Science Hall, where in spite of difficulty of access and the danger of fire she quickly began to acquire a reputation for impressive productions. Plays by Shakespeare, Shaw, Ibsen and Sheridan were effectively presented together with productions by such American masters as O'Neill, Anderson and Wilder. By the time she retired in 1952, Simley had directed over one hundred plays. She was replaced by Jim Carlson, one of her former students who was also a disciple of Eric Bentley. Carlson produced a number of challenging new scripts, among them *The Good Woman of Setzuan* (Brecht), *Blood Wedding* (Lorca) and *The King and The Duke* (Fergusson).

During most of its life, the need for adequate physical facilities at Hamline presented a problem. The fire trap in the attic of the Science Building was finally condemned. In 1947 two World War II quonset huts were assembled to provide reasonably adequate quarters. Then in 1965 Hamline inherited the Edyth Bush Theatre which might have solved the space problems had it not been located several miles away from the campus. Finally, on April 15, 1983, a beautiful campus theatre seating 292 was dedicated. By then three experienced and highly respected staff members were in charge of the program. By 1987 the staff had expanded to seven full time members with Mark Bradley as director of the theatre and William Kimes as chairman of the Department of Theatre and Communication Arts. The aim of Hamline's theatre is to provide students with a stimulating variety of theatrical experience ranging from musicals to classics and including experimental new scripts.

The College of St. Thomas

As in most colleges, the theatre at St. Thomas began as an extracurricular activity when The Players Club was founded in 1907. For the next twenty years plays and entertainments were given on a rather irregular schedule and on a strictly "recreational" basis with men playing the female roles when necessary. With the appointment of Fenton W. Spence to the faculty in 1928 things began to change. A course in dramatic production was added to the curriculum, girls were imported from the nearby College of St. Catherine to play the female roles, and a new standard of dramatic production quickly became apparent. For his production of Channing Pollock's *The Fool*, Spence employed the assistance of a professional actor, Leo Kennedy. Other ambitious productions included *Everyman* and *She Stoops to Conquer*. It was soon apparent, however, that Spence had not only initiated a surge of dramatic creativity, but was also beginning to encounter faculty opposition. The enthusiasm for theatre was spreading beyond control. In May, 1932, Goethe's *Ur Faustus* was translated and produced by a young student, Robert Breen. The following year this incredible young man not only directed an original student musical, *Take Your Medicine*, but later climaxed the year with a production of *Hamlet* in which he played the title role. In general, critics and friends were impressed but certain conservative members of the St. Thomas faculty were not. Neither Breen not Spence returned the following year.

But if conservative faculty members had intended to nip young Breen's career in the bud they were disappointed. Breen's youthful St. Thomas accomplishments were but a small sample of what was to become a truly amazing career. His cast of *Hamlet* was reorganized and reinforced by several outstanding actors from the University of Minnesota. The company then moved into the Minneapolis Shubert Theater in June of 1933, billed as The College Art Theatre. After a week at the Shubert the group toured extensively; this was followed by a season which began in Birmingham, Alabama, in October, and ended in Chicago in May. In the meantime Wilva Davis had joined the company; she was later to become Mrs. Robert Breen and a full partner in most of his accomplishments. In the fall of 1935 Hallie Flanagan Davis enlisted Breen in a project that resulted in Chicago's Federal Theatre No. 1, the first unit of the government-supported WPA Federal Theatre Projects that were soon to dot the nation.

Breen's next striking achievement, in collaboration with Robert Porterfield, director of the Barter Theatre in Virginia, was the promotion of a plan for a national theatre. This eventually resulted in the activation (in 1946) of ANTA, The American National Theatre and Academy, which a decade earlier had been chartered by the U. S. Congress but left without funds. Breen headed the organization as executive secretary during its first five years.

Many of the projects initiated by this restless genius, such as his plan to direct a great Hollywood Bowl production of *Hamlet* starring John Barrymore, failed to materialize, but among the projects that did take place was a production of *Hamlet* at Kronborg Castle, Elsinore, Denmark, with Breen once more in the title role and Walter Abel and Ernest Borgnine in the cast. Perhaps the most successful of Breen's accomplishments was his production of *Porgy and Bess*, which toured the world, including the Soviet Union and other Iron Curtain countries, from 1952 to 1960. It seems unlikely that any other Minnesotan can match Robert Breen's influence on the American theatre nationally.

The College of St. Catherine

As already mentioned, dramatic activity at the College of St. Catherine, an all-women's school, has, for obvious reasons, usually been closely associated with the dramatic activities at the College of St. Thomas. Until 1946 the two colleges maintained a joint extracurricular Players Club; at present, Jo Ann Holonbek serves as chairperson of the Communication and Theatre Department and George Poletes serves as director of theatre at both institutions.

Sister Anna Marie Meyers served as director at St. Catherine's until 1932 when Mary Hart became director. She was followed by Mabel Meta Frey in 1937. Frey installed a program leading to a degree in theatre. In 1940 a gymnasium on campus was transformed into an effective little theatre. In 1970 a fine arts complex was constructed, which includes the O'Shaughnessy Auditorium. Designed by George Izenour, it is an auditorium that can be adjusted to a capacity of either 2,000 or 700. The complex also contains the Mabel Frey theatre seating 125.

With the completion of new theatres, the College of St. Catherine and the College of St. Thomas followed the trend of the times. In addition to majors in theatre, speech, and television, a training program for students frankly contemplating professional careers was established. Jo Ann Holonbek, who had joined the St. Catherine's faculty in 1974, worked with Barbara Barnett, a part-time faculty member, in founding a professional theatre on campus. A number of students who gained experience under their system are now prominent in the numerous professional theatres that dot the Twin Cities and elsewhere. St. Catherine's has been active in the annual American College Theatre Festival, and Poletes himself has been awarded one of the Festival's citations for "outstanding work."

St. Cloud State University

Since about 1950 one of the most energetic and successful college theatre departments in Minnesota has been the one at St. Cloud State University. This was especially true when Art Houseman served as director of the theatre from 1956 to 1968. He was finally lured away from St. Cloud to become head of the theatre at Ohio State University. His departure might have been a disaster for St. Cloud had it not been for the presence of another equally able and talented artist-scholar, Keith Michael, who served at St. Cloud from 1960 to 1971. Together Houseman and Michael founded a successful "professional" summer theatre, Theatre L'Homme Dieu, on a beautiful acreage of wooded property near Alexandria, Minnesota. They also conducted overseas tours: *Wonderful Town* to Iceland and Greenland in 1961 and *Pajama Game* to Germany in 1964. In 1968 a Performing Arts Center was opened on the St. Cloud campus which was clearly one of the best equipped theatre plants in the area. It contains a 430 seat proscenium theatre plus shops, classrooms, offices and dressing rooms.

Nor did the program at St. Cloud die when Michael, like Houseman before him, left to become chairman at another Big Ten institution, Indiana University. Dale Swanson then became St. Cloud's director and has not only continued a solid program of liberal education for students in theatre arts, but under his leadership in 1987 St. Cloud University was selected for one of the nation's most prestigious overseas tours when it took *The Wizard of Oz* to mainland China. This is believed to be the first and only non-professional group to pay such a visit.

Mankato State University

With the appointment of Dr. Theodore Paul in 1950, Mankato State began to attract notice for its theatrical achievements. First he transformed the Mask and Dagger extracurricular student theatre group into the Theatre Guild. Under Paul's direction the Guild became a popular theatre not limited to producing only "unknown Norwegian playwrights." The Guild's success with popular plays led directly to the building of a Performing Arts Center in 1967. The excellent 529 seat proscenium stage theatre was named the Ted Paul Theatre in 1985, at a dedication witnessed by four decades of Mankato theatre alumni.

Paul planned to institute a summer theatre in the new Center, but when the building was not yet completed he rented a huge tent and placed it on the land in front of the new facility. That original tent activity became The Highland Summer Theatre. This is a non-union professional summer stock theatre (now in its 22d season) which offers four major productions during its nine week season. The name reflects its location above the old campus which was on the low land of the river valley.

A master of fine arts degree gained approval in 1980 at which time an independent department of Theatre Arts was also established. Dr. Paul left in 1980 but the department carried on under the leadership of David Jorns, Tom Bliese, and Ronald Olausen. The present chair is Paul Hustoles. The theatre program at Mankato has continued to grow, and is now recognized as a major cultural force in south-central Minnesota. This year (1988) the department hosted the regional American College Theatre Festival. Popular theatre continues to be Mankato's philosophy as touring and children's theatre are a part of the programs.

Augsburg College

One of the last among Twin Cities colleges to overcome the traditional resistance to dramatic production was Augsburg College in Minneapolis. As was the case in so many of Minnesota's really significant theatrical achievements, the leaders responsible for the breakdown of resistance were women, in this case two outstanding teachers, Ailene Cole and Esther Olson.

It was in 1956 that Cole, formerly a high school teacher at Cannon Falls, accepted an $800 reduction in salary to take over the theatrical activities at Augsburg. Olson joined her a few years later. They compensated for the lack of physical equipment for a theatre at Augsburg by being superb human beings and dedicated teachers. At practically no expense to the college, an old church on Riverside Avenue was transformed via hard work into a small theatre. It may not have impressed many with its physical elegance, but it did radiate human warmth and understanding. It was a place where students loved to be—a place where they gained an appreciation of dramatic literature, both by observation and by participation. The plays they produced ranged from popular Broadway hits to the classics. Cole always tried to make certain that students would have at least one chance to see a play by Shakespeare and Olson tried to provide them a chance to see one by Ibsen.

Olson retired in 1975 and Julie Bolton began to teach acting and theatre history in her place. At the same time, Michael Berry became technical director at Augsburg in addition to his position as property manager at The Guthrie Theater. Bolton's professional theatre experience as an actress plus Berry's professional connection with The Guthrie began to change the nature of the Augsburg College Theatre. Gary Parker also joined the staff in 1982.

In the last ten years Augsburg has produced a number of students who

are currently working professionally in various areas of theatre, including design, acting, direction, management and television, in places such as The
Children's Theatre Company, The Guthrie, KSTP-TV, and the Orlando's
Sak Theatre in Los Angeles. One especially enterprising group of graduates
formed their own company called City Stock Theatre, which has been in
operation for three years in Minneapolis.

The theatre facility of Augsburg moved from one old church to another,
but a brand new theatre facility is currently under construction. It is scheduled
to open in the fall of 1988.

St. Olaf College

The theatre developed at St. Olaf in spite of considerable opposition. A
literary society was formed during the 1880's and by 1904 dramatic readings
of Shakespeare were permitted. Finally, in 1921, mainly through the efforts
of George Spohn and Elizabeth Kelsey, *The Merchant of Venice* was presented.
Eventually, Ibsen's plays (in Norwegian) were added to the program and in
1924 St. Olaf broadcast a production of *As You Like It*, which was believed
to be the first radio drama ever aired in the United States. By 1933 the college
was producing a five play season.

In 1949 Dr. Ralph Haugen joined the staff and Patrick Quade was named
director of the theatre. St. Olaf's production of *Godspell* in 1975 was selected
to represent the region at the American College Theatre Festival.

Today (1988) St. Olaf produces six major productions plus a play by its
summer children's theatre institute. Financially all of the work is fully subsidized by the college, and the present staff includes three director-teachers, a
scene designer, a technical director, a part-time costumer and 21 paid student
assistants.

Winona State University

The guiding spirit, as Winona State gradually emerged to become an important influence on theatre activities of southeastern Minnesota, was once
again a woman, Dorothy B. Magnus. As a student, when the college was
known as the Winona State Normal School, she served as president of an extracurricular drama club, the Winona State Players. By 1943 she had returned
to Winona State as a staff member and had established a department of speech
and theatre. She retired in 1970 but others carry on. Being somewhat of a pi-

oneer in the art of thrust staging, Winona State was one of the first colleges to show interest in establishing a relationship with The Guthrie Theater.

A typical season now consists of six plays performed in the Dorothy B. Magnus theatre at the campus Performing Arts Center. In 1976 the University became "host" for the Winona Community Theatre which presents three productions each summer.

Gustavus Adolphus College

Theatre at Gustavus began in 1919 with a production of *The Queen's Husband*. A few years later, however, and under the direction of Evelyn Anderson, Gustavus began to gain a reputation for excellent productions. During most of its years, theatrical activity both on stage and in the classroom at Gustavus took place under the umbrella of the department of speech, a common arrangement at the time, but also one that often led to friction. Gustavus, however, was fortunate. The head of the speech department was Evelyn's husband, Evan. If there was any friction it was not apparent on campus.

A highlight of the distinguished career of the Andersons came about in 1971 when the Schaefer Fine Arts Center opened on campus. It included classrooms, shops, storage facilities and an excellent little 300 seat thrust stage patterned after The Guthrie. It was appropriately christened the Anderson Theatre.

Evelyn Anderson retired in 1977, but the good work that she began has continued. According to a recent leaflet, theatre at Gustavus rests upon two beliefs: first that study and training in theatre opens eyes, minds and hearts — and hence contributes significantly to the development of the liberally educated person; and second, that professional theatre workers — the playwrights, designers, directors, actors and dancers of tomorrow should be broadly educated persons rather than narrowly trained specialists — and hence that liberal arts studies provide the best foundation for a career in theatre.

At present the theatre at Gustavus enjoys fully independent and accredited status. The program is closely allied to dance and other fine arts. Gustavus graduates have an impressive record of success in professional theatre, higher education, and teaching. The present chair of the department is Steve Griffith.

Other College Programs

Several important college theatre programs like those at St. Mary's College (Winona) and at Concordia College (Moorhead) have not been included simply because reliable information was not available. Our requests for information may simply have gone astray. Lack of space has also forced us to ignore some significant work at community colleges, private two year colleges, and some professional schools. We can only hope they will gain appropriate recognition elsewhere.

The High School Theatre

During the nineteenth century it was not the theatrical accomplishments at Minnesota colleges or at its University that first attracted attention; it was the work of Miss Leonora Austin at the old St. Paul High School. As early as December of 1882 Miss Austin joined with Miss Etta Hawkins, a St. Paul professional actress, to present a program of readings at the St. Paul Opera House. In March of 1884, The Debating Society of the St. Paul High School, quite obviously under the direction of Miss Austin, presented *The Sleeping Car* by William Dean Howells. Subsequent productions became even more impressive: they included Shakespeare's *The Taming of The Shrew* (1886) and *Henry IV* (1887). We do not know how well these plays were performed but there is reason to suppose that they were done very well. The fact that they attracted brief newspaper coverage, plus the fact that plays of such quality were unlikely to have been selected unless a reasonably high level of performance could be achieved indicates achievement well above the usual amateur level.

Moreover, either the same or another Miss Austin was still producing high school plays well into the twentieth century. At least, the St. Paul Central High yearbook for 1912 was able to observe with pride, "Not many schools have a Miss Austin." But although not many schools had a Miss Austin, at least one, South High in Minneapolis, had a Miss Helen R. Fish who appears to have been even more gifted. We have already met her as one of the directors of two Minneapolis community groups: The Assembly Players and the Portal Players. She had an impressive background which included a B.A. in both English and Latin from the University of Minnesota plus advanced work at Columbia University and at the prestigious Central School of Speech in London. She also published a book, *Drama and Dramatics*, which was widely used in public schools.

Miss Fish usually tried to produce a classic (old or new) each year plus a musical, usually by Gilbert and Sullivan or Sigmund Romberg. A number of outstanding students were deeply influenced by her work, including Sam Mervis (Michael Loring) and Allen Joseph who eventually enjoyed successful careers in Hollywood.

After such a successful beginning why did the high school theatre fail to develop in the way community and college theatres did? One answer may be found in the type of auditoriums in which high school actors were expected to perform. Beginning roughly in the twenties, architects and administrators discovered that a stage of sorts could be arranged in a basketball gymnasium. This was a disaster as far as intimate legitimate theatre was concerned. Bands and big splashy spectacles could still be effective on a gymnasium stage, but the quiet honest expression of ideas was doomed. A basketball gymnasium is scarcely a more appropriate environment for intimate theatre than an intimate theatre would be for basketball. There is no way, of course, to prove that basketball gymnasiums were the villains, but impressive achievements by a few schools which escaped this general architectural trend seem to support the theory. Two good examples are the schools at St. Louis Park and Hopkins. Each school building included a reasonably intimate theatre seating approximately 400.

That age has no monopoly on talent became abundantly clear when productions at these two high schools, using teen-age actors, were often more exciting and satisfying to their own audiences than were productions of the same plays by college, community, or even professional companies. Some of the effectiveness of these high school productions was, of course, influenced by audience enthusiasm and prejudice, but, as already mentioned, audience enthusiasm and prejudice are legitimate and very real factors in the enjoyment of the thing called theatre. Accordingly some members of the St. Louis Park audiences who saw its high school production of *Fiddler on The Roof* were able to maintain with complete honesty that they had never enjoyed the play so thoroughly even though they had seen the professional production of the same play on Broadway.

There are other secondary schools in Minnesota, of course, that have also done outstanding work. For the most part, however, far too many high school productions are lost in gymnasiums. But productions like those in the little theatres at Hopkins and St. Louis Park are enough to indicate that America's most undeveloped theatrical potential probably lies in its secondary schools.

A Christmas Carol (1975), directed by Stephen Kanee. Nicholas Kepros holding Dwyer Reilly.

Photo courtesy of the Guthrie Theater.

The Misanthrope (1987), directed by Garland Wright. Richard Hicks, Caroline Lagerfelt and Richard S. Iglewski.

Photo courtesy of the Guthrie Theater, Joe Giannetti, photographer.

The Gospel at Colonus (1986), directed by Lee Breuer. Clarence Fountain, Jevetta Steele, and Janice Steele.

Photo courtesy of the Guthrie Theater, Joe Giannetti, photographer.

The Matchmaker (1976), directed by Michael Langham. Barbara Bryne.

Photo courtesy of the Guthrie Theater, Joe Giannetti, photographer.

Costume drawing by Tanya Moiseiwitsch for Pallas Athena, in Guthrie's *The House of Atreus* (1967).

Photo courtesy of Annette Garceau, Leo J. Harris, photographer.

Ma Rainey's Black Bottom (1987), directed by Lou Bellamy. Jack Edwards, Peter Morange, Otis Montgomery, Edna Duncan, Danny Clark, Terry Bellamy, Kahdija Cousins and Marion McClinton.

Photo courtesy of Penumbra Theatre Company, George Heinrich, photographer.

Watercolor drawing for olio drop curtain, from the collection of the Twin City Scenic Company.

Photo courtesy of Performing Arts Archives, University of Minnesota Libraries.

The Adventures of Babar (1983), directed by Myron Johnson. Wendy Lehr and the Children's Theatre Company.

Photo courtesy of The Children's Theatre Company, George Heinrich, photographer.

Strega Nona (1987), directed by Jon Cranney and Tomie dePaola. Blayn Lemke, Cynthia Hechter, and Julie Briskman.

Photo courtesy of The Children's Theatre Company, George Heinrich, photographer.

The 500 Hats of Bartholomew Cubbins (1982), directed by John Clark Donahue. Christopher Passi and the Children's Theatre Company.

Photo courtesy of The Children's Theatre Company, George Heinrich, photographer.

Warp (1981), directed by William J. Norris. Geoffrey Ewing and the Mixed Blood Theatre Company.

Photo courtesy of Mixed Blood Theatre.

The Black Crook (1977), directed by Robert Moulton. Lee Walker.

Photo courtesy of Centennial Showboat, the Theatre Department, University of Minnesota.

PART FOUR

The Great Revival
1963–1988

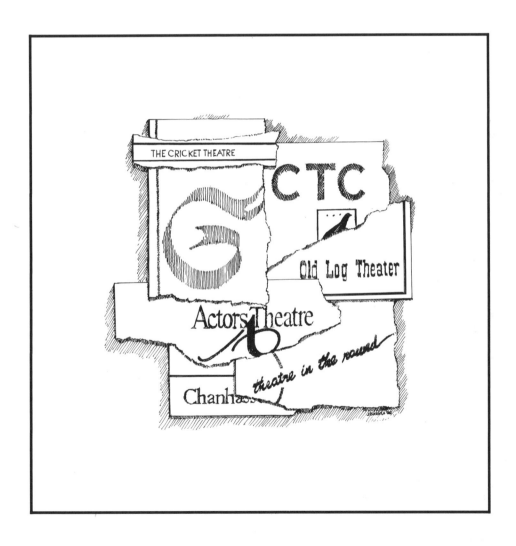

10

Professionals Who Preceded The Guthrie

THE revival of theatrical activity in the Twin Cities area during the sixties and seventies was astonishing. As already mentioned, it was reported at the 1984 Kudos celebration that 106 groups had produced plays in the Twin Cities at some time during 1983. Sixteen of these groups were professional—twenty, if one wished to count Chanhassen as four theatres and the Dudley Riggs theatres as two.

Why and how did such an abundance of activity come about? Some people graciously suggested that the University of Minnesota Theatre had something to do with it, and certainly a number of artists and craftspeople who are prominent today in Twin Cities theatres had attended the University. Moreover, the University's Drama Advisory Service, especially when under the direction of Ray Lammers and Dale Huffington, had considerable influence. Some people, including Tyrone Guthrie, saw the influence of the Theatre-in-the-Round Players and of the Old Log Theater as important. Others maintain that The Guthrie Theater itself was the major influence, and certainly Sir Tyrone Guthrie's example made theatre respectable—no longer need anyone apologize for being connected with the profession. But a more obvious influence has come from a remarkable change of attitude in regard to theatre funding. In L. N. Scott's day the theatre was expected to make a profit; in America until the end of World War II the theatre (including the educational theatre) was, at least, expected to be self-supporting; but today arts councils, foundations, businesses, and individuals contribute to theatres as they do to medicine, education, museums, and other things thought to be good for human civilization. The establishment of the National Endowments for the Arts and Humanities and the state arts boards in the 1960's has also made marketing or development directors important staff members of most professional theatres.

Related to the change of attitude in regard to funding, is a change of attitude toward the size of the building in which legitimate theatre can best be performed. Speaking in very general terms, we can observe that up to and including the first quarter of the twentieth century the "best theatre" was regarded as synonymous with the "biggest theatre." In Minneapolis this meant that Northrop Auditorium on the University of Minnesota campus with almost 5,000 seats was the champion. In contrast to this "bigger is better" philosophy, the present third quarter of the century appears to believe the opposite, for the revival of the legitimate theatre has taken place in small, unimposing playhouses: the original Old Log Theater seated less than 300, the Showboat 210, and TRP about 300. As we shall soon learn, The Cricket Theatre found that even its 384 seat auditorium in the Hennepin Center for the Arts was too big and has shifted to a smaller house seating only 213. Even The Guthrie Theater is considering reducing its seating from almost 1,500 to slightly over 1,000.

Why the change? There are three obvious answers: (1) people, even on the back row, need to hear the actors without electronic amplification; (2) people, even on the back row, need to see the actor's facial expression without using binoculars; and (3) people need to experience a subconscious sensation that the house is packed—that they are lucky to be present at such a successful event!

A small auditorium, of course, means that: (1) companies must remain small and inexpensive or (2) must be heavily subsidized, or (3) must charge exorbitant prices. Even so, the gains apparently outweigh the problems. But whether small intimate theatres, or a change in attitudes toward funding or other factors were responsible, the important fact remains that the living theatre in Minnesota actually did burst into bloom. Because of this astonishing abundance of theatres, Part Four has been divided into three chronological chapters. Chapter 10 is concerned with some of the professional theatres that preceded The Guthrie; Chapter 11 deals with The Guthrie itself; and Chapter 12 discusses some of the theatres which followed The Guthrie. In each chapter theatres are listed chronologically by date of establishment.

The Old Log Theater (1940 to Date)

The story of the Old Log Theater is in many ways an incredible success story. The idea of a straw hat summer theatre in the area was conceived by William S. Ulrich, a dreamer and promoter with an alcohol problem that finally resulted in his expulsion from his own small but tightly-knit family of actors even before the first play opened. It was left to Bob Aden, 19 or 20 years of age at the time, to hold the group together during its birth pains, although it appears to have been Deborah Tighe, a Wayzata woman, who found the backers to provide most of the limited but indispensable funding.

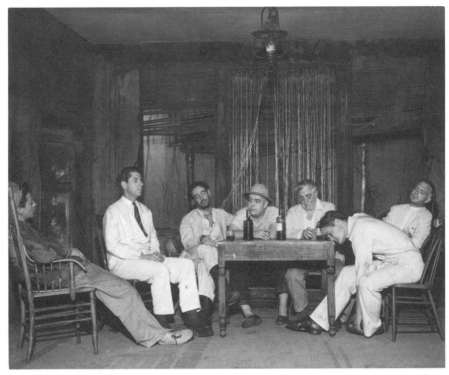

White Cargo (1947), directed by Don Stolz. Don Stolz, Joe Tomos, Bob Aden, Ken Senn, Louis Lytton, Dan Stapleton and Carl Shelton.

Photo courtesy of Old Log Theater, Anthony Lone, photographer.

In any case, it seems doubtful that Henry Van Liew or any other theatrical pioneer ever faced greater or more backbreaking odds than did this handful of stage-struck dreamers who first created the Old Log Theater in Harry Kuechle's barn on the shores of Lake Minnetonka in Greenwood. They had to shovel out evidence that the barn had once housed horses; they constructed a simple but adequate stage, hauled dirt for a sloping floor, built benches, scenery, outhouses, and installed a primitive lighting system — all of this at the same time they were learning their lines for the opening play. They even managed to maintain their courage in the face of an ominous omen for legend insists that early during the Old Log's first season a duck waddled onto the stage and promptly laid an egg.

Their first production, *Pennywise*, opened on the last day of May, 1940, with almost no rehearsal and less direction since Ulrich, the director and instigator of the group, had already been fired. But the company claimed to be "professional" and in its intimate and unique environment the audience seems to have applauded its promise rather than the results. John K. Sherman's review is mainly concerned with the event. He finally states in a review for the

Minneapolis Star-Journal on June 1, 1940, "The play itself is no great shakes; its purpose is entertainment."

The company's lack of a director was partially solved when Tim Ramsland, a gifted director from the University of Minnesota Theatre whom we have already met, agreed to take the job; but Ramsland, accustomed to working leisurely and in depth at the University, found only one week of rehearsal so inadequate that he seldom managed to get to the last act before the day of performance. But this was summer theatre where insane things often happen, and so the company survived. They survived partly because they found an old unemployed pro, Louis Lytton, to play character roles; they not only survived but prospered when June March, a beautiful and talented former burlesque stripper joined them in 1942 to play the lead in *White Cargo*. She became one of the Old Log's mainstays in years to come. But the outstanding addition to the group was an actor-director, a good looking "young kid with an M. A. from Northwestern." This "young kid" was, of course, Don Stolz who has been synonymous with the fortunes of the Old Log ever since.

War interrupted the program in 1942 when Stolz and some of the others were called into military service, but Stolz returned from the navy in 1946, and reopened the theatre. It was not a good season, but in characteristic fashion, Stolz, instead of begging for help, hitch-hiked to Los Angeles to find employment where he could earn enough money to pay off his debts and reopen the Old Log the following summer.

His 1947 season was more encouraging; then in 1948, Stolz came up with an outrageous, but very successful idea: he produced *The Front Page*, a newspaper melodrama, using the local sheriff and a number of Minnesota's most prominent newspaper personalities in the cast. The list included Gideon Seymour, Virginia Safford, Brad Morison, George Rice, Barbara Flanagan, and Sally Luther, plus Minnesota's outstanding drama critic, John K. Sherman. Not only was this project a triumph of publicity, it also resulted in a remarkably good production, although its high quality seemed to prove that community amateurs can be quite as effective on stage as professional actors.

The Front Page, repeated the following season, was joined by another unforgettable performance, this time of a more legitimate nature, when Marie Gale Bainbridge guest-starred in a beautiful production of *I Remember Mama*. By now the Old Log was well on its way to being accepted as one of the nation's important summer theatres. Minneapolis mayor Eric G. Hoyer proclaimed June 13, 1951 to be "Old Log Theater Day." Influential people, including Sinclair Lewis, rallied to the cause. Actors like Ken Senn, Rupert LaBelle, and Maxine Stetson lent loyalty and stability. Both Senn and LaBelle spent over twenty-five seasons at Old Log, establishing records for acting at a single theatre that won't often be equalled. Attendance which had numbered only 8,598 for 13 weeks in 1947, rose to 23,773 for 16 weeks in 1960.

Mister Roberts (1963), directed by Don Stolz. Dave Moore, Angus Duncan and Marcia Crawford.

Photo courtesy of Old Log Theater.

Like all living theatres, the Old Log has had its critics who have tended to question the "literary quality" of the plays chosen and the lack of "adequate rehearsal." Both charges ignore the very nature of a stock theatre. How can any theatre that must rely entirely on its box office for survival fail to maintain an eye toward the popular appeal of its offerings? The remarkable thing about the Old Log has not been that it sometimes produced popular froth like *The Vinegar Tree* or *Under The Yum Yum Tree*, but that it has frequently produced plays like *The Glass Menagerie, Desire Under the Elms, Ah, Wilderness!, A Streetcar Named Desire, Of Mice and Men, Look Homeward, Angel,* and *Waiting for Godot.* In fact, when challenged on the subject, Stolz flatly maintained that the Old Log had produced more "modern classics" (Ibsen to Albee) than any other theatre in America.

Yet regardless of whether the Old Log has or has not deserved to be criticised, all must admit that it has survived—and survived without the usual begging, handouts, and subsidies that most professional groups today demand. And it has been honest. The Old Log has never pretended to be a citadel of "Great Art" or revolutionary techniques. It has simply produced plays

The Odd Couple (1980), directed
by Don Stolz. Charlie Boone
and Roger Erickson.
Photo courtesy of Old Log Theater.

for a popular audience, while its players, like Don Stolz himself, have been decent, good-natured, dependable friends who have paid their bills and made an honest living by acting. The company has usually been a sort of happy family that refused to take itself or the "Great Art" of the theatre too seriously. Some people have been offended by this, but others have found its unpretentious informality appealing. Groups without a sense of reality — without an ability to relax and laugh at themselves and the world occasionally — seldom survive.

Part of the Old Log's attraction, of course, has been its location on the shores of Lake Minnetonka. Its original old log barn was inadequate, colorful, and intimate, accomodating an audience of approximately 240 persons. The company has always claimed to be professional, but it did not actually become an Equity company until 1947. In 1960 a new playhouse, seating 655 persons, was constructed on the site of the old one. The contractor was Herbert Bloomberg who subsequently built his own complex of dinner theatres at Chanhassen. The new building made it possible for the Old Log to become a year-round operation with productions often running six months or longer. The Stolz sons, all five of them, are successfully involved in the theatre business and Don himself was honored as the 1986 "Small Business Person of the Year" by the Minneapolis Chamber of Commerce. His achievement as the owner and resident director of the Old Log was noted as well as his production of industrial shows for companies across the nation. By the time the new Old Log opened in 1960, the company was settled and successful. The question since then has been, can it ever again be quite as colorful and appealing to its own rather special audience as it was during those wonderful wacky, happy, and sometimes heart-breaking years of its youth?

The Paul Bunyan Playhouse
(1951 to Date)

Challenging the Old Log for longevity and success is another Minnesota theater some 250 miles north of it, The Paul Bunyan Playhouse at Bemidji. It began in 1951 with great fanfare when a group of New York professionals led by Robert Gaus established a summer theatre at the Rutgers-Birchmont Lodge, but this first season was barely saved from total failure when several public spirited citizens led by Rowena DeWeese, the wife of a surgeon, and Margaret Lycan, the wife of a hotel owner, conducted a mid-season fundraising drive that netted enough money to enable the company to finish its season—enough money for board and room plus transportation back to New York.

Following the near financial disaster during this first season, a Playhouse board of directors was organized which included some of Bemidji's leading citizens. John Glas, business manager at Bemidji State University and a member of the Playhouse board of directors, has played a vital role in Playhouse business matters since the beginning. Subsequent seasons were less flamboyant, but more successful. Relying mostly on regional talent, a steady record of success has been achieved. Directors who have contributed to this success over the years include Lee Adey, Jay Hornbacher, Laurie Grossman and Michael Brindisi; actors who contributed would have to include Wendy Lehr, Bonnie Urseth, and Joel Hatch. But the group ensemble rather than individual talent has been the factor that maintained The Paul Bunyan's long life and reputation.

The Playhouse season normally lasts from mid-June to mid-August. It usually consists of seven productions of "time-tested popular successes." The 1988 season includes *Enter Laughing*, *Pinocchio*, *Angel Street*, *The Middle Ages*, *Camelot*, and *The Nerd*. Bemidji State University has assisted by coordinating a student workshop, under the direction of Louis Marchand, with the theatre's operation. Cast members and crews are paid on an average of about $135.00 per week. Equity members, of course, receive more. The present artistic director (1988) is Pamela Nice. The Paul Bunyan Playhouse must be rated not only as one of Minnesota's most successful summer theatres, but also as one of the most successful in the entire nation.

Theatre L'Homme Dieu (1960 to Date)

On summer weekends Minnesotans head for their cabins at the lake. These cabins often share lakeshores with camps, resorts and, occasionally, theatres. The Old Log, the Paul Bunyan Playhouse and Theatre L'Homme Dieu are good examples of theatres whose founders liked sylvan settings yet were prepared to deal with the problems, insects and animals which were invariably part of that world. Mosquitoes, of course, are to be expected, but Theatre L'Homme Dieu once had to deal with a scenery-nibbling woodchuck.

Theatre L'Homme Dieu is located by the lake of the same name near Alexandria, 130 miles northwest of the Twin Cities. The company uses buildings originally erected for a resort in the 1920's on five acres of lakeshore property. L'Homme Dieu was founded in 1960 by Art Houseman and Keith Michael from St. Cloud State University, with the goals of providing professional training for their students and offering good entertainment for the people of Alexandria.

The season lasts from mid–June to mid–August with a new play presented each week. Offerings are a typical summer stock mix of musicals and commercial hit plays. The 1987 season played to 81% capacity of the 276 seat house.

Helping L'Homme Dieu get started were members of the Theatre League. The strong association with St. Cloud State University continues. L'Homme Dieu has a paid staff and stock company and provides scholarships for students at the theatre. Artistic director for the past six years has been Susan Speers while a frequent guest director has been Jack Reuler of the Mixed Blood Theatre. L'Homme Dieu alumni are found in the casts and on the staffs of many Twin Cities theatres.

Some Unsuccessful Attempts to Become Professional

With the successful example of the Old Log, plus the abundance of amateur activity in the area it was inevitable that sooner or later some of the Twin Cities theatre units of the forties and fifties would attempt to go professional. Theatre St. Paul's unsuccessful attempt in this direction has already been mentioned. Four other early attempts made brave beginnings but also failed.

The first of these was the North Star Drama Guild organized primarily by Bob Gaus and Tom Scott, who had just returned from military service. Their initial plans and schemes for promotion were impressive: the advisory board, for example, included the name of Hubert Humphrey, Jr. Some notable successes were achieved, thanks mainly to some excellent directing, once again by Tim Ramsland. Fifteen shows were presented during the 1946–1947 season. The climax came during the 1947–1948 season when two Broadway stars, Blanche Yurka and Sidney Blackmer, appeared in Arthur Miller's *All My Sons*. But financial extravagance and the absence of steady, long-range dependability proved to be the North Star's undoing. Unable to control the group's finances, Tom Scott, the business manager, finally resigned. Fortunately, however, he did not leave the area. Instead, he established a theatrical costume business, Norcostco, that is one of the best in the nation—a theatrical business, if not a theatre, in which Minnesotans can take pride. As for the North Star Drama Guild, it was dissolved shortly after Scott's resignation in the spring of 1948.

A similar but slightly less pretentious theatre than the North Star was launched six years later by Robert Corrigan and Phil Gelb. Known as the Star Theatre, it opened in 1954. It managed to produce 24 plays, and burn one theatre building to the ground, before it finally gave up and closed during May, 1955.

A third attempt by former University of Minnesota students to found a professional theatre was also doomed to live a short life. This was the Plantation Playhouse which opened in 1946 in a building on the shore of White Bear Lake that once had been part of an amusement park complex. Kendrick Wilson, Perry Polsky, Allan Livers, Royal Eckert, David and Kenneth Raskin provided most of the inspiration and financial backing for the project. Plays were good and the project a moderate success although it might have lasted longer had not a polio epidemic discouraged audiences from coming. In any case, The Plantation Playhouse closed in 1948.

A fourth attempt to found a professional company was launched in 1960. This was the Minneapolis Repertory Theatre, led by an enthusiastic group of University of Minnesota students headed by Gary Schulz and Sanford Rosen. They rented space at 4217 Bloomington Avenue and managed to turn the building into a small open-stage theatre seating about 125 patrons. The selection of plays was varied and ambitious, ranging from *Medea* through *Look Back In Anger* and *I Am A Camera* to *The Boy Friend*. Most of the plays were directed by Schulz, Robert Hanson, Martha Pierce or Larry Whitely. The group also gained strength from some very talented actresses, including Liz Earl and Joan Eastman. With such a small house, however, it was obviously impossible to continue to pay even minimum salaries. The Repertory Theatre closed in May, 1962.

Semi-Professional Activity

In addition to these early attempts to go professional, there were three semi-professional projects — all of them related to the University Theatre, that merit attention. These were semi-professional in the sense that actors and craftspeople were paid, and paid rather well. On the other hand, membership in one of the groups was regarded as valuable training and experience rather than as professional employment. All three were summer only operations.

The Minnesota Centennial Showboat
(1958 to Date)

The oldest and most enduring of these semi-professional theatres is the Minnesota Centennial Showboat which was born on the evening of June 26, 1958, when Diane Albers — Miss Minnesota of 1958 — smashed a champagne bottle against the steel hull of an old sternwheel river boat, The General John Newton, and rechristened her as The Minnesota Centennial Showboat. A few hours later a wildly enthusiastic audience, including state officials and drama critics, gave the boat's first production, *Under the Gaslight*, a standing ovation, thus launching a history of theatrical success that still continues.

During its Centennial season the Showboat was towed from Minneapolis via tugboat, to St. Paul, Stillwater, Hastings, Red Wing, Lake City, Wabasha, and Winona. Due to Coast Guard restrictions in 1959, the boat remained moored at its landing below the University of Minnesota campus, but in 1960 it once more won its freedom to travel, which it usually did until 1972 when the cost of moving finally became prohibitive.

Centennial Showboat companies tried to play melodramas like *Under the Gaslight* sincerely enough so that audiences not only laughed but also became involved in the suspense and excitement. The 1959 company took pride in the fact that Lee Strasberg, America's foremost teacher of acting, praised *Billy The Kid*. The 1970 company was equally proud when Michael Langham, director of The Guthrie Theater, called *The Lady of Lyons* "absolutely charming." But the 1962 company was probably the happiest of all when Harold Clurman, Broadway director and critic, was so impressed by *Rip Van Winkle* that he recommended it to NBC; a scene from the show was eventually included in Jacqueline Kennedy's one hour television special, "A Stage for Excellence."

Melodramas, however, made up only a portion of the productions seen on the Showboat. Among the classics presented were: *Romeo and Juliet*, *The Merry Wives of Windsor*, and *A Midsummer Night's Dream* by Shakespeare; *The Rivals* and *The School For Scandal* by Sheridan; *The Devil's Disciple* and *Arms and*

The Minnesota Centennial Showboat, formerly known as The General John Newton, acquired in 1957.

Photo courtesy of the University Theatre, University of Minnesota

The Man by Shaw; *The Importance of Being Earnest* by Wilde; *Tartuffe* by Molière, and *The Birds* by Aristophanes. These classics, like the melodramas, almost without exception played to SRO (standing room only) audiences. The credit for this belongs mostly to the talented and enthusiastic young actors. Among them were Joan Eastman, who later played leading roles in the Broadway productions of *Stop The World, I Want to Get Off, Oliver*, and *Cactus Flower* before her untimely death at the age of 32; John Lewin, Richard Hilger, Sheridan Thomas, Lance Davis, and Jon Cranney, among the many who later enjoyed successful careers at The Guthrie; Bob Snook and Evie McElroy, who became mainstays at the Cleveland Playhouse; Loni Anderson, star of *WKRP in Cincinnati*, and Linda Kelsey, the Billie Newman of *The Lou Grant Show*.

During the early years of its existence, the Showboat took a sort of nineteenth century pride in being self-supporting and independent. But all things

Under the Gaslight, (1958) directed by Frank M Whiting. Ray Lammers, Jim Horswill and Julie Hutchison.

Photo courtesy of the University Theatre, University of Minnesota.

change and by the early 1970's the money it earned and the money it required disappeared into, or had to be drawn from, general University of Minnesota budgets. The politics of begging had invaded another theatre. There were advantages, of course. After 1974 the University assumed full responsibility for physical maintenance of the boat: actors specialized as actors and technicians specialized as technicians; seasons were reduced from two shows to one. All these changes were certainly in line with the general trends in modern life. Whether they indicated progress or loss depends upon one's philosophy. In any case, in spite of or because of changes, the Showboat is still afloat and still providing unique experiences for both the performers and for the audiences.

For its 30th anniversary in 1988, Robert Moulton created an original revue of life along the river, *Down-River Ramble: A Mississippi Panorama*. C. Lance Brockman designed a panorama (a nineteenth century type of very long painting on rollers) featuring views and events in the Mississippi's life for the anniversary show.

The Great Git-a-way (1966), directed by Frank M Whiting. Robert Reynolds, Bob Larsen, Jon Cranney, Raye Birk, Linda Kelsey and Loni Anderson.

Photo courtesy of the University Theatre, University of Minnesota.

The Stagecoach Players (1961 to 1979)

During the early sixties Osborne Klavestad—a colorful character who took great pride in his resemblance to Buffalo Bill—decided to add a theatre to his western-style museum and restaurant which was located between Savage and Shakopee, south of the Twin Cities. The result was a charming, old-fashioned "Opera House" seating 235 patrons. The performances, however, that took place in this opera house were the main things that made it important, and these were planned by two University of Minnesota staff members: Wendell Josal who served as managing director, and Robert Moulton who served as artistic director, very ably assisted by their wives, Elizabeth Josal, who handled the tickets, and Maggie Moulton, who provided the publicity.

For the most part, The Stagecoach Players featured melodramas: nineteenth century thrillers like *Ticket Of Leave Man*, and *The Streets of New York*, but these were usually cut, and spoofed unmercifully. Most people loved the result, but others, including most of the younger critics, objected. There was one feature of Stagecoach productions, however, that everyone loved, the Olios—the entr'acte numbers made up of songs, dances and variety. Moulton was a creative genius when it came to these, a gift acquired partly from his early experience in vaudeville, but largely based on his own incredible imagination.

A few of the best productions at The Stagecoach such as *The Merry Widow*, departed from the "Mellerdramer-olio" formula, but these were exceptions. The trite comment of those who wished to be critical was, "If you've seen one, you've seen 'em all." Moulton resigned in 1972 and was replaced by Lee Adey. By the late 1970's, the gasoline crisis made it more and more difficult for people to drive some 20 miles from the Twin Cities to Savage, and The Stagecoach closed its doors in 1979.

The actors, singers and dancers who appeared at the Stagecoach were mostly talented students from Twin Cities colleges. The result was an attractive, enthusiastic group capable of charming audiences on stage and off. Even though their salaries were not extraordinary, the joy of spending a summer at the Stagecoach usually was.

The Peppermint Tent (1967 to 1981)

The Peppermint Tent, which made its appearance in 1967, was a brain child of Willard L. (Tommy) Thompson, dean of the University of Minnesota's summer sessions. With the University's Showboat doing SRO business at its river landing, it occurred to Thompson that a colorful little red and white circus tent on the grassy bank above the Showboat might provide an attractive home for the production of children's plays.

Lee Adey, a University Theatre staff member, was assigned to direct the project. During its first summer three plays were produced: *Androcles and The Lion*, *Daniel Boone*, and *Huckleberry Finn*. This first season was a success, even though the audiences tended to be much younger than anticipated — mostly bright-eyed youngsters from four to ten years of age. Plays like *Huckleberry Finn* were beyond their span of attention. Because of this, during the years to come, plays produced at the Peppermint Tent shifted more and more towards an informal, colorful, improvisational style of performance that invited audience participation. Normally the paid company consisted of about six actors plus a director, scenic technician, and costumer.

During the seventies, because of new regulations of the Minneapolis Park Board, the Peppermint Tent moved from its location on the river bank to a new home in the Stoll Theatre at the Rarig Center. Children were no longer disturbed (or entertained) by mosquitoes, thunderstorms, towboats, automobiles, or the roar of jet planes overhead. Some of the charm, however, of the Peppermint Tent on the river bank had been lost.

Professionals of the Early Sixties

As already indicated, the announcement on May 31, 1960, that Tyrone Guthrie was going to establish his theatre in Minneapolis touched off a surge of theatrical enthusiasm. But the Old Log and at least three other important theatre companies had begun producing before The Guthrie actually opened in 1963.

Dudley Riggs and his Brave New Workshop (1958 to Date)

In the good old days when a drugstore sold drugs and a service station sold gasoline, when a Ford was a Ford and a Buick a Buick, vaudeville was vaudeville, opera was opera and the legitimate theatre legitimate—a place where properly written plays were memorized by actors for presentation before an audience. That has passed. Today drugstores and service stations sell everything from playing cards to Bibles; Fords and Buicks sell everything from luxury limousines to cramped compacts, and so the legitimate theatre also tries to be all things to all people, hesitating not a moment to steal from ballet, variety, burlesque, opera or whatever. Consequently, we can no longer eliminate Dudley Riggs from this book even though his productions are probably no more "legitimate" than were those of Buffalo Bill or Weber and Fields back in the good old days.

Dudley Riggs himself is a fifth generation circus performer. For awhile he attended the University of Minnesota but not long enough to do him much harm. Riggs brought his Instant Theatre Company to Minneapolis in 1958. Its comedy routines were succeeded by political satire of the Brave New Workshop. The Workshop began in 1961, when Riggs and three University friends came up with 100 ideas for satirical, social and political sketches. Performances took place at Dudley's Cafe Espresso, which was located at 207 East Hennepin Avenue (later moved to 2605 Hennepin Avenue South). In 1971 Riggs added his second theatre, the ETC (Experimental Theatre Company) at Seven Corners in Minneapolis. He later formed a touring group that has brought his kind of comedy to Cuba, Morocco, Czechoslovakia, and is now scheduled to invade China.

One purpose of the touring company is to provide training for the Dudley Riggs brand of actors. A typical performer now spends two years in a workshop, two more years on tour, and finally graduates into a regular company after which he usually moves on to glory in Hollywood or elsewhere. According to an article written by Michael Anthony, a former member of the

Dudley Riggs in his office on Hennepin Avenue.

Photo courtesy of Mike Paul/Act Two.

Dudley Riggs Workshop, the number of actors who have at one time or an-
other worked for Dudley could fill a crowd scene in *Gandhi*, and many of
these actors have gone on to make it big in the acting or writing professions.
Neil Thompson, Nancy Steen and Michael McManus played roles in
M.A.S.H. Dan Sullivan became drama critic for the *Los Angeles Times*. Richard
Guindon became a syndicated cartoonist for *The Detroit Free Press*, and Irv
Letofsky became Sunday editor for the *Los Angeles Times* [*Minneapolis Tribune*,
May 8, 1983].

    The type of performance that Riggs presents has a long history. It goes
back at least to the medieval commedia dell'arte and possibly all the way to
the cave men. It usually presents a series of sketches created improvisationally
and then scripted, but never rigidly or formally memorized. Improvisation is
not only always possible, but frequently necessary since Riggs loves to keep
his performers on their toes by locking doors to exits or hiding necessary
properties. The sketches ordinarily present a satire of some phase of human
life, attempting to cover current issues with "promiscuous hostility" as the

Vietnam! the Musical (1987). Michelle Cassioppi, Christine Decker, Peter Staloch, Jim Detmar and Gene Larch.

Photo courtesy of the Dudley Riggs Theatres.

goal of the theatre is stated. They cannot really be written about; they must be seen and heard to be experienced. Among Sullivan's contributions were parodies of Guthrie productions: *Hamlet*, as if written by Tennessee Williams; and *Oedipus*, as if written by Noel Coward. The young husband says to his wife and the mother of his children, "Turns out, Jocasta, you're my mother." "Quite so, will you have tea?" A 1986 satire on the evangelical movement featured a church for secular humanists who instead of praying together doubted together. Such momentary theatre is a tribute to the human spirit. Neither dictators, religious fundamentalists, nor modern pedagogs have been able to crush it. In 1988 the American Association of Comedy Artists presented Riggs with a Charley Award as a tribute to his theatre's longevity and to its success as a training ground.

The Children's Theatre Company
(1961 to Date)

The Children's Theatre Company is a success story with native roots. The story begins with Beth Linnerson, a sensitive young University of Minnesota student with a talent for theatre and a compassion for young people in some of the less fortunate neighborhoods of Minneapolis. Most children's theatres, especially those sponsored by well-meaning, public spirited club women, tend to provide opportunities for the gifted child. This is also true in most school productions where the bright and talented students are naturally the ones selected for extracurricular activities such as plays and programs. In the competitive world we live in, it is rare indeed to find someone who is also concerned about the less gifted and less fortunate—someone with love, patience and understanding—someone concerned about the ugly ducklings, the misfits and the lonelies. Beth Linnerson was such a rare individual. She believed that talent, intelligence, and leadership could be found among the underprivileged as well as the privileged. In 1961 she began working with children on the West Bank, a neighborhood across the river from the main campus of the University of Minnesota. Several friends joined her and together the adults and children—using a combination of creative dramatics and improvisation—created some entertaining and highly original shows, which they presented to the public on Saturday and Sunday afternoons in Mama Rosa's Pizza Parlor.

The Moppet Theatre, as they called their group, soon began to attract audiences; it also began to attract the loyalty of a number of dedicated volunteers. Among them was John Clark Donahue, a high school art teacher, who began working for The Moppets as scene designer and technical director, but who soon became its dominant personality and, finally, its artistic director.

The success of their first season made it necessary for The Moppets to expand into larger quarters, and this became possible when Linnerson and her friend, Martha Pierce, secured the right to move into an old abandoned police station just around the corner from Mama Rosa's. Eager volunteer labor by some forty theatre students and children soon transformed the old station into a humble but adequate home for The Moppets.

By 1964 the group was widely recognized for the high quality of its work. Its staff consisted of Linnerson as educational director; Donahue, artistic director; John Davidson, administrative director; and Sue Kelly, box office and promotion. There were also some extremely talented and dedicated actors, including Bain Boehlke and Wendy Lehr.

Unfortunately it was also during 1964 that a fundamental conflict surfaced. Donahue and the most talented members of the group began to envision a professional art theatre for children of all ages. Linnerson and her friends still clung to a less ambitious dream of a theatre for humanity—for the moppets of an urban society. She saw bigness and importance as a threat; Donahue saw bigness and importance as irresistible goals. When the inevitable split came, Donahue, Davidson and most of the prominent members moved into the lecture hall of the Minneapolis Institute of Arts where they opened a season of plays in 1965 under the new name of The Children's Theatre Company.

Although the lecture hall in the Institute of Arts was a 646 seat auditorium with only a speaker's platform for a stage, Donahue quickly began to display his genius for the visual and aural elements of production. Although sometimes criticised for neglecting the intellectual and story telling qualities of children's theatre, Donahue, with the help of an extremely gifted scene designer, Jack Barkla, soon began turning settings, costumes, choreography, and all other technical elements of a production into shows that were stunning. Children and adults in the audience were usually held spellbound, even though they might disagree as to what it all meant.

In any event, The Children's Theatre Company flourished. A strong educational program was added, and the staff slowly increased. Wages were at first minimal. Prior to 1974, staff members were expected to act in shows, and perhaps also teach classes or serve in administrative capacities. A typical work week was seventy hours long and the salary for nine months was between $3,000 and $5,000. Classics, including John Lewin's translation of Molière's *Le Bourgeois Gentilhomme*, were imaginatively produced, as were new plays—several of them, like *Hang On To Your Head*, were written by Donahue himself.

It was not long before national and international attention began to be showered upon The Children's Theatre. In 1972 the Company was featured at the Association International de Theatre pour l'Enfance et la Jeunesse in Montreal. In 1973 the Company received the Jennie Heiden Award from the American Theatre Critics Association for excellence in professional children's theatre. In 1981, it received an even more prestigious honor, the Margo Jones Award for its production and development of new plays and playwrights. Foundation support became important. Grants were secured from the Minnesota State Arts Council, The National Endowment for the Arts, and the Rockefeller Foundation, plus increasing support from the Minneapolis Society of Fine Arts under whose roof the theatre was housed. The greatest boost came in 1974 when The Children's Theatre Company moved into a new $4.5 million dollar home, designed by Kenzo Tange as a part of the expansion of the museum. Its main theatre has a well-equipped stage and an auditorium

Interior of the Children's Theatre, designed by Kenzo Tange in 1974. The Theatre adjoins the Minneapolis Institute of Arts.

Photo courtesy of the Children's Theatre Company, Warren Reynolds, photographer.

seating 746. There is also a small studio theatre. It is probably the finest playhouse for children's theatre to be found anywhere in the world.

Donahue's genius expressed itself in many ways: first, as already indicated, was his ability to combine dance, music, visual backgrounds and theatre into stunning productions. He also displayed great ability in public relations, working skillfully with foundations, the schools, and the news media. Finally, he demonstrated superb ability as a teacher.

But in spite of his striking talents and achievements, Donahue and his reputation vanished almost instantly when, in April, 1984, he was convicted on charges of sexual misconduct with students. At first, many people feared that The Children's Theatre itself would collapse. Donahue up to that time had been identified as its imagination, heart and soul. But instead of collapsing, The Children's Theatre quickly proved that it had matured into an institution much stronger than any one individual. An interim board made up of members from The Guthrie, the Minnesota Orchestra, the Minneapolis Society of Fine Arts, the Walker Art Center, and the St. Paul Chamber Orchestra was appointed. The theatre school was closed. Jon Cranney, who had been a producer, stage manager and actor at The Guthrie, was selected as the new artistic director. Under Cranney's leadership, and with the help of Bill Connor as executive director, the Children's Theatre Company not only stabilized, but enhanced its reputation for exciting creativity, outstanding productions and daring innovations. Between 1984 and 1987, season ticket sales for the main stage series of seven plays increased 70%. The Theatre's 1986–1987 budget of $3,300,000 ended up with a surplus of some $14,000.

And so past scandals seem to have been forgotten and forgiven. Two world-renowned writer-illustrators, "Dr. Seuss" (Theodore Geisel) and Tomie dePaola have both designated The Children's Theatre as the only authorized producer of stage adaptations of their works. In 1987 Cranney and Connor made a trip to the Soviet Union. As a result an extraordinary cultural exchange has been arranged. Not only does The Children's Theatre plan to visit Moscow, but Moscow's outstanding Central Children's Theatre plans to visit Minnesota. Moreover, Cranney plans to direct a play at the Central while Alexi Borodin, the Russian director, is scheduled to direct at The Children's Theatre. Obviously, The Children's Theatre is one of Minnesota's proudest theatrical achievements.

The Firehouse (1963 to 1969)

Mention The Firehouse theatre to most Minnesotans today and one will normally draw a blank stare of non-recognition. A few pillars of the Establishment will respond with, "Oh, that was that awful theatre that used dirty words and nudity." Only a handful will recall or realize that The Firehouse was one of the most dedicated and significant theatre groups ever to establish a temporary home in the Twin Cities.

Its founders were Marlow Hotchkiss, Jim Faber, James Carlson and Charles Morrison III. At the beginning the theatre was meant to pay its own way, but the drain on Hotchkiss' inheritance led to a change to non-profit status. It opened in 1963 only a few weeks before the opening of The Guthrie. In contrast to The Guthrie with its emphasis on the best of the classics, old and new, The Firehouse, located in an abandoned fire station on Minnehaha Avenue and Lake Street in Minneapolis, was a radical, avant-garde theatre searching for new ways of doing everything. Actors, authors, directors and technicians worked together in workshops, rehearsals, and performances in creative, sometimes bizarre, manners. Sydney S. Walter, who soon became the artistic director of the group, had been a member of the Open Theatre in New York—to some, the most exciting, to others, the most disgusting thea-

Krapp's Last Tape (1967),
directed by Marlow Hotchkiss.
Paul Boesing appearing in the
Firehouse Theater production.

Photo courtesy of Martha Boesing,
Mike Paul/Act Two, Photographer.

tre in America. Many of the new plays produced at The Firehouse were by
authors like Megan Terry and Jean-Claude Van Itallie—playwrights who
were prominent on New York's Off-Off-Broadway.

These were the Vietnam years and the Establishment often regarded The
Firehouse as a revolutionary, political-action group, but the members always
maintained that they were revolutionary towards the theatre itself and towards life in general rather than towards politics. From its own point of view
The Firehouse was a voice crying for sanity and compassion in the wilderness
of an evil, hypocritical, irrational world. From the standpoint of the Establishment on the other hand, The Firehouse was the ultimate in moral
decadence.

In 1969 Walter and most of the company moved to California hoping to
find a more friendly environment for their off-beat ways near the University
of California (Berkeley) campus. Fortunately two of their best actors, Paul
and Martha Pierce Boesing, elected to remain in Minnesota, and since have
wielded a great influence in a number of local groups.

In a story written by Mike Steele when the Firehouse announced its closing, Arthur Ballet was quoted as commenting:

> They've served as a wonderful laboratory for students. The Firehouse has given
> them a chance to see things three or four years before they hit New York and
> several of our students [from the University of Minnesota] have joined the com-

pany . . . And they've done some of this Country's most interesting playwrights when no one else would have touched them. Now these playwrights are big names. They've had extraordinary taste. [*Minneapolis Tribune*, June 15, 1969.]

The names of a few of these playwrights included Samuel Beckett, Harold Pinter, Eugene Ionesco, and Sam Sheppard.

11

The Guthrie Theater

To understand the importance of The Guthrie Theater one must first understand a bit about America's theatrical history. Prior to Tyrone Guthrie's arrival in Minneapolis, almost all of the nation's professional theatres had settled in one location, New York City, a situation which obviously made no more sense than it would have done to localize all symphony orchestras or all art galleries in a single city. Nor was this strange localization of the American theatre its only problem. Guthrie saw others; for example, he preferred a different type of playhouse, one with a thrust stage that would bring audiences and performers closer together, and one that would also provide comparative freedom from the tyranny of technicians, who, in the proscenium theatre with its emphasis on scenery rather than on the play or the acting, had become a disproportionate burden and expense. But Guthrie's chief criticism of the American theatre related to its policy of producing single plays instead of encouraging a group of artists who could produce a series of plays. He disliked America's commercial preoccupation with the production of new plays that could only hit or miss. There was no place in the American theatre for solid but moderate success, and no place where the best of the old plays, the classics, could be seen again and again.

From a financial standpoint the Broadway system had its obvious merits. If the play was a smash hit it could make enormous profits, while if it turned out to be a failure it could be written off as a tax deduction. But from the actors' standpoint, the system was deadly. If the play failed, the actors were denied their chance to develop their skills before a paying audience. On the other hand, if the play was a hit, the initial elation of the actors was destined to degenerate into the boredom of repeating the same thing over and over, eight performances a week for months, or years. Actors, of course, could quit the show when boredom became unbearable, but this did not excuse the system. For actors to develop to their highest potentials either the old stock company routine, or, better still, the repertory system (still common in Europe) had enormous advantages.

Almost everyone connected with the American theatre was keenly aware of these problems, but no one was willing or able to do anything to solve them. Fame and fortune for actors depended upon their ability to succeed in either New York or Hollywood. For them to appear in person elsewhere (other than as guest stars or as a member of a first class New York touring company) was a sure sign that the actors were either "washed-up" or of decidedly second-rate talent. This was an irrational stereotype, but one that even well-established theatre artists dared not challenge. It was a situation that could be challenged only by one of the best, and fortunately Tyrone Guthrie was recognized throughout the world as one of the best, if not the very best. Moreover, Guthrie not only rated at the top of his profession, he was something of a maverick who saw little fun in just directing another hit in New York or London. He had already established an exciting new theatre in the little railroad town of Stratford, Ontario in 1953. Consequently he found the idea of establishing a classic repertory theatre in some city outside of New York quite irresistible. The idea of such a theatre was mentioned in a note by critic Brooks Atkinson on the drama page of the *New York Times*. Representatives of cities interested in such a plan were asked to respond. Replies were received from Boston, San Francisco, Chicago, Minneapolis, Cleveland, Milwaukee and Detroit. Guthrie, his wife, and Oliver Rea, a young New York producer, visited all of these cities to evaluate the proposals. Peter Zeisler, the stage director who was the third member involved in the plan, was unable to join in the trip so, as Guthrie later wrote, he and Rea set off with "spears and blowpipes, with pretty beads, bright shells . . . to bribe the native chieftains."

Fortunately for Minnesota, the location finally selected was Minneapolis, even though other cities, especially Detroit and Milwaukee, were offering much more attractive financial inducements. But Guthrie and his associates were not to be swayed by money alone. He liked Minnesota's healthy climate, its culture, and the level of education. He was perhaps a bit prejudiced by the fact that theatre people, rather than the usual business or political leaders, had been the first to invite him to consider Minnesota. In the end, his decision, like most big decisions, was based not so much on cold logic as on a personal hunch. He admitted that he "wanted" to come, although the final decision in the matter was apparently left to Rea and Zeisler. It was a great day for Minnesota when, on May 31, 1960, Oliver Rea announced that Guthrie's theatre would be built on T. B. Walker Foundation property in Minneapolis.

Three years went by before the theatre actually opened. Ralph Rapson, the architect, and the theatre's steering committee (John Cowles, Jr., Louis Zelle, Pierce Butler III, Justin Smith, Roger Kennedy, H. Harvard Arnason,

Sir Tyrone Guthrie is shown with plans for the Guthrie Theater.
The Theater building, adjoining the Walker Art Center on
Vineland Place in Minneapolis, was designed by Ralph Rapson and
Associates, and opened in May, 1963.

Photo courtesy of The Guthrie Theater.

Philip Von Blon, and Frank Whiting) suffered some anxious moments as the
cost of the building kept rising above the original estimate of $1,500,000. Fi-
nally, after some severe cuts in the plans, it was completed for roughly
$2,200,000. On a brighter side as the opening drew near, public enthusiasm
began to run high, and ticket sales boomed, thanks mainly to the work of
some 700 young women (The Stagehands) who, under the leadership of
Phyllis Wohlrabe and with dedicated volunteers like Sheila Livingston, sold
a record 23,305 season subscriptions. While Guthrie showed great apprecia-

Pictured in Sir Tyrone Guthrie's 1963 production of *The Three Sisters*, the thrust stage of the Guthrie Theater seats 1,437 people, with no seat further than 52 feet from stage center.

Photo courtesy of The Guthrie Theater.

tion for the efforts of The Stagehands, later artistic directors allowed them to feel unimportant and neglected, so this vital organization somehow withered away.

And so the theatre opened on May 7, 1963 with Guthrie's modern dress production of *Hamlet*. George Grizzard played the title role with Jessica Tandy as Gertrude and Ellen Geer as Ophelia. Reviews for *Hamlet* were surprisingly mixed, but reviews for the remainder of the first season: *The Miser* (Molière), *The Three Sisters* (Chekhov), and *Death of A Salesman* (Miller), could be classified as "raves." The hit of the season was Douglas Campbell's production of *The Miser* with Hume Cronyn and Zoe Caldwell playing key roles. As Tom Prideaux, the *Life* critic, expressed it, "*The Miser* . . . busted out like a gay Jacques-in-the-box; it is easily the most entertaining U. S. production of Molière ever given." [*Life*, May 24, 1963.] By the end of the first season everyone agreed that Guthrie, by now Sir Tyrone Guthrie, had scored another daring triumph by establishing a classic repertory theatre outside New York City.

The Miser (1963), directed
by Douglas Campbell.
Zoe Caldwell and
Hume Cronyn.

Photo courtesy of
The Guthrie Theater.

Although The Guthrie Theater is now celebrating its twenty-fifth season,
an impressive life for any American theatre, all has not been smooth sailing.
To begin with, Guthrie's dream of establishing a repertory company was
never more than partially fulfilled and by 1984 had apparently died completely. His dream of making his theatre essentially a classic theatre, where audiences could see the best from past ages, had fared little better. His desire to
break away from proscenium staging and expensive scenery had been over-
ruled. Finally, his hope of establishing a strong relationship to the University
of Minnesota had also come to naught.

Unlike most members of the theatrical profession Tyrone Guthrie was
comfortable in an academic environment as he was an Oxford graduate and
had been the Chancellor of the University of Belfast. During his three years
at the helm of The Guthrie, considerable progress was made in establishing
educational ties. The University of Minnesota officially appointed Sir Tyrone
Guthrie as a visiting professor. In this capacity he conducted student workshops and directed an all-student production of *Six Characters in Search of an
Author*. He also directed a workshop consisting of scenes from *Oedipus Rex*

and another with scenes from plays by Thornton Wilder. His associate directors, Edward Payson Call and Douglas Campbell, also directed student productions and offered workshops. By combining the prestige and resources of the University and of The Guthrie it was also possible to offer summer workshops featuring such celebrities as Dame Sybil Thorndyke, Sir Lewis Casson, Lee Strasberg, Harold Clurman, Alan Schneider, Victor Jory and Arthur Miller.

But the most practical of all The Guthrie - University of Minnesota projects was the McKnight (later the Bush) Fellowship program . The idea was simply to bring ten to fifteen "all-American" theatre students to the University of Minnesota on scholarships. The initial plan was that they would spend fall quarter and most of winter quarter at the University in specialized training, while the remainder of the year would be devoted to practical experience at The Guthrie. At the end of the year The Guthrie might decide to employ a few of the "Fellows" as full members of the company. If not, the "Fellows" could, if they wished, return to the University of Minnesota to complete their academic programs. Unfortunately, this cooperation between the University Theatre and The Guthrie degenerated into rivalry — largely a conflict over the proportion of time that the "Fellows" should spend at each. Actors Equity also provided a coffin nail by decreeing that Fellows could no longer play speaking roles. Guthrie, in contrast, had insisted that the Fellows should be treated as full members of the company. In his opening production of *Hamlet*, for example, Al Rossi and Mike Levin played Rosencrantz and Guildenstern while John Lewin played the churlish priest. After Michael Langham, the last of the professionals to understand the relationship departed, foundations decided no longer to fund the program, and so the McKnight program, which had at first been seen as only one of the beginning steps in University - Guthrie cooperation, came to an end, or at least to a temporary pause.

As to the highs and lows of The Guthrie seasons themselves, the first of the highs occurred during Sir Tyrone's first three years. The success of the first year, 1963, has already been mentioned. The second year (1964) extended the season from 20 to 24 weeks, thus increasing the total possible attendance, and each of the plays (*Henry V*, *St. Joan*, *The Glass Menagerie* and *Volpone*) scored solid, though not spectacular, successes. The third year (1965) maintained a strong aura of success largely because of two productions: a repeat of *The Miser* which played to 84.2% capacity and an unexpected and surprising success, *The Caucasian Chalk Circle* (Bertolt Brecht), directed by young Ed Call. As in the first season's hit, *The Miser*, *Chalk Circle* once more featured Zoe Caldwell and played to 80.6% of capacity.

Guthrie had made it clear from the first that he would be able to serve for only three years as artistic director. By then he assumed that the theatre would be established. Moreover, he was constantly grooming Douglas Campbell as his heir apparent, and since Campbell, already recognized as an outstanding actor, had also scored successes under Guthrie as a director, there was a general feeling of optimism about his ability to carry on after Guthrie retired. Furthermore, as already mentioned, another young director, Ed Call, had scored a surprising success during The Guthrie's third season with his stunning production of *The Caucasian Chalk Circle*. But, in spite of all the precautions for a smooth transition, Guthrie's departure seemed to remove the magic. Attendance for the 1966 season dropped to 66.8%. The production that season of *S. S. Glencairn* (O'Neill) reached an all-time low of 47.1% of capacity. Danger signals began to fly. Things improved in 1967 when Guthrie returned to direct an outstanding production of *The House of Atreus*. This was an adaptation of Aeschylus' *The Oresteia* by a former University of Minnesota student, John Lewin. It played to 96% in 1967 and to 95% capacity when it was repeated in 1968. A new flurry of interest was also added in 1967 when a somewhat smaller company of Guthrie players moved into The Crawford-Livingston Theatre in St. Paul for a winter season consisting of *She Stoops to Conquer* (Goldsmith), *Tango* (Mrozek), and *Enrico IV* (Pirandello). About the same time still another small theatre, The Other Place, was added near The Guthrie. This was devoted to actor training and experimental productions.

But in spite of all the activity — or perhaps because of it — Douglas Campbell decided to resign. Ed Call and Mel Shapiro, with help from guest directors like John Hirsch, tried to carry on, but by 1969 the season attendance had fallen to a mere 60.8% and a worried Board of Directors realized that something drastic would have to be done if The Guthrie were to survive. As Sheila Livingston expressed it, the theatre was "founded by a giant, it takes a giant to make it work." Guthrie himself was deeply concerned, and in desperation the Board tried to persuade him to return, but health and other reasons made this impossible. He died a year later, on May 15, 1971. Michael Langham paid him a fitting tribute: "He was the greatest human being I have ever known . . . his was a life that needs celebrating, not a death that needs mourning." [*Minneapolis Tribune*, May 16, 1971.]

Fortunately for Minnesota, Michael Langham, one of the few living directors who could measure up to The Guthrie Theater's challenge, had already accepted the job of artistic director. A superb director, especially of classic comedy, Langham proved to be the right man at the right time.

Unlike so many modern directors who reinterpret a classic because of a driving desire to make it "relevant and meaningful" plus a desire to display their own cleverness, Langham displayed a deep love and respect for the classic itself and for its author. One, of course, can never be certain what a deceased playwright really intended, but at least Langham tried. And as Aristotle observed some 2,400 years ago, the story (plot), the ideas (thought) and the human beings (character) are the elements of drama that really count. The spectacle (visual and aural) is purely secondary. Langham's productions would have pleased the Greek sage. They made sense. The humanity burned through, and the audience understood why the play had become a classic.

As implied earlier in this book, the Langham approach has enormous practical advantages since its central elements require playwriting, directing, and acting — things that a good repertory company already had, and at no extra bother or expense. Moreover, unlike productions that dazzle audiences with a spectacle (visual and aural), a Langham classic is not forced into deadly comparison (competition) with other spectacles such as opera, ballet, or with films or television. Moreover, Langham was a leader, who quickly restored the confidence and the sense of direction that The Guthrie Theater without Guthrie had been lacking. For the next seven years with the aid of gifted young associate directors like Stephen Kanee and David Feldshuh, The Guthrie enjoyed steady and dependable success.

Langham's first season (1971) with productions like *Cyrano de Bergerac* featuring Paul Hecht, and *The Taming of The Shrew* with Len Cariou and Michele Shay, quickly restored The Guthrie to solid footing. But with Langham's departure in 1977, the theatre once more skidded into perilous danger. Alvin Epstein, like Douglas Campbell an excellent actor, but with comparatively limited experience as a director, was selected as Langham's successor. Perhaps he was an artist rather than an artistic administrator; in any case he seemed unprepared to handle the complex problems of the huge establishment into which The Guthrie had grown. In the middle of his second season (1978) he resigned. Young directors like Stephen Kanee and Richard Russell Ramos with the help of a steady hand from Don Schoenbaum, the theatre's managing director, carried on quite successfully until 1980. Perhaps with solid backing from the Board of Directors and from the company they could have succeeded in creating a steady and lasting program, but the prevailing opinion was that somehow, somewhere, The Guthrie would have to find another giant. Eventually it found one, this time an international giant, the Romanian director and architect, Liviu Ciulei.

Critical acclaim during Ciulei's first season, 1981, was extravagant and The Guthrie received a coveted Tony Award for its success. Ciulei deserved great credit for having increased respect for The Guthrie both nationally and internationally. His popularity with many theatre goers in the Twin Cities, especially with those who had a taste for "modern" theatre, was also high, but his old audience at The Guthrie was unimpressed. Failing to understand what Ciulei's more avant-garde directors like Andrei Serban and Richard Foreman were trying to say, too many theatregoers just no longer bothered to attend. An evaluation of the Ciulei years is, therefore, difficult; many maintain that he won an audience nationally but lost it locally. His first productions, *The*

Tempest (Shakespeare) followed by Richard Foreman's production of *Don Juan* (Molière) were certainly classics by name, but the results were starkly modern. Had Molière been able to attend *Don Juan* he would have been impressed by the blasts of sound and the blinding lights with which Foreman tried to shake modern audiences out of their smug complacency, but Molière might never have realized that the play was his own. Foreman is obviously appreciated and understood at his own Ontological-Hysteria Theater in New York, but too many of his effects simply failed to communicate his, or Molière's ideas, to the rather conservative Midwestern audience at The Guthrie.

Under Ciulei's leadership The Guthrie was often said to have become a director's theatre rather than a playwright's theatre. This statement, however, once again requires modification, for certainly Guthrie and Langham had also emphasized the director's interpretation of the classics. Maybe the difference was only one of degree. Nevertheless productions by Guthrie and Langham, although they usually tried to magnify and lend contemporary meaning to the classics, still tried to be true to what they believed the author intended. On the other hand, some of Ciulei's directors practically annihilated the playwright. Some people felt that Andrei Serban's production of *Figaro* (Beaumarchais) had been written by the Marx Brothers. Many in the audience were simply bewildered and failed "to get it," a problem that plagues modern art and modern music as well as modern theatre. When this happens to people they seldom protest or complain; they just decide to stay home and watch TV or a VCR. As Mark Twain remarked, "people are down on what people are not up on."

The idea of a director's theatre is, of course, nothing new. At the turn of the century an English rebel named Gordon Craig shocked purists with his burning conviction that the director should be all-powerful, a super-director, a super-artist, a genius who could synthesize all the theatre's elements (lights, scenery, sound, script, acting, etc.) into a spectacular, unified whole. Movies have traditionally followed similar patterns. A movie producer usually regards the script (scenario) as only one of the many elements in his production. A popular modern textbook, E. T. Kirby's *Total Theatre*, stresses much the same point. Maybe Ciulei was just ahead of his time, but this did not convince The Guthrie's traditional audience who felt that a primary obligation of a director was to be faithful to what the great playwrights had intended.

But the most obvious departure that Ciulei made from Sir Tyrone's original intent was not his remodeling of the script, but his remodeling of the stage. Ciulei, as a professional architect as well as a director, naturally had ideas as to what the form of the playing space should be. As Mike Steele once pointed out, Guthrie had been primarily interested in the words and the ideas. Ciulei, on the other hand, was primarily interested in the visual elements, including the lights and the scenery. Accordingly, Guthrie wanted a theatre with a "thrust stage" which brought actors and audience closer together so that everyone could see and hear the actors. Ciulei, on the contrary, would obviously have been much happier with an excellent proscenium theatre which would have permitted and encouraged the use of scenic elements. Guthrie's thrust stage, with its essentially neutral background for all productions, seemed inhibiting and uninspiring. Accordingly, one of Ciulei's first acts was to abolish this formal background and thus " open up" a modified inner stage. Unfortunately this "opening up" of the playing space not only added production expenses but also condemned some seats in The Guthrie auditorium to decidedly inferior status. If these seats were sold, their occupants could not see some of the action. If unsold, they were even a greater disaster. Nothing shrieks "failure" in a theatre like a very visible block of empty seats.

Among the outstanding productions during Ciulei's five years (1980–1985) were *The Tempest*, *A Midsummer Night's Dream*, and *Tartuffe*. The shows that packed the theatre, however, were two Broadway musicals directed by Garland Wright; these were *Guys and Dolls* in 1983 and *Anything Goes* in 1984. But many felt that musicals were expensive and out of harmony with the Guthrie tradition. Sir Tyrone, in fact, often referred to American musicals as "vulgar." For most of the other plays during the Ciulei years, except for the traditional *Christmas Carol*, the attendance was disappointing. As early as 1982 the deficit had reached $630,000. In olden days a theatre with such a deficit would have simply disappeared, but not The Guthrie. Times had changed. Unlike commercial theatres of the 1920's, The Guthrie had become an institution, a "treasure" of the community, an object of pride like the symphony, the university, the museums, the Twins, the Vikings, maybe even the Mississippi River itself. Minnesotans civilized enough to realize that quality of life depends on something beyond money alone rallied to The Guthrie's support. Foundations, business interests, individuals, state and national endowments joined forces to provide the funds needed for survival.

Ciulei's term as artistic director ended in 1985. After another intensive search, the Board selected an American director, Garland Wright. Not since Tyrone Guthrie himself launched the theatre in 1963 had a director been given such unqualified support and power. Wright was essentially crowned king. No longer would the Board or a business manager interfere with the artistic director's choice of a season. One of Wright's first actions, for example, was to select a business manager, Edward A. Martenson, with whom he felt certain he could work harmoniously. All this is as it should be. Democracy may be desirable in politics, but in the fine arts, democracy (art by committee) invariably results in mediocrity. On the other hand it should be remembered that Guthrie's skill in working with others (whether students or the Board of

Directors) had been quite as important as his ability to work with actors, a skill which most of the other "artistic directors" between Guthrie and Wright seemed to lack or forget.

Wright came to the Guthrie with impressive qualifications. Although only 40 years old he had, according to Robert Collins, directed at virtually every major regional theatre in the country, including The Guthrie. Moreover, his range was wide and eclectic. He had proven that he could direct everything from popular musicals like *Guys and Dolls* to Shakespeare. Above all he seemed to be dedicated to two ideas that the Board considered very important: (1) the idea of returning The Guthrie to a revolving classic repertory theatre and (2) the idea of establishing an outstanding "permanent" acting company. Permanence (even for one or two years) has been a dream of many American actors, but one that few have ever realized. For the most part, American actors have endured a homeless, temporary, gypsy life. An outstanding permanent rep. company could if successful not only give actors a chance to develop as artists by playing numerous roles; it could also allow them to experience the joy of working together with those they respected. Such a company could also sink roots into its community. The value of having actors evolve into neighborhood friends, into someone you might meet at a shopping center, a church service, a PTA meeting or a wedding reception has obvious importance. Guthrie actors remembered for having developed just such ties with the community have been Paul Ballantyne, Barbara Bryne, Helen Carey, and Peter Michael Goetz.

Wright's first season, especially the three plays he himself directed (*The Misanthrope*, *The Piggy Bank*, and *Richard III*) more than lived up to expectations. They earned rave reviews from critics and a relieved sense of deep satisfaction from most of The Guthrie Board members. The general public was at first slow to respond, but the production of *Richard III* early in 1988 finally removed the skepticism and the crowds have returned.

There are those, of course, who maintain that theatres like The Guthrie will wither away at the first sign of a financial depression just as they did during the 1930's, but one might recall that, even during the Great Depression, the University, the Minneapolis Symphony, and the art museums did not wither away. Like everyone else, they experienced cut-backs and hard times, but they survived. The Guthrie has obviously become another of these ongoing institutions and its twenty-fifth anniversary should be only the first of many such milestones to be honored.

12

Professionals Who Followed The Guthrie

As already mentioned, any fear that The Guthrie Theater would discourage other theatrical units proved to be unfounded. Instead, an amazing burst of theatrical activity has been seen in the area since The Guthrie opened on May 7, 1963; so much activity in fact, that only the more successful groups can be considered here.

The Chanhassen Dinner Theatres
(1968 to Date)

The spark, or is it the muse, that sometimes ignites theatrical achievements can be capricious. For example, powerful organizations like the American National Theatre and Academy, the National Theatre Conference, and the American Theatre Association have long campaigned for more and better theatres; great foundations, including the Ford Foundation and the Rockefeller Foundation plus state art councils and the national endowments have granted dollars and support; scholars, theatrical personalities, and other arts experts have issued pamphlets, made speeches, and written books. The results? Usually nothing.

On the other hand, at sometime during the early sixties, Herbert Bloomberg, a Minnesota businessman and contractor whose only experience in theatre had been his attendance at a few Old Log Theater productions, signed a contract to construct a theatre building for Don Stolz. At about this same time, Bloomberg learned that a new type of restaurant, called a dinner theatre, was becoming popular. That kindled the spark which Bloomberg transformed into the multimillion dollar Chanhassen Dinner Theatre complex which has become known nationally as "The Cadillac of Dinner Theatres." Imagine such a thing happening in a sensible, well-regulated society. Where, but in America!

View of Chanhassen Dinner Theatre main stage.
Photo courtesy of Chanhassen Dinner Theatres.

Bloomberg's achievement is far greater than it at first appears. It would be easy to assume that he was simply an alert businessman, hungry for a quick buck, who saw a chance to make a killing and grabbed it. To anyone making such an assumption, it should come as a shock to learn that on the national scene, the dinner theatre craze proved to be a financial bust. The normal procedure seems to have been for a promoter to move into a city, lease some colorful old attic, train station, or warehouse, equip it for serving food, provide it with a slight stage, import a few entertainers from Hollywood or Broadway, and then present a rather shoddy show. Ballyhoo and advertising usually resulted in a successful opening, but few of the patrons ever returned.

Bloomberg took the opposite approach. He built carefully, solidly, unpretentiously. The prices were reasonable; the food was good but not fancy. Dinner, a massive business in itself which involved the serving of some 1,200 meals in less than two hours, was always served early enough so that noisy dishes could be cleared before the play began. Expensive stars were avoided; the emphasis was on the quality of the play itself, the theory being that if the play was good enough the audience would return even though the names of the actors were not well known. The reliance was primarily on young college or university trained actors—talent with a future rather than talent with a past. But regardless of the reason, the Chanhassen Dinner Theatres have been successful. When Chanhassen's first theatre opened, there were approximately seventy similar theatres in the nation. By 1988, the number had dwindled to twenty-three, with four of these under Chanhassen's ample roof.

Bloomberg's decision to build carefully, relying on steady, unspectacular quality rather than noisy publicity, has paid off. At first he lost money. By 1969 he was even forced to sell some of his property in order to balance the deficit at the dinner theatre. Then in 1970 an old French farce, entitled *A Flea in Her Ear*, proved to be a smashing success. Bloomberg's dinner theatre moved into the black financially and has remained there ever since.

Gary Gisselman, the first artistic director, spent a dozen years at Chanhassen before taking another directorship in Arizona. Gisselman was succeeded briefly by Howard Dallin and, in 1987, by Michael Brindisi. Brindisi had often acted at Chanhassen; he had also directed summer stock at the Paul Bunyan Playhouse in Bemidji, and founded the Minnesota Festival Theatre in Albert Lea before taking on his newest assignment.

The main theatre at Chanhassen seats 600 and presents big shows, mostly musicals. By 1978 three smaller theatres had been added: The Playhouse (130 seats), The Courtyard (160 seats) and The Fireside (250 seats). Shows in each theatre run as long as box office returns warrant. As with so many successful theatres the small size and intimacy of these little auditoriums added greatly to their charm, and to their ability to contain plays with ideas. Backstage space in each of the theatres tends to be cramped and extremely limited, but this has prevented Chanhassen from falling into the trap that has destroyed so many theatres, for technical expense can quickly become an intolerable financial burden. Tom Butsch, Chanhassen's scene designer, has had to rely on imagination, talent and ingenuity instead of space, money, modern convenience and electronic monstrosities to provide the attractive backgrounds that have characterized productions at Chanhassen.

For obvious reasons Chanhassen, like the Old Log, has stressed popular plays such as *Charley's Aunt*, *A Flea in Her Ear*, and *The Matchmaker*. It has also relied upon modern musicals with *My Fair Lady* and *Fiddler on The Roof* being among the favorites. During the spring of 1988, for example, *The Mystery of Edwin Drood* was playing in its main theatre; *Private Lives* could be seen in the Fireside; *The Middle Ages* was featured in the Courtyard; while *I Do! I Do!* was playing in the Playhouse for its record breaking eighteenth year. After *The Middle Ages* closed in May, 1988, the Courtyard space was transformed into a restaurant. Incidentally, David Anders and Susan Goeppinger, the actors who played the husband and wife of *I Do! I Do!* in 1971 and are still playing these parts, were married on stage in 1972. Now, 16 years later, they have teen-age children.

I Do! I Do! (1971),
directed by Gary Gisselman.
David Anders and Susan Goeppinger
appearing at the Chanhassen
Dinner Theatres.

Photo courtesy of
Mike Paul/Act Two.

Hello Dolly (1982),
directed by Gary Gisselman.
Susan Long.

Photo courtesy of
Chanhassen Dinner Theatres,
Betty Engle Levin, photographer.

Gross income at Chanhassen is over $6,000,000 annually. The theatres average 31 performances per week for approximately 6,000 patrons. They employ 6.5% of all Equity actors employed in dinner theatres nationally on any given evening! As the programs proclaim, "Continuity and artistic quality have been credited for Chanhassen's success." It is also a family achievement as daughters Britta and Meta are actively involved in the management of the theatres. The success is also living proof that good art and good business can be harmonious partners rather than antagonists.

The Cricket Theatre (1968 to Date)

In 1968 an energetic actor-manager-promoter by the name of Bill Semans opened the Cricket Theatre in Minneapolis. At the end of its first year The

Cricket produced a locally acclaimed hit, *The House of Leather* by Fred Gaines. In a burst of euphoria the production was transported to New York where it received a severe trouncing, but Semans, although disillusioned with New York, did not lose faith in Minneapolis. He returned to the city determined to establish a theatre that would rate somewhere between The Guthrie and the Chimera in importance. By September, 1971 Semans had acquired and renovated an old 900 seat movie house in north Minneapolis to serve as a home for his Cricket Theatre. The struggle to become firmly established and accepted was not easy. By October, 1971, The Cricket even tried a "dinner package" as a new inducement. Jax Cafe, a nearby restaurant, agreed to provide dinner before the show, dessert after, and two drinks, for a combined price of $8.50.

The Cricket began as a non-professional group, but its aim from the first has been to become fully professional. By 1975 it achieved this aim and became an Equity house. From the first, Semans placed strong emphasis on the production of new American plays; as he told Mike Steele, "Who wants to do the 3,293rd production of *The Cherry Orchard*, which I love, when I can do something American?" Accordingly, not only were new American plays given a chance, but new local playwrights like Eric Brogger, John Orlock and Fred Gaines were also given a chance to see their plays acted by professionals. Local directors, including Jim Wallace and Rosemary Hartup, were given chances to direct; and innumerable local actors like Richard Hilger, Shirley Venard Dircks, and Rosemary Hartup were given chances to act—for a salary!

One of Semans' most spectacular concepts was an agreement with Joseph Papp, the famous New York producer, that allowed The Cricket to acquire scripts Papp had considered but decided not to produce in New York. The project was only partially successful. It resulted in some good publicity, but, for the most part, the Minneapolis productions only indicated why Papp had not produced them in New York.

In 1980, Semans, like Alvin Epstein of The Guthrie, and Gary Gisselman of Chanhassen, decided to resign. The rash of resignations did not appear to be related, just coincidence. Semans hinted that he was tired of the theatre and might try producing movies instead. Lou Salerni assumed control at The Cricket as its artistic director, which by then found itself housed in a comfortable new home, a 384 seat theatre designed especially for The Cricket in the newly renovated Hennepin Center for the Arts. Salerni won Kudos for his directing of *Betrayal* (1982) and for *American Buffalo* (1983).

In addition to its major productions The Cricket offers a Works-in-Progress program under the leadership of Sean Michael Dowse. "Take The Stage," a new program, under the direction of William Partlan, now tries to

House of Leather (1969),
directed by H. Wesley Balk.
Florence Baker, Norma
Jean Wood, and Adrienne
Calhoun appearing at the
Cricket Theatre.

Photo courtesy of
Mike Paul/Act Two.

return the Cricket to its original mission, the development of significant dramatic literature.

In 1984–1985 The Cricket took a holiday; no plays were produced while the management and the board of directors pondered what to do about the $300,000 debt that the theatre had accumulated during its years at the Hennepin Center for the Arts. Finally it was decided that the company might be more successful in a smaller theatre, so the Cricket moved south once again, to 14th Street and Nicollet Avenue. The old Loring Theater, built in the 1920's as a movie house, was remodeled into a modified proscenium stage theatre seating 213 patrons. The new theatre opened in April, 1987, with a production of *Killers* by John Olive and has been a critical success ever since. The objectives of William Partlan, the artistic director, are to continue and strengthen the theatre's commitment to emerging playwrights, to rebuild its audiences, and to retire its debt.

The Playwrights' Center (1971 to Date)

As already indicated, Minnesota's present importance as a theatrical center is based not only upon the abundance of its producing theatres, but also upon their amazing variety. One of the best examples of this is the work of the Playwrights' Center, sometimes known as The Playwrights' Lab. As the title suggests, the Playwrights' Center is not really a producing group. True, scripts may be "read cold" for an audience by professional actors and scenes may be rehearsed. Their primary concern, however, is not the production of plays but the development of playwrights.

The group was first organized as the Playwrights' Lab in 1971 by Charles Nolte, Greg Almquist, Eric Brogger, and Barbara (Nosanow) Field. All were playwrights dedicated to writing, and their first activity consisted primarily of reading plays (mostly original) at coffee houses and local theatres. Since then the group evolved and expanded, and acquired a "theatre"—an old church on Franklin Avenue in Minneapolis. But although the personnel changed and the activities increased, its primary objective, the development of playwrights, has remained the same.

There is nothing else quite like it in America and, above all else, it has been effective. The rapidly growing list of successful playwrights who have worked at the center and who swear by the value of the experience is impressive. The list includes John Olive, Lee Blessing, Barbara Field, John Orlock, John Fenn, Martha Boesing, Lance Belville, Eric Brogger, and August Wilson. The McKnight Foundation, which once offered prestigious fellowships to the University of Minnesota, now gives them to the Playwrights' Center. The Jerome Foundation funds fellowships for playwrights-in-residence, and Jones Commissions support writers of one-act plays. By 1981 the Center could boast that 20 of the 24 Twin Cities theaters that had produced new works, had produced plays by Center writers. Nor is the Twin Cities area the only market for the Center's playwrights. John Olive's *Minnesota Moon* has been produced in New York, Chicago, San Francisco, London, and at the Edinburgh Festival, and has been published in *Best Short Plays of 1982*. Another of Olive's works, *Clara's Play*, has been produced in Louisville and in Chicago, where it won two awards. Yet another of his plays, *Standing On My Knees*, has had similar widespread success. And in 1987, among all of the premieres of plays by American playwrights that opened across the country, 100 were by Playwrights' Center writers.

As valuable as the Playwrights' Center has been to playwrights, it obviously faces a problem of financing. The new works-in-progress that it helps develop are not intended to be staged for paying audiences, and even if they could attract full houses, the Center's auditorium seats only 150. Funding, therefore, becomes a necessity. As early as 1982–1983, operating expenses totalled $392,000; of this amount $268,000 had to come from grants and contributions, primarily from the Minnesota State Arts Board and the so-called "Golden Five" (the Dayton-Hudson, Jerome, Bush, McKnight, and Northwest Area foundations).

In America such a center might logically be expected to find a home in a college or on a university campus. But fears of academic restraints, interference, and regulations outweigh the obvious financial advantages. The

Playwrights' Center therefore remains a unique center for the education (development) of playwrights and will hopefully remain so as long as funding is available. An aggressive fund raising campaign gains power from the fact that, by the fall of 1988, five plays by Center writers could be seen on Broadway; *Fences* and *Joe Turner's Come and Gone* by August Wilson, *The Gospel at Colonus* by Lee Breuer, *A Walk in the Woods* by Lee Blessing, and *The Deal* by Matthew Witten. The director of the Playwrights' Center is David Moore, Jr.

The Palace Theater (1972 to 1984)

The Palace Theater, located on Washington Avenue South in Minneapolis, maintained that its basic aim was to free a company of actors to find the best way of producing new plays with no holds barred. Like The Firehouse before it, the group drew its inspiration from the work of The Open Theatre and Joseph Chaiken's group in New York. It avoided the traditional "author/ director/ actor" division of responsibilities. Everyone was expected to be creative — to contribute to the limit of his or her "cerebral or physical" energy when producing a play.

Nineteen of the plays produced by the Palace troupe during its decade of existence were originals. There were also adaptations of Strindberg, Ionesco, and Pinter as well as boldly physical versions of *Macbeth* and *Uncle Vanya*. The co-founders of the Palace Theater were Ben Krielkamp and Jim Stowell.

Critics wrote of the unique style of Palace productions — the manic physical energy and the humor that sometimes seemed to conceal a lack of deeper meaning. That style attracted loyal, but not large audiences, so financial problems were cited as one of the reasons for closing the theater.

The Palace production of *Macbeth* (1983) won Kudos for its director, Bain Boehlke, and for Jim Stowell who played the title role. Stowell's play, *The Desperadoes* was one of their best known productions. The play was first produced by the Palace in 1975, then revived and presented at New York's Theatre for the New City in 1980. Mike Steele described it as "so wildly active, so noisy and so outrageously risky that it won the troupe a cult following and set its style for the years to come." [*Minneapolis Tribune*, October 20, 1980.]

The Park Square Theatre (1972 to Date)

Unlike The Guthrie Theater which arrived in the area in full bloom, Park Square Theatre is an example of a theatre that appears to be growing slowly from native roots. It began as a community theatre in the fall of 1972 in a tiny 77 seat theatre. It was devoted to the production of classics old and new. Since then it has grown steadily. By 1981–1982 it had moved into a 134 seat theatre in the Park Square Court building. In 1986 it moved again, to a small theatre in the Minnesota Museum of Art's Jemne building. Attendance has increased from a total of 4,756 in 1978–1979 to 17,700 in 1983–1984. By 1988 its artists and crafts people, including actors, were being paid, although Park Square has not yet become an Equity house.

The managing/ artistic director since 1979 has been Richard Cook and the plays have been impressive. The 1987–1988 season consisted of *Hedda Gabler* (Ibsen), *You Can't Take It With You* (Kaufman and Hart), *All My Sons* (Miller), *Mrs. Warren's Profession* (Shaw), *A Touch of The Poet* (O'Neill), and *Twelfth Night* (Shakespeare.) Prices have remained reasonable and its productions have gained recognition. Terry Bellamy's performance in *Waiting for Godot* won a Kudos from the Twin Cities Drama Critics Circle in 1982, while both Bellamy and Faye Price received Kudos for *Boesman and Lena* in 1983.

In The Heart Of The Beast Puppet And Mask Theatre (1973 to Date)

No one, not even Dudley Riggs, represents the wild diversity of present day Twin Cities theatres better than In The Heart Of The Beast Puppet And Mask Theatre (HOBT). Conventional-minded people to whom the "theatre" means the production of a well-crafted script by playwrights like Bernard Shaw or Shakespeare would probably see most of HOBT's activity not as theatre, but as a circus or a carnival. Actually, however, puppets and masks tend to lie at the very root of theatre.

HOBT was organized in 1973 as the Powderhorn Puppet Theatre, but Powderhorn (the name of a nearby Minneapolis park) seemed too military to this peace-oriented group and so a new name was selected. The name comes from the advice of Cuba's Che Guevara, "Stay home and work in the heart of the beast." Had Che only heeded his own advice?

Most of their performances are given in a tiny, 60 seat theatre, where Chicago Avenue intersects with Lake Street, but their puppets, some twenty feet tall, have gained fame by wandering far and wide. For several years now, HOBT puppets have led the May Day parade in Minneapolis. In 1983, from June to October, its troupe of twenty-four adults, five children—and two dogs, traveled from Brainerd to New Orleans aboard an un-Cousteau-like houseboat that they called the Collapso. The troupe paraded and performed the three "plays" that they had developed in 24 communities along the way.

Circle of Water Circus (1983), an outdoor spectacle which toured the Mississippi River by boat.

Photo courtesy of In the Heart of the Beast Puppet and Mask Theatre, John Franzen, photographer.

The Circle of Water Circus was so successful that the players (without Collapso) later traveled to theatre festivals in Stockholm and Gothenberg, Sweden, and Aarhus, Denmark.

HOBT employs a staff of nine full-time artist-actors and two administrators. Sandra Spieler, artistic director, has designed and created many of HOBT's masks and directed the plays in which the masks appear. Its performances and parades have brought its special form of theatre magic to thousands upon thousands—especially to minorities and the disadvantaged. In 1988 HOBT planned to move down Lake Street to the Avalon, a former adults-only movie theatre. After remodeling, HOBT hopes to share its new home with other small theatre groups.

The Plymouth Dinner Playhouse
(1973 to Date)

Although not an Equity company, "Playcrafter's Productions" (now known as Stage Two Productions) at the Quality Inn of Plymouth, Minnesota, is included in this chapter because (1) all the performers are paid and paid very well, and (2) because it has been entirely self-supporting, and (3) because in its area of light musical theatre it has been an outstanding success, especially since 1980 when Curt Wollan became director. During its first year in 1973, the Radisson Playhouse was under the direction of Don Stolz from the Old Log. Stolz abandoned the project after that year, and the theatre experienced its ups and downs until Wollan and scenic designer Jim Johnson, took over. A change in the name of the hotel led to a renaming of the theatre as well.

Curt Wollan, a native of White Bear Lake, had returned to the Twin Cities area after completing the MFA degree at the University of Iowa. Productions by Playcrafters have included *The Last of The Red Hot Lovers*, *Dames at Sea*, and *Play It Again, Sam*, but the real breakthrough came with *Diamond Studs* (1981) which won Kudos for its production, its direction, and its choreography. Another production, *Pump Boys and Dinettes*, a lively, folksy Broadway musical, moved into the intimate informality of the Quality Inn in 1983 and is scheduled to run until September, 1988, when it will be replaced by *Nunsense*. During its last months *Pump Boys* alternated with *Will Rogers' USA*, a one man show starring Gene McFall.

Long successful runs have enabled Wollan to employ his talents elsewhere. For example, by the time *Pump Boys* had opened, he was already beginning to work on *The Little Foxes* at TRP and, as noted, he had also served as artistic director of the Chimera Theatre.

The Illusion Theater (1974 to Date)

The Illusion Theater is a fully professional group that was founded in 1974 by Michael Robins. For two and a half years this company, under the direction of Robins and Bonnie Morris, concentrated on mime, producing such works as *Pioneer Mime Show* and *How The Inventor Took Flight*. Voice was then added to the productions and the company focused its energy on two new primary objectives; the creation of new works relevant to modern problems, and the sharing of these works with a large and varied audience. *Orlando, Orlando*, adapted by John Orlock and the Illusion company from the novel by Virginia Woolf was the Theater's highly praised and financially successful

Becoming Memories (1981), directed by David Shookhoff. Leslie Rapp, Bonnie Morris, Steven Epp, Mary McDevitt, Jo Howarth, Marysue Moses.

Photo courtesy of Illusion Theatre.

transition from mime to a theatre of words. First produced in 1977, it was revived in 1987.

Not all of the company's productions have been originals. Standard plays, however, have usually been adapted to the company's style. Its 1981 production of the German classic, Franz Wedekind's *Spring Awakening*, directed by David Feldshuh, did much to establish the group's reputation. An ambitious touring program soon gave this reputation national importance. *Becoming Memories*, written by Arthur Giron in collaboration with members of the company, caught the attention of New York producers Elizabeth McCann and Nelle Nugent, who gave it an off-Broadway workshop production.

In 1978 the Illusion Theater began focusing on the subject of sexual abuse. Robins and Morris, in cooperation with the Hennepin County Attorney's office and Cordelia Anderson, a specialist in research on such abuse, produced *Touch*, for children, and *No Easy Answers*, for adolescents. These theatre-programs were subsequently toured to schools and other organizations in 33 states. Half of Illusion Theater's time and efforts are now devoted to educational and social service plays.

As already indicated, the Illusion Theater refuses to limit itself to any one type of production. Since 1974 works created at Illusion often result from collaborations between playwrights, directors and the acting company. Ping Chang's *Snow* and Jon Klein's *Southern Cross* from the 1987–1988 season reflected this kind of development. In addition to those already mentioned it is also noted for its colorful and unconventional "entertainments" such as *Cocoanuts*, the old George S. Kaufman romp that was catapulted into fame by the four Marx brothers. The production perhaps proved that the only consistent thing about the Illusion Theater is that whatever it tries to do, it does very well.

Illusion Theater is located in the Hennepin Center for the Arts, the former Masonic Temple building at Hennepin Avenue and Sixth Street in Minneapolis.

At The Foot Of The Mountain
(1974 to Date)

At The Foot Of The Mountain (AFM) was founded largely through the energy and talent of Martha (Pierce) Boesing, who assisted in the establishment of the Moppet Players during the 1960's and was also an active member of the Minneapolis Repertory Theater and the Firehouse. AFM is a women's theatre that tries to "honor women's feelings and nurture women's values as a source of health on our planet." The group does not limit itself to the production of plays. It also provides lectures, workshops, scripts, and tapes which range from biblical themes to subjects such as rape, prostitution and nuclear war. But whatever the medium of communication, the aim is to inspire audiences to "imagine (then create) a just and joyous world."

AFM has its own 90 seat theatre and offices in the Cedar-Riverside People's Center at 20th Avenue and Riverside. Women write, produce, act and manage the theatre whose viewpoint is both multiracial and multicultural. AFM charges a sliding scale of ticket prices to keep its productions affordable. While it was not the first women's theatre, it is now the oldest active women's theatre in the country.

In its earliest plays, *Raped, The Story of a Mother*, and *Junkie!* Martha Boesing and the Company labored together to create works based on everyone's experiences in dealing with isolation, mother/ daughter relationships, and addiction. Audiences were encouraged to "call forth" their own stories as a sharing of the experience. These became what the Company termed "ritual dramas."

Ashes, Ashes, We All Fall Down by Martha Boesing won a best play Kudos in 1983; the play dealt with nuclear madness. Critics have usually been very

Raped (1978),
directed by Phyllis Jane Rose.
Phyllis Jane Rose, Martha Boesing,
Robyn Samuels, Jan Magrane,
Cecilia Lee.

Photo courtesy of
At the Foot of the Mountain.

Vinegar Tom (1988), directed by
Jan Magrane. Andrea Engler, Sarit
Cofman, Regina Marie Williams.

Photo courtesy of
At the Foot of the Mountain,
Kerry Jorgensen, photographer.

impressed by AFM's productions. Peter Vaughan, *Minneapolis Star & Tribune* critic, called AFM "the gutsiest theater in town," and according to Robert Collins:

> By the end of *Junkie!*, a bond has been established between audience and cast. It's a bond whose roots lie in a shared experience and shared beliefs. Millenia ago, theater arose out of this kind of communal experience, and because it doesn't happen very often in today's theater, it's exciting when it does. *Junkie!* has that kind of excitement about it. [*Sweet Potato*, September 17, 1981.]

The production of *Fefu and Her Friends*, written and directed by Maria Irene Fornes, was called "superbly insightful, well acted . . . intelligent and finally haunting" by Mike Steele, who felt that "It might just be one of the most important plays of our time." [*Minneapolis Star & Tribune*, June 24, 1986.]

In 1986–1987 AFM sponsored a residency by Spiderwoman who created their first multicultural production, *Neurotic, Erotic, Exotic*, which dealt with racial stereotyping. Since then the Theatre's goals have been to become a multi-racial, multigenerational group. In 1988 the staff, the five member company and a three member directorship (Jan Magrane, Bernadette Hak Eun Cha and Rebecca Rice) were integrated. Problems over implementing the group's evolving goals seem to have been solved and the important ritual dramas like *The Story of a Mother* and *Raped* have been restaged to reflect the new viewpoint of the Theatre.

The Mixed Blood Theatre (1976 to Date)

Once again, "Sweet are the uses of adversity." A sweeping generalization might maintain that the greatest blot on America's social and economic history has been its treatment of racial minorities. Yet during recent years America's hope for excellence in the arts, as well as in athletics, appears to depend more and more upon its minorities.

The multi-racial Mixed Blood Theatre Company, located in a century old firehouse in the West Bank theatre district of Minneapolis is a good example. It is dedicated to the spirit of Dr. Martin Luther King's dream, and it has five primary objectives. These are, to produce plays using color-blind casting; to take artistic risks in the selection and production of plays; to reach a non-traditional audience; to provide a professional experience for minority actors; and to produce educational programs on racial and cultural themes. In both 1985 and 1986 Actors Equity announced that Mixed Blood was the top employer of professional minority actors in the country.

In less formal fashion, a better personality portrait of the group can be gained from a note by its artistic director, Jack Reuler, which appeared in a 1983 program for *Children of a Lesser God*:

> Right now we are trying to raise the money to purchase and renovate our building, a 1887 firehouse on the National Register of Historic Buildings . . . But don't worry. We won't lose our rustic flavor. The lobby will remain in the former horse stable. The administrative offices will remain in a former bathroom. The prop shop will still be in an old coal bin. We won't lose our sense of humor either. So give a few cents . . . to help support the theatre that's better than the Guthrie, funnier than Dudley Riggs, closer than Chanhassen, and cheaper than McDonalds.

A sense of humor can relax dangerous pressure in a theatre so long as it does not dilute the desire to do high quality work and high quality is something that Jack Reuler, his staff, and eight or nine professional actors have managed to maintain. Since its founding, Mixed Blood has won more than its share of honors and enthusiasm. These honors have included Kudos for *Warp* (distinguished production, 1981) and *Accidental Death of an Anarchist*

A . . . My Name is Alice (1986), directed by Sharon Walton. Sally Ramirez, Shelley Chall, Marvette Knight, Marquetta Senters, and Faye Price.

Photo courtesy of Mixed Blood Theatre, Michael Kissin, photographer.

(distinguished production, 1982). *A . . . My Name Is Alice* was also one of Mixed Blood's popular successes.

The Mixed Blood staff, in addition to Reuler, includes Charlie Moore, as marketing director, associate producer Regina Laroche, and a company of professional actors, including Warren Bowles, Steve Yoakam, Mike Kissin, Marvette Knight, Brian Grandison, Lia Rivamonte, Sanford Moore and Pat O'Brien.

Many of Mixed Blood's productions have been original. None of these have as yet become nationally famous, but a number have been transferred to other theatres and are still alive. Impressive also have been some unusual productions like *One Hundred Years of Solitude*, *Warp*, and the 1983 productions of *Old Time Kanjincho* and *Fishing for a Wife*. These last two were among the first examples of Japanese kabuki theatre to be seen in the Twin Cities.

Penumbra Theatre (1977 to Date)

The founding of Penumbra began at TRP. It was in 1975 that TRP announced that its forthcoming season would include *The Great White Hope*, a powerful drama about Jack Jeffries, the black prizefighter who became the

The Mystery of Irma Vep (1987), directed by Ron Peluso. Warren Bowles and Michael Kissin.

Photo courtesy of Mixed Blood Theatre, Mike Paul/Act Two, photographer.

world heavyweight champion. The leading role went to Earnest Hudson, a black actor from Detroit, who had come to Minneapolis especially to try-out for the role. The production turned out to be a stunning success, but Hudson finally stated that he was "too broke" to continue to the end of the run. As a community theatre TRP dared not begin paying actors and the show closed temporarily until "private contributions" could be found to help Hudson. But it was shocking to realize that with all the professional theatres in the area not one offered any special opportunity for black actors.

Jack Reuler, who had been working towards a degree as a veterinarian, and was also working as a part-time employee at the Center for Community Action, decided to do something about this problem. With help from the Jerome Foundation and others he launched his Mixed Blood Theatre in the summer of 1976. One of his main actors and also one of his directors during that first year was Lou Bellamy. In 1977 Bellamy launched a black theatre of his own in St. Paul's Martin Luther King Center, and named it Penumbra (Latin for half-shadow). While Mixed Blood had emphasized "color-blind casting,"

Penumbra decided to emphasize plays that reflected the black experience in America. Penumbra has presented commissioned works, classics of black literature, and plays from the pens of its playwrights in residence among whom are Horace Bond and August Wilson. One of Wilson's early plays, *Malcolm X*, has long been part of the theatre's touring program. Another, *Jitney*, was the first use by Wilson of material from his own background, a practice he has successfully followed in his later plays. *Ma Rainey's Black Bottom* was produced by Penumbra during May and June of 1987 with great success, and, as almost everybody now knows, Wilson's *Fences*, made a rare grand sweep of New York's theatre prizes in 1987. The city of St. Paul appropriately responded by honoring Wilson as Minnesota's most successful playwright.

Penumbra's schedule calls for five plays a year, each running for one month. Musicals were at first avoided, but the brilliant box office success of *Don't Bother Me, I Can't Cope* changed this policy. This season's (1988) *Black Nativity* could well become Penumbra's *Christmas Carol*. Penumbra's budget is roughly $250,000 per year, about half of which is earned.

As Peter Vaughan observed when summarizing Twin Cities theatre of the 1970's, TRP's *The Great White Hope* was that decade's most significant production, not only because of its near professional quality but because it also established two theatres, Mixed Blood and Penumbra, where black theatre artists had a chance. Penumbra won a Kudos Award in 1984 for its production of *Don't Bother Me, I Can't Cope*.

The Actors Theatre of St. Paul
(1977 to Date)

Theatrical rivalry between Minneapolis and St. Paul has existed ever since they both built opera houses in 1867 and "Grand" opera houses in 1883. One need only recall the indignation with which St. Paul, in 1887, viewed the prospect of having to go to Minneapolis to see Edwin Booth and Lawrence Barrett to realize how deep the feelings ran. During the long reign of L. N. Scott, St. Paul, theatrically speaking, may have held a slight advantage; at least it had the better of the two Metropolitan Theatre buildings, but after the Bainbridge Players established a home in Minneapolis the theatrical lead shifted clearly to the mill city. For a moment Edyth Bush promised to restore the balance to St. Paul with her beautiful little community theatre, but that promise faded. The same thing happened with Rex Henriot's Theatre St. Paul during the 1960's. Finally, after Tyrone Guthrie opened his theatre in Minneapolis in 1963 the balance swung emphatically to the younger sister. In fact, the older sister appeared to feel insulted rather than flattered when in 1967

Blood Knot (1986), directed by Dawn Renee Jones. James Craven and Michael Andrew Miner.

Photo courtesy of Actors Theatre, Connie Jerome, photographer.

the Minnesota Theater Company (the title under which The Guthrie produced at that time) agreed to establish a "second theatre" in St. Paul. To accomplish this, The Crawford Livingston Theatre was remodeled and its seating capacity approximately doubled, but to no avail. St. Paul was no more willing to accept a "second" Guthrie theatre than it had been to accept a "second" Bainbridge company.

As a result Minneapolis, during the late sixties and early seventies, could boast of having professional units at The Guthrie Theater, The Children's Theatre, The Cricket Theatre, and the Firehouse, plus Chanhassen and the Old Log in the suburbs, whereas St. Paul had none. This was a situation that Michael and Jan Miner, both from the Milwaukee Repertory Theatre, decided to correct. In 1977 they organized a small group of actors and found a home for them in the Foley Theatre on the campus of the College of St. Thomas.

From an artistic standpoint the Foley's seating capacity of 260 was excellent even though the potential for income was obviously limited. The Miners, however, had already decided to stress quality rather than quantity. Their group was committed from the start to ensemble acting. They agreed to keep the company small, using only five professional actors in three plays during the first season, although this was increased to seven plays and eight actors for the second. For the most part, The Actors Theatre has chosen either to produce modern classics like Shaw's *Arms and The Man* and Chekhov's *The Three Sisters*, or else it has favored new plays such as *Custer* by Robert Ingram, *Gift Of The Magi* by John Olive and Libby Larsen or *Ten November* by Steven Dietz.

The Actors Theatre does not pretend to be self supporting. Its income from July 1, 1982 to June 30, 1983 totalled $426,000, of which $174,000 was "earned" while the remainder came from grants and contributions. Its strength has come from the quality of its acting and directing, with actors such as David Kwiat, James Cada, James Lawless, Mari Rovang, Sally Wingert and Louise Goetz, and directors like Michael Miner, Jeff Steitzer and David Goldstein.

The work at Actors Theatre is supported by rave reviews generally. Mike Steele, in comparing the St. Paul production of *Tartuffe* to a lavish production of the same play at the Kennedy Center in Washington, D. C. writes, "The St. Paul production was far superior. No double standards. No fake provincial pride. It was on its own terms ten times better than the Washington production." [*Minneapolis Tribune*, June 27, 1982.] And Arthur H. Ballet observed, reviewing *The Grand Hunt* on KSTP-TV, "Most of the cast is endearing, while David Kwiat and Scott Glassner are much more—they are magnificent. The brisk directing and sensitive pacing from David Goldstein, and the rousing old-fashioned play that makes fun of itself gives us (as one of the characters says) another dazzling evening at the Hapsburgs."

In 1985 the Actors Theatre moved to a new facility, an attractive 350 seat auditorium in the Hamm Building, where Miner has intensified his determination to create theatre as well as recreate it. In both 1987 and 1988 a very successful festival of old and new one act plays was produced. One powerful new full length play, *Ten November* by Steven Dietz, about the sinking of a Lake Superior steamer, the Edmund Fitzgerald, was such a success in November, 1987 that it had to be repeated in the following March of 1988. Another indication that the Actors Theatre is not content to stand still is evident from a recently announced exchange with a Russian theatre. During the 1988–1989 season Miner is scheduled to direct *Awake and Sing* at the Yermolova Theatre in Moscow, while Valerie Fakin, the Russian director, is scheduled to direct a play at Actors Theatre in St. Paul. Obviously, Michael and Jan Miner have finally given St. Paul a first class resident professional theatre.

Peer Gynt (1982),
directed by David H. Olson.
Jack Sherman and Elizabeth Pringle.

Photo courtesy of
Cherry Creek Theatre.

Cherry Creek Theatre (1978 to 1988)

All theatres begin with a vision and a mission to create art for the stage in a certain way. Sometimes that vision outlives its founders and sometimes the "customers don't come," as Irving Berlin wrote, but at other times the theatre's work is complete, the vision fulfilled, and the doors are closed. Cherry Creek Theatre shut down its operations in May of 1988 after a decade of accomplishment in southern Minnesota. Its founders felt that they had done what they had wanted to do so it was time to turn to other projects.

Cherry Creek's vision was to be a theatre resource within a community, to find the stories and traditions within that area and bring them to dramatic life. Its founders, David Olson, Marsha Kimble and Lee Hawkins, chose a storefront in an old hotel in St. Peter to start work. Olson taught theatre at Gustavus Adolphus College in St. Peter and several other members of the collective were recent graduates of the college. In 1983 the theatre moved to Mankato's Carnegie Performing Arts Center, a newly transformed library building.

During its ten year existence, Cherry Creek programmed original works, published a magazine called *Theaterwork*, and offered workshops and classes, often as a part of school residencies. A festival conference called the Gathering was sponsored by Cherry Creek in 1981 for workers in the arts.

Cherry Creek's productions have ranged from Brecht (*The Beggar and the Dead Dog* and *The Good Woman of Setzuan*) and Ibsen (*Peer Gynt*) to plays based on the writings of Carl Sandburg and Meridel LeSueur. Story gathering in the area resulted in Cherry Creek's plays *1944!*, *Goosetown*, *Earthbird* and *Ceasefire*. Reviews for Cherry Creek's plays were good; performances were described as engrossing and provocative; its actors termed talented and creative. Cherry Creek leaves a memory of good, interesting productions related to the concerns of people in small-town Minnesota.

The Great North American History Theatre (1978 to Date)

On the surface, one of the most unusual theatres in the area is the Great North American History Theatre (GNAT). The name sounds more like a railroad, or a scholarly academic institution than it does like a theatre. Yet a moment's thought by anyone even mildly acquainted with theatre history, will remind him or her that most of the great playwrights have written plays about history. Aeschylus, Sophocles, Euripides, Shakespeare, Goethe, and Ibsen are all famous for their "history plays." In a larger sense all good playwrights write history, although not necessarily the kind you read in encyclopedias or history books. Some are personal histories, traumatic experiences torn from the lives of their authors (Strindberg, Williams, O'Neill), others are condensed from the lives of the society in which the authors lived (Ibsen, Shaw, Miller). The GNAT is therefore simply a recognition of a basic fact; its use of the term "history" is a matter of emphasis rather than something new.

Lynn Lohr has been the GNAT's guiding spirit—actress, director, manager, ever since it was organized under the auspices of COMPAS. Lance Belville has written roughly one half of the plays which it has produced. Their mission is to present history that is interesting in a style they like to call "prairie realism."

The important thing is that GNAT has produced some impressive new plays. Kudos were awarded to *Scott and Zelda*, *A Servant's Christmas*, and *Plain Hearts*. Among its successful playwrights, in addition to Lance Belville, have been John Fenn, David Wiggins, Lynn Lohr, James Sazevich and Steven Trimble. The plays have sometimes centered on historic figures like James J. Hill, Bronko Nagurski (the football player), and Nina Clifford (a highly successful madam of the saintly city). At other times they have featured a group; for example, *Four Hearts and the Lords of the North*, which examines relation-

Dogs in the Hot Moon (1987), directed by Vern Sutton. Hassan El-Amin.
Photo courtesy of The Great North American History Theatre.

ships between whites and northern Indians. At still other times the drama has centered on an event; *Down to Earth* examines the impact of the Great Depression on the lives of rural Minnesotans.

Exchanges with Russian companies are in the plans of both Actors Theatre and the Children's Theatre but, logically, GNAT brought an Irish group to St. Paul. The Charabanc Theatre Company of Belfast is also a history theatre, specializing in the stories of its own troubled city. Two Charabanc works, *Gold in the Streets* and *Somewhere over the Balcony*, both written by Charabanc founder Marie Jones, were presented in GNAT's first international exchange.

The GNAT has proven to thousands that history can inform and entertain. The theatre tours its productions, but its home base has been the Weyerhaeuser Auditorium in Landmark Center (the restored Federal Courts building) in downtown St. Paul. In the fall of 1988 it hopes to be relocated in the Arts and Science Center, presenting its productions in the Crawford Livingston Theatre.

Traveling Light (1987),
directed by Patty Lynch.
Jim Stowell.

Photo courtesy of
Brass Tacks Theatre,
Lars Hansen, photographer.

Brass Tacks Theatre (1979 to Date)

Brass Tacks was organized in 1979 with the aim of encouraging playwrights to create works that have something to say about modern life and culture. Brass Tacks tries to emphasize the power of language and has built a reputation for the production of funny, stimulating plays. Brass Tacks has no theatre building of its own, but depends on renting performing space at such places as the Southern Theatre (at Seven Corners in Minneapolis) or the Hennepin Center for the Arts. Only 30% of its budget is earned from the sale of tickets.

Patty Lynch, a member of the Playwright's Center, was the founder of this theatre and continues to function as its central core. In 1986 Brass Tacks received a McKnight Foundation Excellence in the Arts award, and hopes to remain "a small, unique jewel in the crown of Twin Cities Theatre."

1929 (1980). Barbra
Berlovitz-Desbois and
Robert Rosen.

Photo courtesy of
Theatre de la Jeune Lune,
F. Desbois, photographer.

Theatre de la Jeune Lune (1979 to Date)

Many Twin Cities theatre-goers if asked to name a sentimental favorite
among the numerous theatres of the area would probably select Theatre de
la Jeune Lune (Theatre of the New Moon) even though some of their more
conservative friends seem to find the theatre's style a bit frenetic, noisy, and
incomprehensible. All, however, would have to admit that it is unique, for it
began by playing half of each year in Minneapolis, and the other half of the
year in Paris, France. The four members of the company who formed its nu-
cleus had a common background; all were trained at the famous Ecole Jacques
Lecoq in Paris. Their style of performing tends to be delightfully different; an
uninhibited, imaginative style that borrows inspiration from the medieval
commedia dell'arte, from mime, the circus, Molière, and from the avant-
garde. Yet in spite of their youthful irreverence toward traditional realistic
theatre they are mature and skillful performers. One feels that they could, if
they wished, give superb performances of classics by Aristophanes,
Shakespeare, Molière or Shaw.

The two members of the troupe primarily responsible for its creation are
Barbra Berlovitz-Desbois and Dominique Serrand. Berlovitz-Desbois is a

Minneapolitan, one among a number of talented performers who were first lured into theatre by the work of Gary Parker at North High School. Barbra graduated from the University of Minnesota, and then went to Paris where she met Serrand. After graduation from the Lecoq school they formed a drama duo and toured for several years. Travel finally brought them back to Barbra's home town of Minneapolis, where the idea of an international theatre seems to have been born. They were joined in 1979 by two other Lecoq graduates: Vincent Gracieux from Paris and Robert Rosen from Minneapolis, to form the company which was to become the Theatre de la Jeune Lune.

The talent of these four permanent members of the troupe is supplemented by a number of others, some paid and some volunteers. The quality of the company's work is indicated by the fact they have won six Kudos for outstanding achievements. Only The Guthrie Theater, The Children's Theatre Company, The Cricket Theatre, and the Actors Theatre of St. Paul have won more. The credo of the group reads: "We are a theatre of directness, a theatre that speaks to the audience, that listens to it, and needs its response. We believe that theatre is an event. We are a theatre of emotions—an immediate theatre—a theatre that excites and uses direct language—a theatre of imagination." Many of Jeune Lune's productions have been created by the company, such as *Cirque de Molière* and the incredibly titled *Yang Zen Froggs In Moon Over A Hong Kong Sweatshop*. More recently they have turned to Michael de Ghelderode, Alain Gautre, and Peter Barnes, whose *Red Noses* closed the 1988 season.

Red Eye Collaboration (1983 to Date)

Red Eye Collaboration is one of the newest, smallest and most unusual theatre groups in Minnesota. Its home is a 60 seat theatre located in the warehouse district of Minneapolis. Its three co-founders (Steve Busa, Miriam Must and Barbara Abramson) met through the Playwright's Center in 1982, but their decision to establish their own theatre came later as the result of a series of long distance telephone calls at red eye rates (hence the theatre's name).

At first the tiny group tried to produce only its own rather avant garde works such as Steve Busa's *Geography*, which won a Kudos in 1984, but the group soon found it advisable to expand. Lee Breuer's *Shaggy Dog Animation* (1985–1986) was a critical and box office success, as was Busa's own *Blue Moon* which integrated film, music and plot into a rather startling production based on *The Scarlet Letter*. With *Blue Moon*, Red Eye members felt they had found the direction which future work should take. In 1988 they plan to take *Blue Moon* to a theatre festival in Poland, while *Shaggy Dog Animation* is presented in Atlanta. The production is also scheduled to play at Cafe La MaMa in New York City in 1989. Skill in fund-raising as well as in playwriting and production seems to account for Red Eye's rapid success.

Minnesota Festival Theatre (1984 to Date)

Theatre in Minnesota is far from limited to the Twin Cities. The town of Albert Lea, 100 miles south of the metropolitan area of Minneapolis-St. Paul, has long been home to a thriving community theatre; since 1984 it has also supported a professional summer theatrical operation. Michael Brindisi and Michelle Barber were the founding artistic managers of Albert Lea's straw hat Minnesota Festival Theatre. Brindisi and Barber had worked together at Chanhassen and then spent three summer seasons at the Paul Bunyan Playhouse at Bemidji. In the fall of 1983 they came to Albert Lea to direct a production of *The Pirates of Penzance* for the community theatre. Something about the town, its interest in theatre and its support for the arts led them to propose a professional summer theatre and by the following June it was open for business.

The Minnesota Festival Theatre uses an airconditioned 260 seat playhouse that once was a Masonic temple. Initial funds for the theatre came from the city government, the chamber of commerce, downtown businesses and the state office of tourism which had helped to promote the theatre as an arts attraction in a wider region than southern Minnesota. The short distance from the Twin Cities makes it possible to attract actors and audiences.

Productions for the opening season were *The Matchmaker, Side by Side by Sondheim, Private Lives, She Loves Me* and a Sherlock Holmes tale. Barber and Brindisi shared directing duties; their casts were half-Equity and half non-union performers. In 1986 David Hawley wrote that one of the major problems in any summer theatre is that of casting. Rehearsal times are often so short that actors must "know their stuff." He felt that the Minnesota Festival Theatre cast of *The Rainmaker* played with "stock competency" and that the theatre was becoming one of the best in the state. [*St. Paul Pioneer Press*, June 25, 1986.]

By 1987 Barber and Brindisi had moved on to new jobs at the Chanhassen Dinner Theatres. The Festival Theatre faced the difficulties of replacing them and retaining the local support and enthusiasm that had brought the Theatre into being. Its new artistic director is Ron Peluso, a University of Minnesota graduate in directing who had directed in the Twin Cities and in Iowa. The schedule for the summer of 1988 lists *The Little Shop of Horrors, The Glass Menagerie, Tartuffe* and *Oliver*. Theatre supporters say proudly that Minnesota

Festival Theatre is in the black and that they plan to continue producing plays in Albert Lea for many summers to come.

Theatre 65 (1985 to Date)

A number of other professional groups have started up, enjoyed considerable promise, but have as yet failed to prove that they can become permanent. A good example is Theatre 65. The idea of a theatre for those chronologically disadvantaged is an excellent one. The group, organized in 1985 by George Farr and Marjorie D'Aguila, made a brave beginning. Its opening production, *Taking My Turn*, received good reviews. Subsequent lack of sufficient funding, however, has caused them to cautiously withdraw from the battle of survival. At present Theatre 65 is either defunct or enjoying a temporary vacation.

Some Final Thoughts About the Theatres

And so these professional groups all have a mission and a message. They are entertaining, yes. They have to be in order to exist. But beyond the fun and the laughter is usually a surprisingly serious note—a hunger to examine life and the human condition—to do or say something that might indirectly make us a bit wiser, a bit more prepared to cope with this absurd and dangerous world in which we live. Theatre originated in religious ceremonials. Perhaps theatre and religion, although usually bitter enemies on the surface, both arise from a similar primitive urge—an urge to find meaning and purpose in human existence. But any impulse to draw pat conclusions about the theatres of our own age or about the nearly 157 years of theatrical highlights from the first soldier shows at old Fort Snelling to this year, 1988, of theatrical anniversaries, could only be doomed to failure. Until human life itself can be summarized into pat conclusions, the theatre as life's imitation, must also resist pat conclusions. We only know that for thousands of Minnesotans life has been and continues to be a bit more enjoyable, a bit richer, sometimes a bit more understandable, because of the theatre.

The Critics and the Theatre

On the surface drama critics and theatre artists (mostly actors) appear to be deadly enemies. A closer look, however, reveals that they need one another. A good critic, as John K. Sherman once observed, is the voice of "the discriminating audience." [*Minneapolis Sunday Tribune*, August 15, 1948.] Woe unto the actor who prefers to rely only upon the voices of fawning friends or doting relatives.

During the nineteenth century Minnesota critics seldom signed their reviews. It was roughly at the time of World War I that names like James Gray and Frances Boardman began to appear. The two most influential critics prior to the appearance of The Guthrie were probably John Harvey (St. Paul) and John K. Sherman (Minneapolis). Both were intelligent, knowledgeable, and a bit tender hearted. Their encouraging comments probably did more than most people realize to stimulate the renaissance that occurred with the arrival of Guthrie.

Critics not only serve as a sounding board—an audience of one—their written words often remain as the only link we have with the past. Moreover, the critic by the very nature of his or her profession is not as concerned with the welfare of any one theatre as with the welfare of a community of theatres. How to encourage theatre artists to work together for the good of the whole has been an age old problem. In the 1950's, for example, some of us made a brave beginning in this area by establishing The North Central Theatre Association, but it died within a few years. Other attempts have had little more success. As far as the Twin Cities are concerned, one of the wisest recent attempts to instill some sense of community among theatre artists was the organization of an annual Kudos celebration sponsored by the Twin Cities Drama Critics Circle.

Although it lasted only from 1981 through 1984 the annual Kudos awards celebration was a giant step in the right direction of recognizing excellence and increasing community awareness of the theatre. The celebrations were launched by local critics Peter Vaughan (*Minneapolis Star*); Mike Steele (*Minneapolis Tribune*); Dave Hawley (*St. Paul Pioneer Press*); Robert Collins (*City Pages*); Carla Waldemar (*Twin Cities Reader*); and Mike Phillips (*Minnesota Daily*). Jon Cranney directed the celebrations and numerous theatre artists participated in the programs. The awards were called *Kudos* after Kudos of Syntax, the first recorded regional drama critic (who didn't cover Athens).

From the community's standpoint it was a great idea, but it faced the obvious problem that haunts all events subject to human judgment. One has only to imagine what would happen to the popularity of athletic contests like football if the "winner" and "loser" were determined by a panel of judges! And so even though these critics made heroic efforts to emphasize excellence rather than winning or losing there were the inevitable disappointments. Moreover, Kudos celebrations require time and money. In any event, 1984 marked the end of an excellent idea which should be revived. A partial list of Kudos winners is given at the end of this chapter.

The critics selected the Kudos list, but a separate committee chose the annual winners of two other awards. The John K. Sherman Award (named after the late *Minneapolis Tribune* critic) was given for outstanding achievement in theatre to The Jerome Foundation, Jack Barkla, John Clark Donahue and Frank M Whiting. The Veda Hyde award, given only twice, went to Annette Garceau and James Bakkom. It was voted for achievement in the technical aspects of theatre.

In addition to these awards by the critics, both community and educational theatres stage competitions. In Minnesota, the community theatres have organized a competition festival every second year. The Minnesota winner then competes in the regional level and, if successful, goes to the national competition. Minnesota's competition began in 1973. The winners to date have been as follows:

1973 — *An Unknown Soldier* — Theatre in the Round.
1975 — *No Mourning After Dark* — Centre Stage.
1977 — *Today a Little Extra* — Centre Stage.
1979 — *Hopscotch* — Minnetonka Community Theater.
1981 — *Public Eye* — Minnetonka Community Theater.
1983 — *Actor's Nightmare* — Theatre in the Round.
1985 — *Tennessee* — Theatre in the Round.
1987 — *Quien Sabe . . . Quien Soy* — Teatro Latino.

A Partial List of Kudos Awards

Some of the Kudos awarded between 1981 and 1984 include:

1981

DISTINGUISHED PRODUCTIONS:

Wings (Cricket Theatre).
Ubu for President and *Cirque de Molière* (Theatre de la Jeune Lune).
The 500 Hats of Bartholomew Cubbins (Children's Theatre).
Warp (Mixed Blood Theatre).
Journey's End (Trinity Films Theatre Perspectives).

DISTINGUISHED ACHIEVEMENT IN DIRECTION:

Howard Dallin, *Wings* (Cricket Theatre).
John Clark Donahue, *The 500 Hats of Bartholomew Cubbins* and *Falling Moons* (Children's Theatre).

Jeff Steitzer, *How the Other Half Loves* (Actors Theatre).
Gary Gisselman, *Annie Get Your Gun* (Chanhassen Dinner Theatres).
Bain Boehlke, *Journey's End* (Trinity Films Theatre Perspectives).

DISTINGUISHED ACHIEVEMENT BY AN ACTOR:

Gary Rayppy, *Richard II* (Theatre in the Round).
Michael Goodwin, *Wild Oats* (Guthrie Theater).
Vincent Gracieux, *Ubu for President* (Theatre de la Jeune Lune).
Steve Benson, *Hello and Goodbye* (Performers Ensemble).
Clive Rosengren, *A Streetcar Named Desire* (Cricket Theatre).

DISTINGUISHED ACHIEVEMENT BY AN ACTRESS:

Patricia Fraser, *Wings* (Cricket Theatre).
Mim Solberg, *Happy Days* (Olympia Theatre).
Wendy Lehr, *Cinderella* (Children's Theatre).
Barbara Bryne, *Mary Stuart* (Guthrie Theater).
Peggy O'Connell, *Annie Get Your Gun* (Chanhassen Dinner Theatres).

DISTINGUISHED ACHIEVEMENT IN PLAYWRITING:

Nancy Beckett, *The Women Here Are No Different* (Women's Theatre Project).
Timothy Mason, *The 500 Hats of Bartholomew Cubbins* (Children's Theatre).
Barbara Field, *Camille* (Guthrie Theater.).

1982

DISTINGUISHED PRODUCTIONS:

The Tempest (Guthrie Theater).
Don Juan (Guthrie Theater).
Eve of Retirement (Guthrie Theater).
Tintypes (Cricket Theatre).
Diamond Studs (Radisson Playhouse).
Accidental Death of an Anarchist (Mixed Blood Theatre).

DISTINGUISHED ACHIEVEMENT IN DIRECTION:

Liviu Ciulei, *The Tempest* (Guthrie Theater).
Richard Foreman, *Don Juan* (Guthrie Theater).

Larry Whitely, *The Crucible* (Theatre in the Round).
Curt Wollan, *Diamond Studs* (Radisson Playhouse).
Lewis Whitlock, *Tintypes* (Cricket Theatre).

DISTINGUISHED ACHIEVEMENT BY AN ACTOR:

Ken Ruta, *The Tempest* (Guthrie Theater).
Dominique Serrand, *1929* (Theatre de la Jeune Lune).
Roy Brocksmith, *Don Juan* (Guthrie Theater).
William Newman, *Our Town* (Guthrie Theater).
Terry Bellamy, *Waiting for Godot* (Park Square Theatre).
Pat O'Brien, *Strider* (Mixed Blood Theatre).

DISTINGUISHED ACHIEVEMENT BY AN ACTRESS:

Louise Goetz, *Hedda Gabler* (Actors Theatre).
Jessica Tandy, *Foxfire* (Guthrie Theater).
Lynn Musgrave, *Same Time Next Year* (Theatre in the Round).
Susan Long, *Tintypes* (Cricket Theatre).
Betty Miller, *Eve of Retirement* (Guthrie Theater).

DISTINGUISHED ACHIEVEMENT IN PLAYWRITING:

Frank Pike, *Smaller Heartaches* (Out-and-About Theater).
Erik Brogger, *Northern Lights* (Cricket Theatre).

1983

DISTINGUISHED PRODUCTIONS:

The Dance and the Railroad (Cricket Theatre).
Ashes, Ashes We all Fall Down (At the Foot of the Mountain).
Tartuffe (Actors Theatre).
Candide (Guthrie Theater).
Force of Habit (Dudley Riggs Brave New Workshop).

DISTINGUISHED ACHIEVEMENT IN DIRECTION:

Jeff Steitzer, *Tartuffe* (Actors Theatre).
Andrei Serban, *Marriage of Figaro* (Guthrie Theater).
Garland Wright, *Candide* (Guthrie Theater).

Lou Salerni, *Betrayal* (Cricket Theatre).
Bain Boehlke, *Macbeth* (Palace Theater).

Distinguished Achievement by an Actor:

James J. Lawless, *Betrayal*, *Clarence Darrow*, and *Dear Ruth* (Cricket Theatre).
Bob Breuler, *True West* (Cricket Theatre).
David Warrilow, *As You Like It* and *Marriage of Figaro* (Guthrie Theater).
Mark Davis, *Poor Murderer* (University of Minnesota).
James Stowell, *Macbeth* (Palace Theatre).
Richard Ooms, *Candide* and *Room Service* (Guthrie Theater).

Distinguished Achievement by an Actress:

Barbara Kingsley, *Tartuffe* and *Fallen Angels* (Actors Theatre).
Sally Wingert, *Tartuffe* and *Fallen Angels* (Actors Theatre).
Louise Goetz, *Fallen Angels* (Actors Theatre) and *Dear Ruth* (Cricket Theatre).
Jana Schneider, *Marriage of Figaro* (Guthrie Theater).
Anne Enneking, *Pippi Longstocking* (Children's Theatre).
Bonnie Lee, *Present Laughter* (Theatre in the Round).

Distinguished Achievement in Playwriting:

Lance Belville, *Scott and Zelda,* and *The Beautiful Fools* (Great North American History Theatre).
Marisha Chamberlain, *Snow in the Virgin Islands* (Theatre Three).

1984

Distinguished Productions:

Cloud Nine (Cricket Theatre).
Don't Bother Me I Can't Cope (Penumbra Theatre).
Plain Hearts (Great North American History Theatre).
The Seagull (Guthrie Theater).
The Secret Garden (Children's Theatre).
Secret Traffic (The Loft).

DISTINGUISHED ACHIEVEMENT IN DIRECTING:

Edward Payson Call, *The Entertainer* (The Guthrie Theater).
John Clark Donahue, *The Secret Garden* (Children's Theatre).
Kevin Olson, *Translations* (University of Minnesota).
Lou Salerni, *American Buffalo* (Cricket Theatre).
Binky Wood, *The Unseen Hand* (Children's Theatre).

DISTINGUISHED ACHIEVEMENT BY AN ACTOR:

Terry Bellamy, *Boesman and Lena* (Park Square Theater).
Thomas Freiberg, *Boy Meets Boy* (Out-and-About Theater).
James J. Lawless, *The Entertainer* (Guthrie Theater) and *Terra Nova* (Cricket Theatre).
Dominique Serrand, *The Caprices of Marianne* (Theatre de la Jeune Lune).
Frederick Winship, *American Buffalo* and *Cloud Nine* (Cricket Theatre).

DISTINGUISHED ACHIEVEMENT BY AN ACTRESS:

Shirley Venard Diercks, *The Constant Wife* and *Cloud Nine* (Cricket Theatre).
Pauline Flanagan, *The Entertainer* (Guthrie Theater).
Jane Murray, *Cloud Nine* (Cricket Theatre).
Faye Price, *Boesman and Lena* (Park Square Theatre).
Barbara Sharma, *Guys and Dolls* (Guthrie Theater).
Sally Wingert, *Translations* (Actors Theatre).

DISTINGUISHED ACHIEVEMENT IN PLAYWRITING:

Frank Kinikin, *Man in the Bath* (Primary Vision Performances).
Thomas W. Olson, *The Secret Garden* (Children's Theatre).

Notes and References

PART ONE - The Early Years
(CHAPTERS 1–4).

The vast majority of the information in Part One comes from three un-published Ph.D dissertations:

Hermann E. Rothfuss. *The German Theatre in Minnesota*. Ph.D dissertation (University of Minnesota) 1949.

Frank M Whiting. *A History of the Theatre in St. Paul, Minnesota from its Beginning to 1890*. Ph.D dissertation (University of Minnesota) 1941.

Donald Z. Woods. *A History of the Theatre in Minneapolis, Minnesota from its Beginning to 1883*. Ph.D dissertation (University of Minnesota) 1950.

Each of the above works is based primarily upon articles in newspapers of the period, although each also contains an extensive bibliography of secondary sources.

Among other sources referred to in Part One are the following:

Ernst H. Behmer. "Seventy Years of the Swedish Theatre in America" *in* Eric Westman, Ed., *The Swedish Element in America*. Chicago: Swedish American Biographical Society, 1934. Vol. 4. 111–120.

Theodore C. Blegen. *Minnesota. A History of the State*. Minneapolis: University of Minnesota Press, 1963.

Roy A. Boe. *The Development of Art Consciousness in Minneapolis and the Problems of the Indigenous Artist*. M. A. thesis (University of Minnesota) 1947. Materials concerning Peter Gui Clausen are found on 109–126.

T. Allston Brown. *History of the American Stage*. New York: Dick & Fitzgerald Publishers, 1870.

Oral Sumner Coad and Edwin Mims, Jr. *The American Stage*. New Haven: Yale University Press, 1928. Vol. 14.

Randolph Edgar. "Early Minneapolis Theaters". *Minnesota History*, 9:3, (March, 1928) 31–38.

William Watts Folwell. *A History of Minnesota*. St. Paul: Minnesota Historical Society Press, 1926. Vol. III.

The Fuller Papers. Collections of the Minnesota Historical Society.

Anne Charlotte Harvey. "Swedish-American Theatre" *in* Maxine Seller, ed., *Ethnic Theatre in the United States*. New York: Greenwood Press, 1983. 491–524.

Anne Charlotte Harvey and Richard H. Hulan. " 'Teater, Visafton Och Bal': The Swedish

American Road Show in Its Heyday". *The Swedish American Historical Quarterly*, 37: 3 (July 1986) 126–141.

Lawrence J. Hill. *A History of Variety - Vaudeville in Minneapolis, Minnesota from its Beginning to 1900*. Ph.D dissertation (University of Minnesota) 1979.

Clinton M. Hyde. "Danish American Theatre" *in* Maxine Seller, ed., *Ethnic Theatre in the United States*. New York: Greenwood Press, 1983. 101–118.

Joseph Jefferson. *The Autobiography of Joseph Jefferson*. New York: The Century Company, 1897.

Beatrice Morosco. "Famous Visitors". *Hennepin County History*, 31: 3 (Summer, 1972) 5–13.

Clara Morris. *Life on the Stage*. New York: McClure Phillips and Company, 1901.

Germain Quinn. *Fifty Years Back Stage*. Minneapolis: Stage Publishing Company, 1926.

Hermann E. Rothfuss. "The Early German Theater in Minnesota", *Minnesota History*, 32: 2 (June, 1951), 100–105; 32: 3 (September, 1951), 164–173.

Hermann E. Rothfuss. "Criticism of the German-American Theater in Minnesota". *The Germanic Review*, 27: 1 (February, 1952), 124–130.

Hermann E. Rothfuss. "Theodor Steidle, German Theater Pioneer", *The American-German Review* 17: 3 (February, 1951), 17–19, 33.

John K. Sherman. "Music and Theater in Minnesota History" *in* William Van O'Connor, ed., *A History of the Arts in Minnesota*. Minneapolis: University of Minnesota Press, 1958. 3–63.

Maud and Otis Skinner. *One Man in His Time. The Adventures of Harry Watkins, Strolling Player*. Philadelphia: University of Pennsylvania Press, 1938.

Charlotte Ouisconsin Van Cleve. *Three Score Years and Ten, Life-Long Memories of Fort Snelling, Minnesota, and Other Parts of the West*. Minneapolis: Harrison and Smith, 1888.

Donald Z. Woods, "Playhouse for Pioneers. The Story of the Pence Opera House." *Minnesota History*, 33: 4 (Winter, 1952), 169–178.

PART TWO - The Big Business of Show Business (CHAPTERS 5–7).

Material in Part Two is based upon another group of Ph.D dissertations, as follows:

Thomas Owens Andrus. *A History of the Legitimate Theater in St. Paul, Minnesota from 1918 to 1939*. Ph.D dissertation (University of Minnesota) 1961.

Francis E. Drake. *A Study of the Personality Traits of Students Interested in Acting*. Ph.D dissertation (University of Minnesota) 1949.

John Myles Elzey. *Professional Legitimate Theatre in St. Paul, Minnesota, from 1890–1918*. Ph.D dissertation (University of Minnesota) 1972.

Audley Mitchell Grossman, Jr. *The Professional Legitimate Theater in Minneapolis from 1890 to 1910*. Ph.D dissertation (University of Minnesota) 1957.

Also the following Master's theses:

Evelyn Cecile Anderson. *A History of the Theatre in St. Peter, Minnesota, from its beginning to 1930*. M. A. thesis (University of Minnesota) 1946.

Truly Trousdale Latchaw. *The Trousdale Brothers Theatrical Companies from 1896 to 1915*. M. A. thesis (University of Minnesota) 1948.

James Robert Thompson. *Influences of Modern Painting on the New Stagecraft*. M. A. thesis (University of Minnesota) 1951.

The papers of L. N. Scott and Theodore Hays are found in the collections of the Minnesota Historical Society and the Bainbridge players Papers are contained in the Performing Arts Archives, University of Minnesota Libraries. Other sources of information are:

Michael Conforti. "Orientalism on the Upper Mississippi. The Work of John S. Bradstreet." *The Bulletin of the Minneapolis Institute of Arts.* LXV, 1981–1982, 2–35.

George Grim. "For Marie Gale, Stage was the Happy Life". *Minneapolis Sunday Tribune*, August 22, 1965.

Andrew F. Jensen. "Two Decades of Trouping in Minnesota, 1865–85", *Minnesota History*, 28: 2 (June, 1947), 97–119.

Ward Morehouse. *Matinee Tomorrow, Fifty Years of Our Theatre.* New York: McGraw Hill, 1949.

L. N. Scott. "Memories of Local Stage", *The Minneapolis Journal*, Editorial Section, June 22, July 6 and August 31, 1924.

Jerry Stagg. *The Shubert Brothers.* New York: Ballantine Books, 1968.

Frank M Whiting. "Theatrical Personalities in Old St. Paul", *Minnesota History*, 23: 4 (December, 1942), 305–315.

——. *Popular Entertainment 1895–1929. The Twin City Scenic Collection.* Minneapolis: University of Minnesota Art Museum, 1987. [Exhibition Catalogue.]

——. Hiz Honor, Part VIII. *Hennepin County History.* 26:3 (Winter, 1967), 26–27.

PART THREE - Interlude: The Amateurs Come of Age (CHAPTERS 8–9).

PART FOUR - The Great Revival (CHAPTERS 10–12).

Material in Parts Three and Four is based on information from two unpublished doctoral dissertations and three master's theses. They are:

Douglas Proctor Hatfield. *A History of Amateur Theatre in St. Paul, Minneapolis, and their Suburbs, 1929–May 1963.* Ph.D dissertation (University of Minnesota) 1969.

Michael Erwin Pufall. *A History of the Old Log Theater in Greenwood, Minnesota, 1940–1970.* Ph.D dissertation (University of Minnesota) 1974.

Donald Borchardt. *A History of Theatre Touring at the University of Minnesota.* M. A. thesis (University of Minnesota) 1958.

Robert Frederic Gee. *A History of the Theatre at the University of Minnesota from its Beginning to 1937.* M. A. thesis (University of Minnesota) 1949.

William Joseph Grivna. *The history and the development of the Paul Bunyan Playhouse.* M. A. thesis (University of Minnesota) 1968.

Other published and unpublished materials used in these two Parts are as follows:

Bob Aden. *The Way It Was. A Highly Personal Account of the Old Log's Early Years.* Unpublished manuscript, 1987.

Michael Anthony. "When Dudley Riggs' Brave New Workshop was New". *Minneapolis Sunday Tribune* (picture magazine), May 8, 1983.

John A. Baule. "Broadway in Bloomington: The Bloomington Civic Theater". *Hennepin County History* 46: 3,4 (Fall, 1987) 18–19.

Harold Wesley Dixon. *Regional theatre profile: decentralized theatre in America; comparative survey and critical analysis of two regional centers: Minneapolis/ St. Paul and Los Angeles.* Ph.D dissertation (University of Minnesota) 1976.

John Clark Donahue and Linda Jenkins, eds. *Five Plays from the Children's Theatre Company of Minneapolis.* Minneapolis: University of Minnesota Press, 1975.

Deborah Dryden. "Chanhassen, the Cadillac of Dinner Theatres". *Theatre Crafts*, 14: 5 (October, 1980) 25–26, 78–79.

Tyrone Guthrie. *A New Theatre.* New York: McGraw Hill, 1964.

David Hawley. "The Man Who Came To The Dinner Theater." *St. Paul Pioneer Press-Dispatch*,
    January 24, 1988.
David Hawley. "Chimera had to move on or die". *St. Paul Pioneer Press-Dispatch*, October 14,
    1987.
D'Arcy Mackey. *The Little Theatre in the United States*. New York: Henry Holt & Company.
    1917.
Fred William Meitzer. *The Duluth Playhouse: a case study in community theatre structure, policy and
    practice*. Ph.D dissertation (Ohio State University), 1966.
Thomas W. Miller. *Heroes and Clowns - A History of the University Theatre*. Minneapolis: Univer-
    sity of Minnesota Department of Theatre Arts, 1973.
Bradley Morison and Kay Fliehr. *In search of an Audience. How an Audience was found for the
    Guthrie Theatre*. New York: Pitman. 1968.
Peter Vaughan. "70's and Drama". *Minneapolis Star*. December 24, 1979.
Peter Vaughan. "Dinner Theaters serve steady diet of entertainment for a profit." *Minneapolis
    Star*. November 25, 1975.
Frank M Whiting. *One of Us Amateurs*. Provo: Stevenson's Genealogical Society, 1980.
Joseph Ziegler. *Regional Theatre: The Revolutionary Stage*. Minneapolis: University of Minnesota
    Press. 1973.
——. "Special Report: The Twin Cities." *Theatre Crafts*, 17: 7 (August/ September, 1973.)

Papers relating to the Eastside Theatre and the Bloomington Civic Theatre are in the collection of the Performing Arts Archives, University of Minnesota Libraries. Materials relating to Chimera Theatre and Theatre St. Paul
can be found in the archives of the Minnesota Historical Society. A series of
taped interviews with important figures in local theatrical history (recorded
by Barbara Brown) may be consulted at the Minneapolis Public Library.

Index